Voices of the Enslaved
in Nineteenth-Century Cuba

A book in the series
Latin America in Translation /
en Traducción / em Tradução

SPONSORED BY THE CONSORTIUM
IN LATIN AMERICAN STUDIES
AT THE UNIVERSITY OF NORTH
CAROLINA AT CHAPEL HILL
AND DUKE UNIVERSITY

Voices of the Enslaved in Nineteenth-Century Cuba

 A DOCUMENTARY HISTORY

Gloria García Rodríguez

Translated by Nancy L. Westrate

Foreword by Ada Ferrer

The University of North Carolina Press
Chapel Hill

This book was published with the assistance of the Anniversary Endowment Fund of the University of North Carolina Press.

Translation of the books in the series Latin America in Translation / en Traducción / em Tradução, a collaboration between the Consortium in Latin American Studies at the University of North Carolina at Chapel Hill and Duke University and the university presses of the University of North Carolina and Duke, is supported by a grant from the Andrew W. Mellon Foundation.

© 2011 The University of North Carolina Press
All rights reserved
Set in Whitman and Quadraat Sans
Manufactured in the United States of America

Originally published in Spanish by Centro Investigación Científica "Ing. Jorge L. Tamayo," A.C., in Mexico, as *La esclavitud desde la esclavitud: La visión de los siervos*, © 1996 Centro Investigación Científica "Ing. Jorge L. Tamayo," A.C.

The paper in this book meets the guidelines for permanence and durability of the Committee on Production Guidelines for Book Longevity of the Council on Library Resources.

The University of North Carolina Press has been a member of the Green Press Initiative since 2003.

LIBRARY OF CONGRESS CATALOGING-IN-PUBLICATION DATA
García Rodríguez, Gloria.
[Esclavitud desde la esclavitud. English]
Voices of the enslaved in nineteenth-century Cuba : a documentary history / Gloria García Rodríguez ; translated by Nancy L. Westrate ; foreword by Ada Ferrer. — 1st ed.
    p. cm. — (Latin America in Translation/en Traducción/em Tradução)
    Includes bibliographical references and index.
    ISBN 978-0-8078-3218-9 (cloth : alk. paper)
    ISBN 978-0-8078-7194-2 (pbk. : alk. paper)
    ISBN 978-0-8078-7767-8 (ebook)
1. Slavery—Cuba—History—Sources. 2. Slavery—Cuba. I. Title.
HT1076.G3713 2011
306.3'62097291—dc22   2011005515

Contents

FOREWORD BY ADA FERRER xi   TRANSLATOR'S PREFACE xv

Introduction 1
    The Growing Hegemony of the Plantation 4
    Slaves and More Slaves 7
    The Sociodemographic Imapact of the Plantation 11
    The Plantation Community 15
    The Informal Structure of Plantation Life 23
    Family and Kinship 29
    Plantations and Commerce 36
    Slaves in the City 40
    Slave Rebellions 43

1. Slavery and Its Legal Regulation: The Slave Code 47
    Royal decree and instructional circular for the Indies on the education, treatment, and work regimen of slaves. May 31, 1789. 47

2. Slaveholders and the Slave Code 55
    Statement from Havana's ingenio owners to the king. Havana, January 19, 1790. 55

3. Toward a New Slave Code 74
    3.1. Survey by Captain General Gerónimo Valdés. Havana, February 23, 1842. 74
    3.2. The hacendado Jacinto González Larrinaga explains his methods. San Antonio de los Baños, April 14, 1842. 76
    3.3. Excerpts from the slave code. November 14, 1842. 80

4. Slavery and Family Life 85
    4.1. Excerpts from the proceedings against Ildefonso Carabalí, slave owned by Don Diego Francisco de Unzaga, for attempted suicide. Havana, September 11, 1807. 85

4.2. The tragic fate of Rita Gangá: Excerpts from the case against Juan Gualberto Toledo for theft of the slave woman. Remedios, June 25, 1835. 87

4.3. Carlota Moreno, morena, brings suit against her sister. Havana, March 8, 1836. 88

4.4. José Agustín Cepero petitions for the freedom of his daughter Juana. Havana, July 12, 1836. 89

4.5. Petition filed by María de los Dolores Frías, native of Africa and resident of Barrio de Guadalupe, requesting that her daughter be allowed to change masters. Havana, September 11, 1837. 90

4.6. Official request by the freedman Romualdo García to free his wife. Havana, October 17, 1837. 90

4.7. Official request by Juan Pablo Sobrado seeking authorization to redeem an unborn child. Havana, April 7, 1853. 91

4.8. Complaint filed by Dominga Gangá, slave owned by Don Pedro Macías, seeking visitation with her children. Havana, April 14, 1853. 91

4.9. Official request by María Belén Medina to free her son Simón. Havana, July 25, 1853. 92

4.10. Petition of Miguel Moreno, slave owned by Doña Merced Polo, to free his daughter Tomasa. Havana, August 6, 1853. 92

4.11. Antonio Cuesta, free moreno, purchases the freedom of his son, a slave on the ingenio Santiago. Havana, January 18, 1854. 93

4.12. Luciano Gutierrez petitions to purchase his daughter's freedom against her master's wishes. Havana, January 28, 1854. 94

4.13. Canuto Houssin wants to free Juliana and then marry her. Havana, February 14, 1854. 94

4.14. Petition by Antonio Abad Palomino requesting that his daughter officially be granted her freedom. Havana, May 26, 1854. 95

4.15. Juana Evangelista Suazo requests that her sister change masters. Havana, September 3, 1860. 96

4.16. Antonio Sánchez demands freedom for his wife Lucía Carabalí. Havana, March 21, 1862. 97

4.17. Juana Sánchez y Sánchez demands freedom for herself and for her son. Havana, August 12, 1862. 98

4.18. Benigna Rendón requests a revised coartación of her son Félix Cantalicio Linares. Havana, March 27, 1863. 98

4.19. Juana Valenzuela files a complaint against her master and husband. Havana, October 6, 1864. 99

4.20. Manuel Valerio, Congolese, agrees to change owners, providing that he is permitted to see his children. Havana, June 13, 1864. 99

4.21. Emilio Piñeiro demands his money or his freedom. Havana, December 1864. 100

4.22. Dolores Roca's ordeal to have her daughter Teresa appraised. Havana, August 30, 1866. 101

4.23. Carlota Polo defends the rights of her stepdaughter and demands freedom for her stepdaughter's son. Havana, October 5, 1866. 102

4.24. Juana Socarrás charges that her mother and son are unjustly enslaved. Havana, November 6, 1866. 103

4.25. The dramatic struggle of Dimas Chávez to free his mother. Havana, December 7, 1866. 104

5. The Plantation Social Network 105

5-I. SLAVES AND MAYORALS 105

5.1. The slaves on the cafetal Catalina walk out on their mayoral in protest and run off into the scrub. Guanajay, July 12, 1828. (Excerpts from the suit.) 105

5.2. Savad Carabalí Bibí assaults the carter from the ingenio San Juan Bautista. Puerta de la Güira, July 1, 1831. 109

5.3. Gaspar Lucumí injures the mayoral on the cafetal Nuestra Señora del Rosario. San Luis de la Ceiba, July 27, 1835. 111

5.4. The contramayoral Benigno Lucumí leads a revolt against the ox herd from the ingenio Intrépido. Macurijes, August 14, 1835. 113

5.5. Slaves belonging to San Juan de Manacas flog their mayoral. Guaminao, Santiago de Cuba, June 23, 1840. 115

5.6. Fermín Lucumí, a former African chieftain, kills his mayoral on the ingenio Balear. Rancho Veloz, July 31, 1840. 118

5.7. The mysterious death of Alejo Criollo on the ingenio Santa Teresa. Bahía Honda, February 18, 1863. 119

5-II. CONFLICTS WITHIN THE PLANTATION SLAVE COMMUNITY 121

5.8. Ceferino Mandinga kills Pantaleón Carabalí in an attempt to collect a debt. Guanabo, November 25, 1823. 121

5.9. The contramayoral Francisco does his duty and is murdered by a fellow slave for his trouble. Aguacate, November 11, 1829. 122

🍀 5-III. FUGITIVE SLAVES CANNOT ALWAYS RELY ON HELP FROM THEIR FELLOW SLAVES 123

5.10. Cirilo dies at the hand of a runaway slave. Bauta, March 4, 1831. 123

5.11. A sentry gambles with his life fending off fugitive slaves. Guanabacoa, August 13, 1834. 124

5.12. Pedro Criollo confesses to the murder of his sweetheart María del Rosario Gangá. Pipián, April 2, 1837. 125

5.13. Chinese colonos murder a black slave. Matanzas, September 9, 1865. 126

🍀 5-IV. SOLIDARITY IN THE FACE OF INJUSTICE 127

5.14. The adult men defend the youth Nepomuceno. Güira de Melena, October 23, 1827. 127

5.15. Juan Bautista and Ceferino, both Minas, abet their countryman Rafael. Tapaste, July 28, 1830. 130

5.16. The Lucumís of Arratia rise up in solidarity with their fellow slaves to protest their punishment. Macurijes, July 22, 1842. 132

6. The Labor Relations of Coartado Slaves 136

6.1. José Antonio Avilés Congo cannot pay his mistress the day wages that he owes her. Havana, October 5, 1837. 136

6.2. Gumersinda requests an accurate appraisal of her skills. Havana, August 8, 1853. 137

6.3. María Magdalena's mistress uses her to pay off a debt. Havana, September 18, 1853. 137

6.4. Manuel Córdova wants to use his day wages to purchase his freedom. Havana, February 13, 1854. 138

6.5. María de Jesús intercedes on behalf of her daughter, a day laborer. Havana, March 9, 1854. 138

6.6. Pedro Real Congo, capataz of the Congo association, intervenes on behalf of his compatriot, María Luisa González. Havana, April 21, 1854. 139

6.7. José Isabel Galainena offers his services as lien. Havana, April 19, 1861. 140

6.8. Nicolás de Azcárate intercedes on behalf of an ingenio slave. Havana, February 5, 1862. 140

6.9. Manuel Congo protests the control that the syndic exercises over his money. Havana, February 13, 1862. 141

6.10. An elderly slave is subject to a flagrant injustice. Havana, April 4, 1862. 141

6.11. Pedro Criollo buys his freedom and wants to continue working on the ingenio. Havana, July 13, 1864. 142

6.12. Taking up a collection for Mamerto Salas. Puerto Príncipe, May 17, 1865. 143

6.13. Antonio Quesada Congo cannot earn his daily wages due to illness. Havana, November 21, 1866. 143

7. The Master's Violent Hand 145

7.1. A local commissary intervenes in a case of brutality. Havana, September 25, 1818. 145

7.2. A modern version of the chastity belt. Havana, November 1834. 146

7.3. The dungeon on the hacienda La Cuaba. Santiago de Cuba, November 11, 1834. 150

7.4. Domingo Verdugo, lieutenant governor of Cárdenas, takes action. February 1861. 152

7.5. A humanitarian writes to Captain General Francisco Serrano concerning atrocities he has witnessed. July 1862. 156

7.6. Excerpts from the proceedings of a lawsuit executed in Sagua la Grande on April 28, 1864, against Andrés Mena and his son Justo for atrocities. 159

8. Freedom Road 161

8-I. THE RIGHTS OF SLAVES WHO TRAVEL TO COUNTRIES WITHOUT SLAVERY 161

8.1. The syndic rules that Catalina is free. Havana, January 13, 1852. 161

8.2. Manuela de la Guardia represents the slave José and gives testimony on his behalf. Havana, November 26, 1861. 162

8.3. The mulatto Dámaso sails for Mexico and freedom. Santiago de Cuba, September 6, 1864. 163

8.4. The slave girl Ángela Díez and her visit to Venezuela as grounds for petitioning for her freedom. Havana, January 20, 1865. 164

8-II. MAROONS AND PALENQUE DWELLERS 164

8.5. Account by Francisco (Pancho) Mina, captain of the maroons. Cayajabos, August 31, 1835. 164

8.6. Fugitives from the ingenio Santísima Trinidad. Guanajay, August 1837. 166

8.7. The inhabitants of El Cedro talk about palenque life. Santiago de Cuba, August 1838. 168

8.8. Alejandro Congo recounts his experiences as a maroon. Candelaria, August 21, 1844. 169

🌿 8-III. WAGING WAR, WINNING WAR 171

8.9. Insurrection on the coffee plantations of Matanzas. June 1825. 171

8.10. War in the lands of Mariel. Banes, August 13, 1833. 176

8.11. The terrifying rebellion on the ingenio El Triunvirato. Santa Ana, Matanzas, November 5, 1843. 180

8.12. An aborted general insurrection. Cimarrones, February 16, 1844. 187

NOTES 193   BIBLIOGRAPHY 205   INDEX 209

Foreword ADA FERRER

The translation of Gloria García Rodríguez's *Voices of the Enslaved in Nineteenth-Century Cuba: A Documentary History* (first published as *La esclavitud desde la esclavitud: La visión de los siervos* in Mexico in 1996 and then in Havana in 2003) marks an important moment in the scholarship on Cuban slavery. It provides for English-language readers the first substantial glimpse into the very rich — and still very underutilized — material on slavery available in Cuban archives: tomes and tomes of slave judicial testimony, hundreds of slave denunciations against their masters, and countless appeals to authorities for the recognition of rights theoretically guaranteed by law. García, who has done decades of archival research on Cuban slavery, has chosen these documents with care, organized them thematically, and then prefaced them with a pioneering essay on the history of Cuban slavery, one that draws on decades of her and others' scholarship but that also brings fresh insight garnered from her reading of the documents in the collection and undoubtedly of thousands more like them. The result is more than a comprehensive overview of slavery in Cuba and more than an assortment of revealing documents. It is rather a sophisticated and bold entrée into a whole world, little known in the United States and, to some extent, still little known in Cuba.

With fewer than a handful of exceptions, all the documents in the book are from the nineteenth century — that is, from the period during and following the entrenchment of a full-fledged system of large-scale plantation slavery intimately tied to the world economy. This transition was both gradual and brutal, impelled most dramatically by events both local and world historical. These included the opening of the slave trade to Spanish possessions beginning in 1789; the destruction of sugar production in Saint-Domingue as a result of the slave revolution that began there in 1791; the closing of the British and American slave trades in 1807 and 1808, respectively, which, rather than severing supplies of new Africans, redirected them to then burgeoning systems like Cuba's; and the building of Cuban railroads starting in 1837, which greatly increased the amount of land under cultivation, the tons of sugar produced, and the number of slaves consumed by the system.[1] It is from this period of large-scale, slave-based agriculture that the documents in this book are chosen. It is arguably the best-known period of Cuban slavery — treated in classic works of history and anthropology, from Fernando Ortiz's important works on the history of Afro-Cuban culture to Manuel Moreno Fraginals's path-breaking study of the Cuban sugar mill, first published in 1964 and presented to even wider audiences in reeditions of nineteenth-century Cuban literature as well as in important films such as *La ultima cena* (1976) and *El otro Francisco* (1975).

Yet the picture afforded us of that system by Gloria García's collection is new and fresh. She presents, as do these older works, a world that is populated by enslaved people who resist the system of slavery and violent masters and overseers who brutally enforce it. Thus her thematically organized chapters include extensive sections with documents on relations between slaves and their masters and overseers, on the physical violence of plantation owners and administrators, and on rebellions and maronnage among the enslaved. But García's collection richly documents other aspects of slavery as well. She includes, for instance, extensive material on the slave family and more generally on social relations among the enslaved.[2] Numerous documents provide evidence of freed slaves laboring and attempting to avail themselves of recourses promised by the law to free family members still enslaved. Other documents suggest networks of kin, ethnicity, and friendship that were mobilized on plantations to confront authorities or simply to lessen the burdens of enslavement. Many, thankfully, provide evidence of women's experience of slavery, from a group of slave women who cheer their male companions as they beat a particularly brutal overseer to the case of Florencia Rodríguez, who, facing certain sexual torture at the hands of her master, flees to Havana only to have her appeals to the governor rejected and to be returned to her master.

Aspects of García's depiction of plantation slavery may at first surprise North American students. For example, one theme that emerges clearly in the selection of documents is the sometimes significant level of physical mobility of rural slaves, who often appear in the documents traveling between plantations and between city, town, and countryside. Students might likewise be initially surprised to read about a vibrant and complex slave economy, in which slaves acted as proto-owners of provision grounds and as petty merchants, traders, and consumers who used their modest profits in pursuit of their or their loved ones' freedom. To reveal these understudied aspects of Cuban slavery is not to lessen the reality of domination but rather to suggest the ways in which the very demands of labor and production necessitated a kind of mobility and economic agency that could also serve slaves in their efforts to organize community and even at times to promote overt political resistance.³

Another important feature of the collection is García's attention to the intersection of slavery and the law, an area that is receiving renewed attention.⁴ She includes here some of the legal documents that in theory governed the purchase, holding, and treatment of slaves. At the same time, she includes numerous examples of the enslaved turning to and using the law in attempts to mount challenges to the slave system, from slaves' invocation of the free soil principle to denunciations of masters for illegal treatment to suits for family members' freedom to cases involving disputes over self-purchase. In fact, the enslaved's almost ever-present pursuit of freedom by various means is a strong current throughout the documents. But another strong current is one that emphasizes the perils and pitfalls of that pursuit. In one document, we see a slave winning a juridical appeal for freedom; in the next, a master violently flaunts his disregard of the law, boasting, for example, that to him the law and the Síndico mattered nothing. And alongside García's attention to legal avenues for freedom available to slaves is her equally significant attention to better-known extralegal avenues — from overt rebellion to quotidian forms of sabotage, physical attacks on plantation authorities, and group and individual cases of flight. By paying attention to legal as well as extralegal avenues taken by slaves and, importantly, to the unpredictable and inconsistent results of slaves' efforts, Garcia is able to lay bare both the purposeful initiatives of the enslaved and the violence of the system of slavery in nineteenth-century Cuba.

The guiding principle at work in the collection is a commitment to trying to recuperate — in a necessarily imperfect way — the voices, thoughts, and actions of the enslaved. Of course, García recognizes the difficulties inherent in that project. For example, in the judicial documents so amply reproduced in the volume, the words of the enslaved are recorded by scribes who paraphrase them in the third person, thus intervening in what was recorded, remembered, and now available to us as scholars and students. Similarly, the very format and requirements of legal petitions for freedom on various grounds also necessarily shaped the ways in which slaves narrated their own enslavement. García is not trying to give us an unmediated voice of the enslaved; she knows that is likely impossible. But she does succeed in laying before us a view of enslavement from within the confines of the plantation, in the process giving us a much fuller and richer picture of the interior world of Cuban slavery than any yet available.

NOTES

1. On this transition, the classic work is Manuel Moreno Fraginals, *El ingenio* (Havana: Editorial de Ciencas Sociales, 1978). An abridged translation was published as *The Sugarmill: The Socioeconomic Complex of Sugar in Cuba, 1760–1860*, trans. Cedric Belfrage (New York: Monthly Review Press, 1976). An important recent treatment of the transition can be found in Dale Tomich, *In the Prism of Slavery: Labor, Capital, and World Economy* (Lanham, Md.: Rowman and Littlefield, 2004); and Jorge Ibarra, *Marx y los historiadores ante la hacienda y la plantación esclavistas* (Havana: Ciencias Sociales, 2008).

2. These topics have become more visible within Cuban scholarship on slavery in recent years. See especially Aisnara Perera Díaz and María de los Angeles Meriño Fuentes, *Esclavitud, familia y parroquia en Cuba: Otra mirada desde la microhistoria* (Santiago: Editorial Oriente, 2006); María del Carmen Barcia, *La otra familia: Parientes, redes y descendencia de los esclavos en Cuba* (Havana: Casa de las Americas, 2003) and *Los Ilustres Apellidos: Negros en la Habana Colonial* (Havana: Ciencias Sociales, 2009); Manuel Barcia Paz, *Con el látigo y la ira: Legislación, represión y control en las plantaciones cubanas, 1790–1870* (Havana: Ciencias Sociales, 2000); and Manuel Barcia Paz, "Fighting with the Enemy's Weapons: The Usage of the Colonial Legal Framework by Nineteenth-Century Cuban Slaves," *Atlantic Studies* 3, no. 2 (2006): 159–81. Three important recent treatments published in the United States are Alejandro de la Fuente, "Slave Law and Claims-Making in Cuba: The Tannenbaum Debate Revisited," *Law and History Review* 22, no. 2 (2004): 339–69; de la Fuente, "Slaves and the Creation of Legal Rights in Cuba: Coartación and Papel," *Hispanic American Historical Review* 87, no. 4 (2007): 659–92; and María Elena Díaz, *The Virgin, the King, and the Royal Slaves of El Cobre: Negotiating Freedom in Colonial Cuba* (Stanford: Stanford University Press, 2002).

3. For a very effective development of this theme, see Aisha Finch, "Insurgency at the Crossroads: Cuban Slaves and the Conspiracy of La Escalera, 1841–1844," Ph.D. diss., New York University, 2007.

4. See especially the works of Alejandro de la Fuente, Manuel Barcia Paz, and María Elena Díaz cited in note 2.

Translator's Preface NANCY L. WESTRATE

I have translated many and varied things over the years: journal and magazine articles, books, all kinds of documents, even the résumé of a Chilean pig farmer. The level of difficulty in this translation far surpasses anything that I have ever done: the archaic Spanish, the syntax and sentence structure, the unfamiliar context, the sometimes impenetrable prose. Even I did not fully appreciate the degree of complexity of these documents until I had produced a few unsatisfactory English versions. This book is the end result of that long and arduous process.

Without realizing it, I have accrued a number of slavery-related credentials. I was probably most influenced by a course I took on slavery taught by Eric Wolf in the City University of New York many years ago. There we met and listened to Herbert Gutman, Sid Mintz, and Peter Worsley, among others. A fellow student introduced me to the shadowy world of Santería. Years later, my familiarity with slavery in Latin America served as an invaluable resource when I translated Arturo Warman's *Corn and Capitalism: How a Botanical Bastard Grew to Global Dominance*.

What intrigues me most about this translation process is not unusual words or obscure colloquial expressions or improbable usages but the social forces informing the events and occurrences related in the text. It is quite impossible for me to translate anything unless I have a firm grasp of the social context behind the printed page. I am an anthropologist by training, more a social historian than a linguist per se. I like to think that this, rather than any formal training I may have received, is the key to any good translation.

One linguistic issue tempered by social history was that of race. The documents specifically identified an individual slave by his name, and often his tribal affiliation and occupation, naming his owner and place of residence. They also provided the slave's racial designation. Those mixed-race slaves were referred to by the terms *pardo* or *parda* and their plural forms (brown, brownish-gray, gray, drab brown), *moreno* or *morena* and their plural forms (brown, black, dark brown, or mulatto), black or Negro (synonymous with slave), mulatto, colored, and so forth. At first, I attempted to find English-language equivalents: yellow, high yellow, quadroon, octoroon, darkie, or simply colored. However, in the course of perusing the documents, it became clear that in some documents moreno or pardo meant one thing, and in later documents the term meant something else. Alejandro de la Fuente pointed out that the use of racial designations in Cuba varied over the years, as reflected in various official census reports. In addition to this, and as anthropologists are well aware, neither self-reporting nor the subjective designations made by others (such as the scriveners taking testimony) were consistently reliable. For all these reasons and in the interest of historical accuracy, I ultimately decided to simply replicate the terms recorded in the original Spanish text. A somewhat similar process took place as I pondered the equivalents of various legal posts and administrative and civic positions. In almost all instances, I initially recurred to clumsy equivalents in English before I decided that the best course was to return to the original Spanish term. This collection is not meant as a definitive reference for serious researchers. They must recur to the original documents for that. But the use of the contemporary terms at least imparts a sense of time and place.

It is important to remember that the late eighteenth and nineteenth centuries were, in general, violent times. Whether slave or free menial labor, working conditions were harsh and punishment was meted out in a brutal and often preemptory manner. In the United States, the situation for free labor was far from enviable. The Lewis and Clark expedition, which set out to explore the far reaches of the Louisiana Purchase in the first years of the nineteenth century, provides some poignant examples. Expeditionary soldiers convicted of military offenses could be sentenced to hundreds of lashes over a period of days, lesser floggings, repeated runnings of the gauntlet, and even death. While all this was in considerable excess of the Spanish Crown's twenty-five-lash limit on floggings for slaves, it is not a legitimate source for comparison. Slaves were stripped of a constellation of freedoms governing all aspects of their lives. And as the documents demonstrate, many of the punishments they received far surpassed any putative legal restrictions and controls. The psychological state attaching to the mentality of many slave owners and their subordinates bordered on the pathological. One owner's attempts to insert a chastity belt into the flesh of his female slave or another's tolerance of slaves' maggot-infested wounds left to fester as the victims lay confined in a basement cell provides gruesome testimony to this effect. Many of the documents reproduced in the following pages stand out as profound examples of slaves' capacity to act on their own or other's behalf as they sought redress through the auspices of the local syndics and the courts. This they did in an environment where the threat of violence was hulking nearby in the person of their overseers, superintendents, and owners, ever present and sinister.

It is in this context that I forewarn readers that, as they delve into the documents, they will come upon terms and expressions that will seem an affront. Slavery as subject and object is an ugly, repugnant phenomenon. There are sections of this manuscript that are rife with demeaning treatment, outright torture, and degradation. That is the nature of subjecting one human being to the behest of another. The inclusion of gender-specific and racial terms was a deliberate choice: negro, negress, pickaninny, negrito, and boy, among others. I include English slave dialect to reflect the imperfect grasp many slaves had of Spanish in those instances where it is so represented in the original documents. This is not a political treatise and is unrelated to today's politically correct linguistic wars. Rather, it is a book of historical documents, and given the chance, I purposely used the less gentle terms in order to remain true to the times. My job is to bring the reader as close as possible to the pathos, the anguish, and the injustice of the times.

I am grateful to many people who contributed to the final version of this book. The staff of Duke University's Perkins Library, as always, offered superb information and advice, especially the Reference Department and the Circulation Department. Early in the process, Ada Ferrer readily responded to my inquiries. Later on, Teresita Martínez Vergne delved into the book's challenges with enthusiasm. I appreciated Alejandro de la Fuente's comments and his timely responses to my many questions. The book is a better piece of scholarship for his pointed criticisms and suggestions. Gloria García Rodríguez's intimate acquaintance with these documents proved invaluable in the final version of the manuscript. I would like to commend the patience and encouragement of my editor, Elaine Maisner. As she came to appreciate the true degree of difficulty of this particular translation, she endured the repeated postponements of the final manuscript with remarkable grace and good-natured patience.

Lastly, I am especially grateful to my mother-in-law, Zulima Degastaldi de De Luca. Zulima took on the unglamorous chore of following along in the original as I read an abbreviated, off-the-cuff Spanish retranslation of the English manuscript and verifying the gist of my translation. Every morning she asked with a smile, "When are we going to work on the book?"

On more than one occasion, she demonstrated a good deal more enthusiasm for that day's chore than I did. It is a rare eighty-five-year-old who remains so undaunted in the face of such a challenging task. In addition to her valuable contribution to the translation itself, Zulima tirelessly cooked, cleaned, did laundry, and tended my rather bereft husband and children so that I could work in an uninterrupted fashion. Heartfelt thanks, Zulima.

**Voices of the Enslaved
in Nineteenth-Century Cuba**

Introduction

Only infrequently do we ourselves have the occasion to listen firsthand to the voices of slaves. In both contemporary and historical literature, the slave voices we routinely hear have been distorted, mediated. We have depended on others, on persons who have never been slaves themselves, to discern these slave voices and to speak on the slaves' behalf. Acting out of benevolent concern, these interpreters produce slave voices that serve either to exemplify authentic cases of social iniquity or to embody the interests of an omnipotent mercantilism. The slave voices they hear are object rather than subject. These voices are of slaves incapable of apprehending the reality in which they live, of slaves unable to cope with life's challenges. More than a result, slaves are a product of the interaction of counterpoised forces. The history of slave societies is presented in terms of decisive and almost single-handed actions on the part of the planter class, while slaves respond to this dominant dynamic with mere token resistance, intermittent and spontaneous outbreaks of rage, or desperate and ill-fated rebellions.

There are numerous obstacles to overcome in the historical analysis of the initiatives taken by American subaltern classes in general and by slaves in particular. How can we approach the motivations, the ideas, and the feelings that informed the day-to-day existence of these men and women, reduced as they were to the most brutal class of persecution? The clues allowing for the reconstruction of that belief system are few. There was little concern with compiling such testimonials in Cuba. Autobiographies do not exist. What family correspondence there may have been remains undiscovered. Nevertheless, there are numerous court proceedings in which slaves figure as witnesses, defendants, petitioners, or advocates. There are letters written by slaves to the island's governor, demanding their rights or alleging abuse and injustice. These documents are unusually accurate in revealing their subjects' intents. So much so, that this process in and of itself calls out for further scientific inquiry.

Most slaves were illiterate. Those friends or family members who were free were scarcely any better off in this respect than their less fortunate compatriots. Court cases could not be taken at face value, given the potentially activist role that notary publics who prepared the documents were in a position to play. Notaries could stylistically alter the form and content of any testimony they took, distorting, interpreting, or reconstructing the accounts. Nevertheless, and even allowing for probable inaccuracies or deliberate misrepresentations intended to conceal more than they revealed, the slaves' real world somehow relentlessly emerged.

The claims transcribed here allow us to appreciate a new facet of slavery. They aptly demonstrate forms of resistance available within the existing legal system. Systematically pursuing redress in the courts is far less spectacular than seeking a safe haven in a *palenque* (remote fugitive slave settlements with a defensive stockade around the perimeter) and less public than *cimarronería* (the fugitive slave phenomenon). However, seeking legal recourse remains an equally significant alternative in slaves' tenacious, fundamental, resolute struggle to surmount injustice in their everyday life. Rebecca J. Scott, for one, makes use of these documents in order to demonstrate the key role of the apprenticeship system in the final years of slavery, which led to the ultimate demise of the entire system. Resorting to legal means is not limited to the years immediately before abolition. The large collection of claims in the Archivo Nacional de Cuba (Cuban National Archive, or ANC) illustrates, on the contrary, that legal recourse and strategies associated with this practice are just one part of a larger long-term trend. The bulk of these documents cover the golden age of slavery and the period leading up to its final debacle, the period from 1820 until slavery's dying days in 1886. Cases from the late eighteenth and early nineteenth century also survive, although they are relatively few in number.

Through these writings, it is possible to appreciate more fully the arsenal of resources and arguments that the slaves themselves and their families, friends, and advocates make use of in order to improve their living and working conditions, to gain even the conditional freedom of *coartación* (slaves' legal right to be appraised for a fixed value and to pay down their balance over time until they are free), or even to attain manumission itself, a status realized only by some and longed for by all.

Recourse to effective legal action reveals the contemporary social and psychological profile of slaves who have such legal documents drawn up. These official depositions, petitions, and suits faithfully reflect an impeccable sense of individuality, qualities of personal dignity issuing from the claims for their inalienable rights, and a determination to maintain family ties. The family — even in the face of threats of its imminent demise — is shown to be an institution whose very existence and continuity are stubbornly affirmed, even under the most dissimilar and tentative circumstances. Such cases help us assess why the relentless attempts to commodify slaves fall far short of their objective. On the contrary, the documents reflect the spiritual world and code of conduct of individuals who, acutely aware of their subordinate status and vulnerability, remain determined to maintain and expand their human dimension.

Another aspect of these writings is the invaluable information they supply concerning the enforcement of laws that bestow an ensemble of rights — limited but significant, nonetheless — pertaining to slaves. A colonial legal structure is superimposed on a preexisting medieval legal system, expanding its original scope. Such is the case with coartación, which in the mid-nineteenth century incorporated aspects that were almost certainly the result of social confrontation historiography has yet to address.

The rule of established law, on the other hand, is a reflection of colonial policy toward slaves and free blacks. The attitudes, favorable or unfavorable, toward the claims presented here clearly illustrated an evolution in the treatment of problems related to slavery at diverse historical moments by successive colonial governor generals. Local syndics, the legal advocates officially charged with acting in the best interests of the slaves, conspicuously figure in these proceedings. They necessarily must be familiar with court proceedings involving slaves and be capable of rendering initial decisions as to the merits of individual cases. Prominent persons typically fill these positions — José Morales Lemus and Nicolás Azcarate, among others. Both the legal precedents and judicial proceedings to which they recur serve to illustrate the behavior of a nucleus of intellectuals who play a decisive role in the political history of the island.

Each and every case brings the reader closer to the daily lives of slaves, lives subject to subtleties that are both more dreadful and more lavish than we customarily assume. The documents, letters, and the records of judicial proceedings reproduced in this book allow us to penetrate the inner workings of the slave system in greater depth and detail from a unique perspective. Even now, the documents reposing in Havana's historical archives patiently await a more systematic examination.

The Growing Hegemony of the Plantation

Slavery in Cuba was a social institution of long standing. The concurrent presence of large-scale production of export crops and a servile labor force to produce them was no happy coincidence. Rather, these two elements were indispensable for a crucial sector of the island's productive system dating from the sixteenth century. From the colony's earliest days, large numbers of slaves herded cattle and tanned leather. Those products became important commodities that were the source of foreign exchange in this initial period. Slaves produced sugar in primitive *trapiches* (sugar mills), and slave labor likewise played a substantial role in tobacco production. Over the centuries, the comparative import of each of these products shifted in their relative share of foreign exchange, but export trade and slave labor persisted as essential characteristics defining the essence of the colony's productive scaffolding.

Meanwhile, slave labor insinuated itself into more and more areas. The daily provisioning of cities and domestic commerce depended, in good part, on slaves working as muleteers, hucksters, small craftsmen, or in any of the myriad marine and port-related tasks. Their labor fueled the distribution network linking producers and consumers. In cities as well as in the countryside, the slave as a social type was firmly ensconced as a productive force, supplying the widest-ranging services, and to the same extent was the almost-exclusive source of domestic laborers. Despite slaves' crucial role in colonial life and demographic significance, it was not until the late eighteenth century that slavery was particularly prominent, becoming the most dynamic factor in the development of *criollo* (Cuban-born) society.

Around 1770 or 1780, this development already was discernible, and there was a growing awareness of such a trend. At that time the export economy became firmly established, and it subjected the island to a rhythm of rapid expansion. Concomitantly, the number of slaves associated with those activities rapidly and inexorably increased. Both of these developments conferred an entirely new quality on the former integral elements of colonial society. Suddenly, the transformative impact of those elements was subjected to new, adverse circumstances. That impact affected all colonial social forces and, despite the obstacles to regular and sustained access to foreign trade, prompted those forces to move in that direction thanks to the diffusion of mercantile relations. Cautious liberalization of commerce between the metropole and its American colonies encouraged Cuba's mercantile trade, both domestic and foreign. The Antilles had especially benefited from various concessions. The Regulation of 1765 opened island markets to the entire Iberian Peninsula. Up until that time, all trade was restricted to the port of Cádiz.

The immediate consequence of those measures for Cuba was the increase in the number of embarkations from Havana, the island's only authorized port. Commercial traffic became regularized. Products now were exported on a more reliable timetable and in greater volumes. The legislation still fell short of the expectations of Cuban exporters. They believed that the colony possessed all the necessary conditions and resources to enable it to become fully integrated into the more widespread commercial traffic that had begun to reach critical mass in western Europe. To accomplish such integration required only two things: a more liberal trade policy that facilitated contact with those expanding markets and, especially, more workers to increase production. These requests constituted the principle demands of the powerful group of landowners who were in the forefront of the changes coming to the island at century's end. In this moment of remarkable articulation, the interests of the metropole and the demands of producers converged to remove whatever impediments there were to the transformation of Cuba into a major exporter. It also explained the speed and depth with which the transformation process took place.

Free trade legislation promulgated in 1765, in 1778, and yet again in subsequent years promoted such an evolution. This process already was well underway in the island's agrarian sector. At the heart of this process was the restructuring of rural holdings. This rural shake-up involved the subdivision of large landholdings that were a carryover from livestock's dominance of the economy earlier in the century.[1] The insatiable European appetite for colonial goods mobilized colonial reserves, provoking a reorganization of the elements of its entire economic system.

Because *haciendas* (large rural estates) monopolized the vast majority of arable land in this initial productive period, the only way that new forms of agrarian production could be established was by displacing the reigning hacienda system. Haciendas were broken up into smaller parcels of a thousand acres or more in order to establish *ingenios* (sugarcane plantation and processing complexes) and *cafetales* (coffee plantation and processing complexes). This did not exactly portend the imminent demise of large rural properties. It was, first and foremost, a socioeconomic transformation of its constituent elements. While the total acreage of ingenios and cafetals constituted a mere shadow of the former livestock-driven haciendas, those operations, nevertheless, came to dominate the surrounding countryside. Due to the hacienda's economic clout, it became the prototype of the large rural holding. The subdivision of lands strengthened the hand of landowners, catalysts of change, because they still controlled large, fertile, well-situated agricultural extensions. Those holdings, while smaller than the livestock enterprises, were more productive and generated even greater incomes for their owners, who continued to occupy their traditionally dominant position by new means. Since 1780, the number of ingenios, cafetals, and tobacco operations — excluding, for now, other farms unrelated to export trade — rapidly expanded into separate tracts of arable land on the western end of the island. The centers of this growth, although stronger in those areas bordering the colonial capital, were not limited to it. In the south-central part of the island, specifically in Trinidad, another enclave would develop on the fertile plane in what later came to be known as the Valley of the Ingenios. The area ringing the port city of Santiago de Cuba, in a band extending beyond the mountainous cloister of that city, farther east — toward Guantánamo — and the formerly wild reaches northward, were dotted with ingenios and cafetals.

From 1770 to 1810, the pronounced increase in the export of sugar, tobacco, and coffee initiated a new stage in Cuba's colonial economy. All that growth in the island's export sector coincided with the demise of the role of Saint-Domingue (modern Haiti) in the world export economy. Not only were new lands brought under cultivation, but also the exploitation of these properties was now for intensive agricultural production rather than extensive livestock production. The technical aspects of the production of sugar, coffee, or tobacco for consumption were still relatively primitive, not demanding a highly trained labor force. Essentially, the greater volume of production resulted from expanding the area under cultivation and working it with a growing number of agricultural workers.

The issue of the availability of a regular supply of labor became a key problem in keeping pace with Cuba's transformation. *Hacendados* (hacienda owners) concentrated on ensuring a steady supply of workers to apply to the production process en masse. The number of those laborers had to be readily renewable over the short term as a logical consequence of their labor-intensive role. The importation of workers had to be rapid and allow for the exploitation of the favorable economic climate without unwarranted delay. Francisco de Arango y Parreño, knowledgeable spokesman for a powerful group of hacendados, clearly articulated the quandary of the times: in order to assure an adequate supply of labor, was it preferable to depend on the servile population's natural reproductive pace or to bring in additional laborers where they were most sorely needed?[2] The obvious formula for success was "wealth equals slaves." One only needed to contemplate the palpable growth of the Caribbean colonies belonging to England and France in order to become convinced that such a formula would guarantee the successful expansion of the sugar and coffee production and accelerate the profit rates they so fervently sought.

The struggle to remove that obstacle particular to the commercial system focused on those mechanisms regulating the supply of labor. A search for a massive wave of cheap labor was underway, seeking enough workers to fulfill the demands of an increasingly intensive labor regimen in regions recently incorporated into agricultural production. The island's new economy was underwritten by the inclusion of previously unexploited regions that had easy access to roads and ports. Sugar, coffee, and tobacco easily dislodged the old livestock-based economy that previously dominated the island's rural landscape.

Slaves and More Slaves

Up until 1789, when the slave trade was deregulated, the Crown controlled the commerce in slaves by awarding contracts to suppliers from Spain and elsewhere. Such tight control adversely affected the labor supply, and *colonos* (sugar planters, large and small producers alike) complained of chronic labor shortages. Eliminating such barriers assumed that the means existed to increase the number of laborers and to dependably acquire replacement workers at regular intervals. With this incentive, determined producers waged a fierce battle with the metropole for the deregulation and removal of trade barriers standing in the way of their objectives.[3]

By 1775, if we consider the number of agricultural units and the array of activities utilizing slave labor, the situation in Cuba seemed to support producers' arguments. Although new slave shipments arrived regularly every six months, their numbers were barely adequate to cover replacement purposes. Such paucity in numbers meant that the opening up of any additional new acreage to production was simply out of the question. Before 1790, no more than twenty-five hundred slaves a year were imported, a figure woefully inadequate to serve the entire colony's needs. After deregulation, supply improved significantly and from then on was interrupted or contracted only occasionally as a vagary of any of the several wars between European powers that flared up over this period.

Table 1 illustrates trends in the supply of slaves over nine five-year periods, both before and after liberalization of the transatlantic slave trade. Over the three five-year periods before 1789, as many as 34,000 slaves were imported. In the three five-year periods after that date, the growth rate exploded. Nearly 98,000 slaves entered Cuba between 1790 and 1804, and almost 159,000 more over the following three five-year periods. In addition to these direct purchases, the tally had to be adjusted to account for the contraband slave trade with other Caribbean islands and also for the arrival of immigrants from Saint-Domingue. Some of those colonos were able to flee that island and seek refuge in Cuba, bringing their slaves with them.

A similar migratory wave came from the sale of slaves from Louisiana and Florida. Later, the Latin American wars of independence also prompted an influx of another indeterminate amount of servile labor to the island. Although the lack of hard data made it difficult to quantify the impact of these immigrants on the island's population with any precision, anecdotal and other references seemed to confirm that their numbers were appreciable. While not a part of the licit slave trade, the numbers of blacks coming to the island by other, less apparent routes should not be underestimated.

The conclusion of the 1817 treaty that abolished the transatlantic slave trade—effective in 1820—did not mean an end to the trade itself. The planters continued to enjoy a regular supply of slaves and, in many cases, even experienced an increase in their labor supply, although at somewhat higher costs. For decades after the end of the legal traffic in slaves, blacks continued to arrive in Cuba.

Between 1820 and 1829, estimates put the number of black slaves arriving in Cuba at 68,388, at 110,446 over the subsequent ten years, and at no less than 60,000 between 1840 and 1849.[4] The tentative nature of these figures, estimates based on figures of known contraband, lead us to believe that the actual number of smuggled slaves was much higher. The striking growth of Cuba's export market over the same period supports suppositions of an ongoing, flourishing black market in slaves. There are records of the seizure of contraband Africans off the Cuban coast as late as 1870.[5]

The impact of such a migratory torrent had a tremendous effect on the island's demographic trends. Those responded to Cuba's new productive system, which now was subject to the fluctuations of an international market. That productive system favored the importation of able-bodied adult slaves, preferably men, available to begin to work immediately in an agricultural setting subject to seasonal adjustments in the application of labor. Such a productive system favoring adult men predictably resulted in a sexually asymmetrical population on the island. For decades, such a situation

TABLE 1. Known Figures on Importation of Slaves, 1775–1819

Year	Total per 5-Year Period	Yearly Mean
1775–79	11,970	2,394
1780–84	9,847	1,969
1785–89	12,068	2,414
1790–94	32,713	6,543
1795–99	24,238	4,848
1800–1804	40,650	8,130
1805–09	16,519	3,304
1810–14	31,308	6,262
1815–19	111,146	22,229
TOTAL	290,459	6,455

Source: Statistical appendix in Instituto de Historia de Cuba, *Historia de Cuba*, vol. 1, 472–73.

prevailed in cities and was the preferred circumstance on rural properties. Just as predictably, this scenario created obstacles to normal cycles of the reproduction of the island population.

The demographics of Cuba's slave system experienced changes over the course of the years. After 1825, planters tried to compensate for the disproportionately male slave population by acquiring more female slaves and, somewhat later, by improving living conditions for slaves—even in those areas where slave birthrates did not warrant it. The results were marginal at best. None of these measures had the effect of stabilizing the servile population living within a structure subjecting them to extremely high mortality rates. The birthrates of slaves in Cuba never approached those in the southern United States, where the slave population reproduced itself without recourse to the periodic importations of new slaves. That phenomenon in the American South was the lone exception among the ensemble of American slave-holding societies.

The island's population continued to be overwhelmingly male, and that sexual asymmetry was to become even more pronounced. Around 1850, as part of a search for alternatives to slave labor, agents contracted free labor from Spain and also imported Yucatecans and Chinese colonos. Those contingents of workers were almost always exclusively male.[6]

The most lasting effect of such demographic trends was, nevertheless, the rapid change of the social composition of the island's population. Even though slaves had constituted a substantial segment of the colony's popu-

TABLE 2. Total Resident Population according to Racial Categories, 1775–1862

Year	Population Totals	Per 100 Inhabitants			
		Whites	Chinese and Yucatecans	Free Population	Slaves
1775	171,652	56	—	18	26
1817	553,033	43	—	21	36
1827	704,487	44	—	15	41
1846	898,752	47	—	17	36
1862	1,359,238	54	3	16	27

Source: Population censuses.

lation for centuries, their incidence in the island's overall population did not seem to have reached an overly high proportion. At the time of the first census, slaves represented only some 26 percent of Cuba's inhabitants. Gradually, over the course of successive five-year periods, that situation shifted in favor of the slaves. Between 1817 and 1841, Cuba's servile population grew at an accelerated rate and went on to constitute something more than one-third of the island's total population (table 2).

The overall figures, underscoring the surge in a slave population that increased at a relentless pace, obscured the unequal regional distribution of that phenomenon. In areas where commercial agriculture had become entrenched, the proportion of slaves was much higher than in those areas where the former economic system endured. This trend appeared early on. In Güines around 1813, for example, there were forty-seven whites, four free blacks and mulattoes, and forty-nine slaves per one hundred inhabitants.[7] Five years later, in wide swaths to the east, west, and south of Havana, sugar and coffee cultivation came to saturate the area with slaves. The situation was comparable in Trinidad and in the regions surrounding Santiago de Cuba and Guantánamo located in the far eastern section of the island.

The magnitude of this social transformation prompted the appearance of entirely new enclaves that included almost no free population whatsoever. This was exactly what occurred around 1817 in the ten districts located in the sugarcane and coffee regions surrounding Havana, which were expanding rapidly at that time (see table 3). Slaves easily made up 50 percent of that population as a whole.

It came as no surprise that, where the sociodemographic structure possessed those characteristics, slavery imprinted some specific practices on all aspects of local social life. That came about primarily because a pre-

TABLE 3. Slaves per 100 Inhabitants in the Greater Havana Area

Districts	Number of Slaves per 100 Inhabitants
Cayajabos	81
Batabanó	73
Aguacate	72
Guayabal	70
Bahía Honda	68
Mariel	65
San Antonio	64
Puerta de Güira	63
Madruga	63
Alquízar	62

Source: Census of 1817 in ANC, *Donativos y Remisiones*, 357/1.

requisite for the new agricultural system was a creation of a substantial permanent nucleus of labor as compared to the meager labor requirements typical of other types of agricultural regimens. The most prominent characteristic of the new system was the tendency for intensive labor practices, rather than the previously extensive work force, radically modifying the rural population. The increase in the number of inhabitants, however, did not depend on the normal process of reproduction, not even in previously settled areas. On the contrary, operations dependent on slave labor appeared as specific types of settlements springing up out of nowhere on newly cleared lands or competing with older, less stable settlements.

The Sociodemographic Impact of the Plantation

The ingenio and cafetal were part of a colonization process that, unlike others, concentrated a relatively large number of workers within the limited confines of a medium-sized farm. Compared with primitive livestock ventures or small farms, the new enterprises had a population density that made them unique among other colonial agrarian operations. Around 1800, that settlement pattern energized the economic and social evolution of the western part of the island.

At that time, out of 213 ingenios for which records exist, 40 percent had more than ninety workers, both slave and free, living on the farm on a more or less permanent basis.

TABLE 4. Distribution of Slave and Free Labor on Western Ingenios in the Vicinity of Havana in Western Cuba, 1800

Laborers	Number of Ingenios	Total Laborers
0–30	43	757
31–60	42	1,873
61–90	41	3,197
91–150	63	7,463
151–250	22	4,227
251 and above	2	706
TOTAL	213	18,223

Source: Population censuses.

Slaves overwhelmingly made up the bulk of the workers on these farms, and more than 60 percent of them lived together in large groups of between ninety and three hundred persons.[8] Taking into account that in 1800 there were more than 400 ingenios in the region, one could appreciate the social impact of this forced colonization. On many occasions, the ingenio, possessing a larger population and greater resources, compared favorably to some squalid neighboring towns (table 4).

Those farms, whose settlement pattern was later to be mimicked by cafetals, popped up one after the other and came to cover a wide geographic area only recently opened to commercial agriculture. It was common for three or four ingenios to appear on the perimeter of a former cattle ranch, separated only by woodlands that served as their reserve productive acreage. That was why, in this type of region, population density could not be calculated on the basis of numbers within the boundaries of one isolated plantation. Plantations tended to cluster together, and population figures, such as in the case of the ten districts in table 3, reflected an almost absolute predominance of slaves, even in those areas that had been settled previously.

In this way, the sugar and coffee enterprises imposed their particular sociodemographic structure, characterized by a small nucleus of free settlers within a large mass of slaves in the surrounding area. By 1800, this organizational model had taken shape and, with few if any changes, endured over the course of the century.

A high proportion of free laborers appears in the first two categories of ingenios in table 5 because they represented recently established enterprises. It was customary in such operations to entrust clearing the land

TABLE 5. Slave and Free Labor on Ingenios in Güines and Managua, 1800

Laborers	Number of Ingenios	Free	Slaves	% Free Laborers
0–29	9	23	147	15.6
30–60	10	30	412	7.2
61–90	21	63	1,516	4.1
91–150	18	72	2,035	3.5
151–250	8	41	1,518	2.7
TOTAL	66	229	5,628	4

Source: Population censuses.

and construction of facilities to free labor specifically contracted for those tasks. The rest of the table clearly shows a pattern of settlement specific to plantations and the social effects that this type of colonization had on the colony.

What made the plantation unique as an agricultural operation was something other than its extensive acreage, or the markets for its products, or the primary crop to which it was dedicated. The cluster of such particular inseparable characteristics reflected the specific mode of social organization for the production of each commodity. In addition, the social nexuses linking their human components transcended productive relations, given that stable coexistence presupposed the realization of activities that go far beyond that sphere.[9]

The fact that the plantation was a social institution more than anything else explained its capacity to reorder the communities within its sphere and to reshape and integrate them as parts of its functional mechanism. When the plantation attracted free settlers to carry out specialized labor or administration, it subjected them to its own norms and hierarchical principles. A plantation region was a microcosm, crisscrossed by a multitude of ties that united its segments, and it was not conceivable to analyze any single one of those segments in isolation.

There was an ebb and flow of population as former settlers were displaced by concentrations of laborers, slave and free, and new social relations associated with plantation economies became established in the surrounding area. Plantations could well attract the services of a certain number of salaried laborers from neighboring population centers. They could also have precisely the opposite effect, because the social practices deriving from relations of servitude penetrated well into the surrounding areas, insinuating themselves into every aspect of community life. Although those negative effects have yet to be studied, indicators of that perverse evolution left their mark on contemporary testimonials. Free laborers, especially blacks and mulattoes, frequently protested their treatment. They complained of the strong tendency for them to be subject to the same handling as slaves in terms of their social treatment — including physical punishment. This was perhaps the best indicator of the negative influence of the plantation on free workers and townsfolk. Likewise, it was one of the most powerful factors pushing the free population of color toward the cities or toward areas where slave-driven enterprises had yet to appear.

In the 1820s and 1830s, fewer and fewer areas in the western part of the island were left untouched by plantation life. By that time, the number of plantations had multiplied to such an extent that they almost completely blanketed the present-day province of Havana and the eastern part of Pinar del Río. Toward the east, plantations had begun carpeting Matanzas Province. A document prepared by the Church on the payment of tithes illustrated that incredible expansion for the period from 1804 to 1834.[10] Growth was marked by all the characteristics first seen in its early development in the late eighteenth century. Although the document was incomplete, the geography of the plantation showed a considerable degree of concentration of the slave population on the ingenios and cafetals of the diocese. Unlike the data presented in table 4, this document did not include free laborers in its count of workers.

The increase of sugar and coffee plantations was associated with the growing number of hired labor on each type of establishment. Those with fewer than sixty slaves were recently established operations, as in the case of all the sugar ingenios. Table 6 summarizes the available legible data from each plantation in order to compare these results with those from 1800.

At the beginning of the century, slaves lived on *fincas* (rural agricultural estates) on which a relatively large number of people already resided. At that time, nearly 68 percent of slaves lived on sugar establishments comprising more than ninety persons. Around 1830, the percentage of slaves living on ingenios rose to 74 percent. In any case, more than half of table 6 shows small communities of approximately 100 or more inhabitants. If free workers, whose numbers were small in any case, were added to that figure, it would be evident that the plantation was, in and of itself, a colonizing vehicle of the first magnitude, structuring a social order superimposed on a productive foundation that completely changed the rural space of entire regions.

Two fundamentally dissimilar bases prompted those demographic trends.

TABLE 6. Slave Labor on Farms in Western and Central Cuba, 1834

Personnel	Ingenios	Slaves	Cafetales	Slaves	Total Fincas	Total Slaves
0–30	102	1,601	604	8,941	706	10,542
31–60	100	4,959	231	10,419	331	15,378
61–90	78	6,018	89	6,732	167	12,750
91–150	124	14,743	79	8,948	200	23,691
151–250	70	13,792	22	4,237	92	18,029
250 plus	22	7,400	2	558	24	7,958
TOTAL	496	48,513	1,024	39,835	1,520	88,348

Source: ANC, *Miscelánea de Expedientes*, 3772/Añ.

One responded directly to a productive process and had to be replenished annually. The other organized the social reproduction of the people living on those establishments.

The Plantation Community

The historian Moreno Fraginals left us a very precise description of the sugar plantation as an economic mechanism.[11] The productive aspect alone did not address the many thorny issues associated with this phenomenon. As far as the sugar planter was concerned, the plantation existed essentially as a business enterprise, and his actions and decisions responded to that consideration. The ensemble of relations between master and slave — just as those between the slaves and the free hired help who also lived there — was structured around an economic base, responding to production needs. The realization of this primary objective could not be separated from other determining factors through which that interest materialized. That is, the normal development of activities specific to the cafetal or the ingenio assumed a satisfactory interrelation between the human components that carried out those activities.

The daily routine on both the ingenio and the cafetal depended on such a delicate equilibrium and not simply on blind obedience to the owner. Contemporary descriptions were overwhelmingly one-sided and distorted in that matter. Even appeals to violence were limited for fear of affecting the uneasy coexistence of the different sectors on the plantation. The owner had at his disposal only a limited set of devices to maintain an atmosphere

TABLE 7. Geographic Distribution of Plantations: Ingenios and Cafetales in the Diocese of Havana and Their Slave Labor

Parishes & Districts	Ingenios Established before 1804	Slaves	New Ingenios
Artemisa	—	—	3
Bahía Honda	—	—	7
Cabañas	10	1,642	1
Cayajabos	11	1,965	2
Guanacaje	—	—	1
Guanajay	13	2,229	—
Guayabal	8	468	—
Mariel	5	770	2
Puerta de Güira	3	484	—
Quiebrahacha	13	2,341	—
San Diego de Núñez	—	—	16
Santa Cruz de los Pinos	—	—	—
PINAR AREA	63	9,899	32
Alacranes	—	—	20
Alquízar	1	150	—
Bainoa	2	280	—
Batabanó	8	614	3
Bejucal	3	226	—
Ceiba del Agua	2	120	—
El Cano	—	—	—
El Corralillo	5	890	2
Guanabacoa	8	793	—
Guanabo	9	1,403	—
Guara	8	622	5
Guatao	—	—	1
Güines	20	1,735	2
Güira de Melena	8	1,290	—
Jaruco	3	363	—
La Catalilna	5	612	3
La Salud	1	300	—
Madruga	7	1,236	2
Managua	4	259	—
Nueva Paz y Bagáez	—	—	9
Pipián	1	161	4

Slaves	Cafetales	Slaves	Total Fincas	Total Slaves
486	39	2,535	42	3,021
746	13	215	20	961
100	—	—	11	1,742
171	73	3,071	86	5,207
100	29	2,072	30	2,172
—	29	1,391	42	3,620
—	54	631	62	1,099
340	5	170	12	1,280
—	57	3,088	60	3,572
—	—	—	13	2,341
3,300	33	434	49	3,734
—	13	292	13	292
5,243	345	13,899	440	29,041
741	16	231	36	972
—	117	5,993	118	6,143
—	6	Illegible	8	Illegible
230	20	1,005	31	1,849
—	7	—	10	331
—	28	—	30	1,598
—	2	—	2	21
86	3	—	10	1,039
—	1	—	9	853
—	2	—	11	1,491
364	15	—	28	1,475
60	8	—	9	483
68	16	—	38	2,222
—	67	—	75	6,468
—	5	—	8	487
397	—	—	8	1,009
—	12	—	13	960
380	7	—	16	2,109
—	7	—	11	550
559	13	—	12	909
228	9	221	14	610

TABLE 7 (continued)

Parishes & Districts	Ingenios Established before 1804	Slaves	New Ingenios
Quivicán	4	350	1
San Antonio Abad	—	—	—
San Antonio de las Vegas	10	1,015	—
San José de las Lajas	10	1,062	—
San Martías de Río Blanco	3	810	—
Santa María del Rosario	1	70	—
Santiago de las Vegas	2	199	—
Tapaste	6	464	—
Vereda Nuevas	—	—	—
Wajay	1	88	—
HAVANA AREA	132	15,112	52
Cabezas	—	—	19
Camarioca	—	—	10
Ceiba Mocha	7	553	4
Corral Nuevo	9	1,438	2
Guamacaro	—	—	24
Guamutas	—	—	11
Lagunillas	—	—	15
Macurijes	—	—	37
Matanzas	2	157	1
Sabanilla	—	—	19
Santa Ana	6	462	19
MATANZAS AREA	24	2,610	161
Barajagua	1	14	—
Ceja de Pablo	—	—	1
Jagua (Cienfuegos)	2	156	3
Palmarejo	1	400	14
Sancti Spiritus	2	53	—
Trinidad	22	3,016	11
Villa Clara	8	56	22
CENTRAL AREA	36	3,695	51
TOTAL	255	31,316	296

Source: ANC, *Miscelánea de Expedientes*, 3772/Añ.

Slaves	Cafetales	Slaves	Total Fincas	Total Slaves
142	35	1,875	40	2,367
—	22	835	22	835
—	3	280	13	1,295
—	20	813	30	1,875
—	1	30	4	840
—	4	70	5	140
—	8	315	10	514
—	16	Illegible	22	Illegible
—	7	114	7	114
—	6	294	7	382
3,255	483	22,318	667	40,685
957	14	388	33	1,345
705	31	670	41	1,375
259	19	685	30	1,497
511	2	16	13	1,965
2,063	85	2,448	109	4,511
1,000	24	216	35	1,216
1,390	—	—	15	1,390
3,055	43	1,058	80	4,113
20	2	6	5	183
2,621	—	—	19	2,621
1,466	19	300	44	2,228
14,047	239	5,787	424	22,444
—	—	—	1	14
140	2	16	3	156
303	—	—	5	459
2,237	—	—	15	2,637
—	—	—	2	53
665	12	404	45	4,085
181	—	—	30	237
3,526	14	420	101	7,641
26,071	1,081	42,424	1,632	99,811

that facilitated production. Even then, he often was faced with volatile situations which demanded highly flexible conduct on his part.

An incident involving the Count de la Fernandina in June 1844 effectively illustrates the daily realities of plantation life. While visiting a tract in San Diego de los Baños, the count came upon a conflict that had flared up between his partner and administrator, Pedro González, and a slave crew of ten women and twenty-two men. Lined up before their master in order to air grievances, a time-honored tradition, they objected to the new administrator's policy of forcing them to spend the night under lock and key. The women also complained that their children frequently died because González did not take "good care of their sons and daughters."

In the face of such protests, the planter's attitude reflected a reaction typical of those of his social class:

> . . . as due deference from my servitors, I reminded my slaves that they must obey blindly whatever the administrator ordered them to do, and that I would speak with him about those issues. This was the typical strategy used by farmers before addressing the repeated complaints of slaves, buying [the master] a little time to inquire into whether such grievances were justified or baseless. As soon as the slaves left and I was alone with González, I attempted to minimize the effect that I knew those accusations had made on him, fearing that he would harbor a grudge against his accusers. I reminded him that those wretched slaves had no other consolation [in life] than grumbling to their masters, and that any disciplinary measure, such as forcing them to spend the night enclosed in the barracks, a new restriction to which they were entirely unaccustomed, had to be introduced gradually and using a great amount of discretion . . .[12]

The master and administrator expected that a submissive slave crew would placidly await the owner's decision and, as a result of the master's compassion, their treatment probably would improve. But the slaves were determined to have their demands met no matter what. They sought redress through the intervention of a third party to serve as an advocate on their behalf and went out to an adjoining tobacco field belonging to the count.

The master, by this time visibly irritated, scolded them and demanded that they obey the administrator and peremptorily ordered them "back to work." Nevertheless, that night the slaves refused to sleep in the barracks. Informed of this turn of events, and unable to contradict González's policy "in order [to maintain] . . . intact the chain of command absolutely necessary on the farms," the count ordered the administrator to compel the slaves to obey his command. From the count's standpoint, the slaves' attitudes were "highly pretentious, their ignorance leading them to believe that they [would] get their own way."

The administrator, frustrated once again and feeling himself to be the object of ridicule, assailed the unarmed slaves, and the incident ended in disaster: three slaves dead at the hand of the administrator or one of his sons, four more lynched, and several more wounded.[13]

This incident faithfully reflected the complex nature of decision making that was necessary at every level in order to maintain a stable equilibrium of opposing forces. On the one hand, it was necessary to preserve the authority of the master himself and that of his surrogates, the hired help, even if the means they were forced to use were improvised or inadequate. On the other hand, the slaves clearly were anything but docile. Almost without exception, they openly protested without fear of repercussions or even death in order to defend what they considered to be their rights, limited as though those might be. The fact that the final result of the confrontation was ill fated did not diminish their demonstrated capacity to take the initiative. In spite of the deaths and punishments meted out to the slaves, the outcome was not encouraging for the count, either. The partnership with González was dissolved, work was disrupted during the investigation, and especially the deaths of seven slaves represented a considerable financial loss.

Although we do not know how such an incident might have affected the subsequent treatment of slaves on the farm, other similar cases over the years suggest that in some way the demands of the slaves were taken into account.

The collection of documents transcribed here provides unmistakable evidence that treatment within the confines of a particular plantation somehow has to accommodate the outcomes of these periodic confrontations, although it is virtually impossible to determine the exact extent of such accommodations retrospectively.

It was in the owners' best interests to seriously consider anything and everything related to the complicated management of their slave crews. Failure to do so effectively entailed a loss of workers and endless legal hassles. The slaves knew full well that concerns over such issues resulted in a certain amount of restraint on the behaviors of individual property owners, and the slaves ably manipulated the situation in their favor. A case in point was that of Benito, a thirty-year-old slave, something of an organic intellectual, owned by the ingenio Quevedo in the province of Cimarrones. He expressed exactly that sentiment, when he glibly responded to a threat of punishment by noting that "he had cost his master a pretty penny and now his master could not simply throw his money away."[14]

The slaves' struggles were far from confined to issues of food, clothing, or time off. They also openly opposed certain labor practices, especially those affecting the rhythm and intensity of work. In many places, there was more or less open opposition to the installation of steam-powered machinery to grind sugarcane, because the slaves were acutely aware of just how much the work pace was likely to increase. One slave attempted to organize a protest to stop the menace heralded by the installation of the new machinery. Francisquillo, hailing from the ingenio Soledad in Cimarrones, claimed that the slaves "did not want to grind sugarcane with steam but with oxen, because their numbers were inadequate and therefore would increase slaves' individual workload."[15] There were other recorded cases of rebellions against new overseers wanting to prove their worth at the expense of overworking the slaves.

The examples reproduced here do not deny or aspire to deny the existence of labor mechanisms and management techniques imposed on farm slaves. This labor regimen lent itself to modification only in part, and that part only with great cost and effort. However, the daily routine of the plantation could not rest exclusively on the indiscriminant use of naked violence. Rather, it was workable only to the degree that an understanding was reached to settle conflicts between opposing interests. Eugene Genovese showed, in circumstances specific to the American South, precisely how this process worked.[16] And although he had the tendency to overemphasize, in our opinion, the periods of equilibrium and stability in plantation life, it was no less certain that slaves developed the means to survive under brutal conditions, making the most of a bad situation, or ably and tenaciously resisting in order to prevail.

What becomes apparent from this collection of data is that on each plantation a sort of complex modus vivendi emerged in which the master was allowed to get what he wanted out of the slaves and in which the slaves themselves understood what was reasonably expected of them. Because each party had a precise appreciation of their respective rights and obligations, any breaches of that mutual understanding caused heightened tensions and even open conflict.

The white hired help as well as black slaves were equally subject to the strict observance of those norms. For this arrangement to work, a progressive hierarchy of hired help on the plantation operated subject to the discretion of the property owners' delegation of authority. At the apex of that hired help pyramid were three authority figures: the administrator, whose presence was required only if the operation was substantial enough to merit it; the *mayoral* (overseer), a key hired man who attended to the day-to-day productive operations and management of the work force; and, lastly, the *boyero* (ox herd or drover), who substituted for the mayoral as needed. The remainder of the salaried workers — carpenters, blacksmiths, and woodcutters — followed in this descending hierarchical order, and the slaves were obliged to obey their orders blindly.

To the hired help fell the direction and execution of specific tasks. In order to differentiate those paid employees, their lodgings usually were separated spatially from the slave quarters, just as the master was in the big house and the slaves were removed to huts or barracks. Such spatial distribution of housing precisely replicated the difference and distance in status between the various components on the finca.[17] At the end of a long day's work, the plantation dwellers went their separate ways as members of entirely different communities.

The Informal Structure of Plantation Life

Underlying the obvious chain of command governing the ingenio or cafetal lay another structure, one less apparent but just as effective as the first. Within the plantation slave community, there was an order all its own that emerged from a social and cultural foundation completely unrelated to the plantation's economic objectives.

The plantation slave community was not simply an aggregate of identical units. Operating as such units, slaves responded to a chain of command in which they were counted and distributed in order to successfully complete their daily tasks. Every slave, subject to the directives of the mayoral and other hired help, suffered the onus of the same subordinate status and was considered nothing more than a mere purveyor of manual labor. From the perspective of the big house, slaves existed only to the extent that they were part of a machine sui generis, a piece of equipment made out of flesh and blood, that functioned solely in order to serve the productive necessities of the farm. Such an image, a product emerging from travelers' accounts and nineteenth-century literature, was in stark contrast to the images of a heretofore unknown and complex world depicted by contemporary documents and legal cases.

The boundaries within which that "community" could develop naturally were set by the actual physical perimeter of the plantation itself. The very condition of "being the possession of another" drastically limited slaves' social initiatives and life circumstances. It compelled slaves to define themselves in terms of the precarious nature of their lives and those of their family members, friends, and countrymen. Nevertheless, despite all such obstacles, some patterns emerged which were vaguely reminiscent of African traditions. In colonial Cuba, those components became integrated into a new system, one created out of the fervor of experiences on that island. Obviously, the varied ethnic composition of plantation slave communities did not make such integration easy, and cultural differences worked to create distance between groups rather than to unite them.

The coordinates around which individual members of the plantation slave community clustered respond to a body of highly diverse relations. Subsequent research will confirm whether such apparent diversity was an external manifestation of a unified content that for now remains obscured. What was certain was that slaves generated a hierarchy of subordination to which they all submitted, regardless of tribal origin, age, or gender.

The black *contramayoral* (slave gang boss or foreman) figured prominently as a unifying figure, bringing together the internal and external structures that governed life on the plantation. It was common for the contramayoral to remain on the job to see to it that all of the day's work was carried out properly. In general, his responsibilities included supervising the daily routine on the farm, including the very important task of making sure that his fellow slaves slept under lock and key in order to prevent overnight outings or escape attempts. The mayoral served as a general manager and, at least on the larger establishments, only rarely stooped to the contramayoral's level of closely supervising workers' tasks.

The choice of the contramayoral, therefore, was an extremely important one. The outcome affected whether work and social activities were carried out within stable, socially acceptable limits. The contramayoral was comparable to a pivotal pulley, enjoying the trust of his superiors but, at the same time, counting on the acquiescence of the plantation slave community because his ability to exercise control could not rest solely on delegated authority or, for that matter, on the threat of violence by his superiors. Because of that, whenever possible the contramayoral was chosen on the basis of the respect he enjoyed from his fellow slaves.

Contramayorals were expected to conduct themselves in such a way that they occupied the middle ground, equidistant between the submissiveness of a slave and the reproof of a master. They were obliged to carry out orders, including the disagreeable task of administering punishments. Any slave with a degree of autonomy in carrying out daily plantation chores typically was dubbed with the offensive nickname "whitey's snitch." Any contramayoral so characterized was looked down upon by everyone, as hated as he was scorned, and he lost his capacity to act as a mediator between his superiors and the slaves.

This was a common cause of disturbances and tensions on the farms. Just as there was visceral opposition to decisions made by the master and his hired help, warranted or not, there were also confrontations with the contramayoral. Violence even could break out over objections to a particularly undesirable *capataz* (foreman). Cristóbal Carabalí ("Carabalí" is an African tribe, whose name was used as a form of surname to distinguish between slaves with the same first name) from the ingenio Loreto in Managua, was the object of one such incident. The contramayoral José, Cuban born, received twenty-five lashes and was ordered restrained with ball and chain for an unspecified period of time as punishment for responding disrespectfully to a mayoral. Cristóbal was named in José's place. But it was an ill-fated decision. After the punishment had been administered, the plantation slaves remained in the *batey* (centrally located courtyard surrounded by a farm's outbuildings, equipment, and processing facilities), a sure sign of imminent conflict. Once the throng of slaves was dispersed, according to an eyewitness account by one of the hired help, the slaves refused to go to sleep or to work at their assigned tasks. Then the mayoral, handing his whip to Cristóbal — a symbol of his new authority — ordered Cristóbal to menace the rest of the slaves. "And by the time he had cracked his whip three or four times, the slaves began stoning Cristóbal and the Carabalí had to run for his life."[18]

José Criollo recounted how the slaves rebuked the wretch. "You, Cristóbal, are you perchance our new mayoral? Why do you punish us?"[19] The words of Pablo Gangá (another tribal name used as a surname) perfectly captured the prevailing state of mind when he said that everyone had become "indignant toward him."

Whites sometimes interpreted such episodes as products of tribal antagonisms. The slaves themselves never missed an opportunity to encourage such an idea. Surely, conflicts of that nature took place as frequently in the rural countryside as in the cities. Regardless, the general impression was that such outbursts were more likely the result of contradictions arising from social practices than from tribal rivalries. Slaves were acutely conscious of their individual place and respective responsibilities. Strict observance of their positions and roles prevented clashes. It was possible for a conflict to be exacerbated by old tribal grudges, but only rarely did the cause of a clash originate in cultural issues.

An incident on the cafetal Perserverancia could be interpreted as one such example of a dramatic confrontation in which diverse ethnic origins exacerbated a situation. Two weeks earlier, Dionisio Gangá appeared on the plantation as the gang boss for a work crew contracted as seasonal labor during the harvest. It was not long before there was a confrontation with another contramayoral, the middle-aged Andrés Lucumí ("Lucumí" was yet another tribal name used as a surname), which caused the rest of the slaves to unanimously rebuff Dionisio. The Gangá contramayoral recounted the incident:

> Two or three days after arriving, the contramayoral Andrés Lucumí told Dionisio that no one on that farm trusted mayorals, that they trusted only their master. The deponent [Dionisio] responded that he was accustomed to obeying the mayorals and to trusting them, because the master had put those individuals into that position. With this, the contramayoral Andrés became visibly agitated, and from then on spoke in his native language whenever they worked in the fields and whenever he was able with others of the Lucumí nation who the deponent [Dionisio] brought with him, because he had noticed that those blacks were very humble and good workers. . . . Lately, Dionisio had begun to notice that [those slaves] only grudgingly obeyed orders, in solidarity with Andrés, their former shipmate, who was always speaking to them in their native language and turning them against the deponent [Dionisio] because the blacks on that farm love Andrés very much.[20]

It was clear that differences arose from clashes between the mayoral and the slaves, and not from tribal differences or antagonisms. Dionisio was, evidently, somewhat of a snitch and had only himself to blame for becoming an outcast among his fellow slaves. That situation was in no little means encouraged by invidious comparisons with another contramayoral, who most decidedly enjoyed the affection and respect of his fellows.

The masters and their more able hired help chose slaves for those positions who already wielded substantial influence over their former shipmates. Such influence sprang from several different sources. Some slaves immediately stood out from their fellows for their natural leadership abilities. Others were chosen for the prestige they continued to enjoy as former leaders in their native lands, retaining the stature associated with those positions, at least among others from the same tribe. Similarly, still others had been religious leaders who, with their powers of witchcraft, maintained the ancestral cults and attended to the spiritual needs of the slaves.

For those reasons, the removal of a contramayoral could be quite destabilizing because it altered the balance of power within the plantation. These contramayorals had to respond to conflicting agendas that were byproducts of ongoing tensions. In the contramayorals' defense, it is worth mentioning that they quite frequently came down on the side of their fellow slaves. This contradicts the widespread belief that they automatically were accomplices of the system. They frequently were the very ones who organized, led, and promoted riots and uprisings, or those who, because their job allowed them to move about freely without arousing undue suspicion, maintained communication with bands of runaway slaves, allowing them onto the plantation in search of food or refuge. From the late eighteenth century until the last recorded conspiracies and uprisings in the mid-nineteenth century, contramayorals were implicated as active participants and leaders of those movements. Given the organization of plantation work and security on the farm, it was extremely difficult to organize protests or escape without counting, at the very least, on the neutrality of those slave leaders.

Just as important for the plantation slave community as the slave who was chosen as contramayoral were the leadership positions of *taita* (venerated black leader) and *brujo* (witch doctor). Both were accorded great prestige and exercised great influence in times of crisis. As was the case with the contramayoral, there tended to be several of those on the same plantation. A taita was not necessarily an elderly man, as contended by Esteban Pichardo.[21] On the contrary, the term was reserved for those who, in the eyes of the plantation slave community, symbolized restraint and good judgment.

The figure of the taita appeared in documents under the widest array of circumstances: as a sentry keeping watch on the edge of the plantation, or as someone carrying out specialized tasks, whether as a domestic in the big house or in the home of the mayoral. The presence of the brujo, however, was more elusive. Only rarely did he clearly figure in his role as protector of his fellow slaves, such as the moment a revolt broke out or when he cast magical spells and mixed life-saving potions or recited incantations ensuring victory. In the course of the many criminal proceedings initiated after the conspiracy of La Escalera, that figure emerged on every plantation as one of those implicated in the plot. His influence went far beyond the physical confines of the plantation perimeter and even occasionally reached neighboring towns. His underground network included the free colored population that maintained close contact with the plantation slave community as they furtively worshiped together under cover of darkness in remote secret meeting places.

Beyond that hierarchy of sorts governing the most important aspects of the plantation slave community were some other practices that were observed rather strictly. One of these was associated with the sexual division of labor that, in contrast to labor practices on the plantation, remained consistent with practices in Africa. Once women completed their assigned tasks, they were in charge of food preparation and laundry. Men and women ate dinner at the same time, but separately, even in those cases in which they lived together in their own huts rather than in barracks.[22] The documents made absolutely no reference to the care of young children, but when a riot broke out or a revolt erupted, children stayed with their mothers, who looked after them on their escape routes or out in the brush. Also, during those incidents of open insubordination, the women shouted encouragement to the rebels or trailed behind them, but there is no direct evidence that they actively participated in the actual fighting.

In addition to such a strict sexual division of labor, there was differentiation according to age. Usually the plantation slave community was divided into crews that were formed on the basis of age. Nevertheless, the slaves themselves adopted a point of view that considered other factors as well. Slaves descriptively identified both young and old, those categorizations taking priority over other social factors. The youngest slaves, for example, were the first to be excluded from all planning of conspiracies, and they were sheltered from fighting and, hence, protected from any allegations of cowardice. On the other hand, youths were expected to defer to decisions made by their elders and to obey their commands concerning plantation work and any extra responsibilities they were assigned.

Factors distinguishing between age grades or statuses were imprecise. At times, according to the documents, youths between eighteen and twenty years old were regarded as children. Naturally, age categories were influenced by individual physical traits and emotional maturity, because very few of the slaves actually knew their precise age.

Other differentiations within the hierarchy of the plantation slave community coincided or supplemented the distinction of chronological age. What were known as "new" slaves were distinguished from "old" slaves or, rather, slaves only recently arrived from Africa were differentiated from established slaves who had been on the island quite some time. Those well-seasoned slaves were capable of socializing newcomers and familiarizing them with routine practices and customs particular to the estate. In a similar vein, the terms *bozal* (an African-born slave or any slave who does not speak Spanish well) and *ladino* (an African slave who has learned to speak Spanish and is more or less culturally adept) were denominations that communicated varying degrees of assimilation to the social medium of the plantation slave community. The newcomers and the bozals were expected to learn quickly from the old-timers and those who already knew some rudimentary Spanish. On the other hand, the most experienced slaves immediately commanded the respect of any new arrivals to the plantation.

All of these nexuses that crisscrossed and organized the black masses arose, as we have seen, at the fringes of the structure contained within the plantation's physical boundaries.

Family and Kinship

Similarly complex relations came to bear on family life. Family connections were kept alive despite the impediments inherent to the servile status of slaves. There was no doubt as to the precarious nature of families' existence. Slavery conspired against the very formation and stability of the family. The nature of slavery promoted an imbalance of the sexes on large farms, subjected family members to the constant onus of separation, and created a thousand-and-one other obstacles to family life. The tenacity, the unqualified importance, and the innumerable sacrifices that slaves had to develop and impart in order to maintain and preserve those ties truly were admirable. The documents reproduced here constitute a limited sample of that struggle which, across time and place, included attempts to rescue family members, obtain their freedom, or seek to protect them from the abuses of masters and mayorals alike.

Reconstructing the family trees of plantation slaves is no easy task. The detailed records that allowed Herbert Gutman to trace strategies used to preserve the family in the United States simply do not exist in Cuba.[23] The only resources available in Cuba are isolated bits of data and passing references to the transatlantic voyage. The paucity of information permits us only to point out certain characteristics and propose hypothetical scenarios that subsequent researchers must substantiate.

Determining the number of couples married by the Church on any given plantation with any precision was not possible. Such marriages clearly did take place and were duly noted in the documents reviewed here dating from the late eighteenth century onward. The provision of independent housing for couples — *bohíos* (primitive huts made of guano, royal palm, and other readily available materials with a gable roof) — or, later, barracks erected with special areas reserved for couples reflected the acknowledgment of such relationships. Nevertheless, those who were married formally by the Church were not the only established couples living together. In practice, the slave community gave comparable recognition and respect to less formal consensual unions. The colorful slave expression, "married by the *manigua*" (generic term for jungle brush), was a reference to those unions. Such unions constituted the institutionalization of a bond that enjoyed a status comparable to formal marriage and did not necessarily imply informal relationships of only a transitory nature. There were numerous legal cases that frequently arose as a result of the violation of those norms and almost always concerned the demise of the offending party.

The case of Pedro Criollo is illustrative. Presumably jealous of the continual flirtatious behavior of his woman, María del Rosario Gangá, Pedro killed her. She already effectively had dissolved their bond, and the slave community supported her action. For that reason, her lover, Fernando Lucumí, dared approach her in the first place, because "she was a free woman and she told him that, yes," she welcomed his attentions. In the course of the legal proceedings, other slaves testified against the ostensible husband, indicating that the marriage no longer existed.[24] Although standards associated with entering into and dissolving a marriage were secondary issues, it did not necessarily mean that the slave community lacked norms concerning the rules governing those familial relationships it otherwise respected.

As couples were constituted on the plantation, rules concerning minor sons and daughters were not as clearly established. Apparently, it was customary to raise children away from their parents in a separate, specially designated area, usually the plantation infirmary. The Regulation of 1842 did no more than bless this already established practice. Mothers attended to their little ones on previously agreed-upon schedules, usually after the completion of their daily tasks. This arrangement remained in place until the children reached a certain age, which some pinpoint at between five and seven years old. It has not been possible to determine if families at some point during the day spent other time together. The documents were for the most part silent on this issue and referred to infancy only in passing and usually in regard to the need for slave mothers to regularly breastfeed their infants.

Slaves conceived of the family not only as blood relatives but also in more wide-ranging, flexible terms. Couples typically adopted adolescents and new arrivals from Africa, making them members of the family unit and forming mutually enduring affective ties. The origin of such a practice was attributable both to African cultural heritage and to those specific conditions which were by-products of the slave system. Countless references showed how such newcomers were mentored and protected until they were transformed into true members of a composite family unit. The testimony of Ramón Mandiga (another African tribal name) was typical. In the middle of the clamor of the rebellion of Sumidero, he did not hesitate to face danger and try to retrieve the body of his friend Juan, whom "he look[ed] upon as a father," in order to give him a proper burial.[25] The respect those youths had for the adults who took them in, especially for the men who served as father figures, was tremendous. In fact, it inspired such loyalty in those youths that they joined their mentors in rebellion unreservedly, although they personally considered such undertakings to be sheer lunacy.

Fathers, sons, and brothers, separated by the very same vicissitudes of slavery, nevertheless maintained close relations, visiting each other on their respective plantations and even, when possible, on fairly distant settlements. At times, they risked leaving the plantation without formal permission, taking advantage of the carelessness of some hired hand and walking for miles in order to effect a fleeting encounter. At other times, they acted in complicity with the contramayoral, who fomented such late-night meetings. Neither time nor distance worked to diminish those familial feelings or presented obstacles to family contact.

Not even the possibility of freedom, longed for and precious, was sufficient cause to abandon the family. Pedro Criollo, a slave from the ingenio belonging to Gutiérrez y Casal, managed to save five hundred pesos (old silver coin of Spain and Spanish America equal to eight reals [coin worth one-fourth of a peseta or twenty-five cents]) for his manumission. Pedro reserved the right for his former masters to hire him as a worker on that selfsame ingenio, where he wished to remain because he had three children living there.[26] Many other slaves were willing to withstand a prolonged separation by working elsewhere, if it provided the financial wherewithal to liberate family members remaining on the plantation.

The family was only one component of a kinship system particular to the island setting and deriving from the singular circumstances of slavery. Groups of slaves united by reciprocal rights and obligations built on the basis of a common ethnic origin, coexistence on the same plantation, and/or the institution of *padrinazgo* (sponsorship or patronage, religious and/or civil) also constituted kin. Each of those served as a vehicle to establish a type of kin relationship that survived manumission and was found just as often in the rural countryside as in Cuba's colonial cities.

Undeniably, ethnic origin was a strong unifying element and provided a group identity for slaves on particular farms and cities. Spontaneous relationships arose between Africans and were reinforced by the colonial authorities through the establishment of *cabildos de nación* (ethnic associations) in urban areas. The connections between members of the same ethnicity were strong and presupposed mutual aid and common activities. For this reason, slaves in Cuba always referred to their compatriots with the simple denomination "kin" or "relative." Juan Télles, a slave from Bayamo, an ethnic Mina (another African tribe), did precisely this when he said that in a neighboring house "his relatives the Mandingas and the Minas [were] found gathered together."[27] There were many other similar references in that same vein. Pablo Mayorga, a Carabalí, alluded to a circumstance in which the free black Carabalís were accustomed to being fed every Sunday by one of their relatives.

On the same farm, slaves designated individuals related by this ethnic bond indistinguishably with the word *carabelas* (shipmates on the transatlantic voyage) or simply "relatives" or "kin." Group activities naturally included those who worked to preserve their cultural traditions. On ingenios in Trinidad, it was customary to celebrate the drum dances of different tribes on the same day, dances spatially differentiated according to the African origin of the members of the plantation's slave community. In 1838 José Iznaga, a Gangá from the ingenio Mainicú, declared that he would be attending his relatives' dance at the same time that the ingenio Congos had organized theirs.[28]

Evidence of such relations was a source of concern for the colonial government, which considered them a breeding ground for conspiracies and uprisings. The fiscal for the Real Audiencia (Royal Court) of Puerto Príncipe advised officials there to be on their guard. There was special concern over the area in the vicinity of the slums of Santo Cristo, "composed almost entirely of freedmen who [were] on good terms and in communication with rural agricultural slaves," because those "ha[d] their fellow slaves and friends there, and they stay over at their houses on holidays," such occasions were especially apt times for the much dreaded revolts.[29] The warning served as an example of the large-scale kin network that united rural slaves with those in the slums and cities. Even recourse to discredited repressive practices never served to weaken, much less eliminate, such networks.

The institution of padrinazgo was just as robust and widespread as ethnically based kinship and became an important and long-lasting vehicle for solidarity. The custom of naming a slave as "godfather" to a recent arrival for purposes of baptismal rites prompted a complicated range of relations within the rural slave communities and between urban slaves. Some individuals served as godfather to many. The slave José María, a Gangá from the ingenio Alcancía, had no fewer than four godsons on that particular farm.[30] Vicente Criollo, a cart driver from the ingenio La Trinidad, maintained very close relations with a freedman in the neighboring town, in that "he ha[d] with him a spiritual kinship because he [was] baptized as his son," more than thirteen years ago.[31]

The godfather Vicente was referring to was Jacinto Roque, who stood accused of witchcraft and of organizing a revolt on the ingenio. This brought up yet another aspect of that type of relationship that raised serious doubts. The relationship between a godfather and his godson was Catholic in origin, but those terms also reflected African religious practices. In both the Regla de Ocha, better known as Santería, and the Congolese system of religious beliefs known as Regla de Palo, the priest who administered rites and the recent converts who received them were known, respectively, as godfather and godson. Both were subject to reciprocal obligations.

It would be safe to say that the use of those terms in almost all rural slave cohorts and in the very midst of urban slave communities was more likely attributable to African beliefs than to those associated with Catholicism. In any case, there was nothing to stand in the way of juxtaposing both practices. It is interesting to point out that each of the two types of bonds, especially those originating in Africa, supposed the systematic exchange of assistance extending to all spheres of life and, therefore, by definition, included the multiform and varied universe of slave kinship.[32]

The complex network of relations that, as we have seen, underlay the everyday life of rural slave communities constantly eroded the norms established by the planter class and other authorities. The illusion of transforming the slave into a singularly efficient human machine ran up against effective resistance, even under the most unfavorable circumstances. Not even the exhausting shifts of the sugarcane harvest diminished the slaves' capacity for creating a system that allowed them to preserve some of the social network that they considered so indispensable. Tremendous obstacles stood in the way of organizing such a system, as both hacendados and colonial authorities grew increasingly fearful of the possibility of devastating revolts.

One such revolt took place in the early 1840s, as a campaign to guarantee security for the plantation slaves at all costs intensified. A series of riots and rebellions, such as the unexpected sociopolitical movement of the free population of color, prompted the appearance of the so-called barracks system, which consisted of depriving the slaves of their freedom of movement once the day's work was done. According to Article 25 of the Regulation of 1842, slaves had to gather in a designated location or building that allowed them to spend the night under lock and key.[33]

The construction of those buildings would prevent any misconduct because the blacks "take advantage of routine rest periods and venture out at these times; they communicate with other plantation slaves, choosing to meet on farms with careless guards, and, emanating from these gatherings and discussions, the riots, lootings, and similar dreadful things one can imagine come about . . . ," according to the opinion of the captain of the Macurijes district in the 1830s.[34] It was a long-standing belief, because some of the riots in the 1820s were products of an initiative of certain masters and mayorals to force plantation slaves to sleep under lockdown. Captain General Gerónimo Valdés put the regulation in place that made such a practice widespread, and the effect on slaves everywhere was the same.[35]

Noncompliance with the regulation prompted an order on July 20, 1843, which reaffirmed the directive and set a deadline of four months hence for owners to build or reconstruct secure locations. While the planter class was in open agreement on the desired ends, it was divided concerning the assessment of the most efficient methods to assure the tranquillity of the slaves. Many considered the establishment of such enclosures as counterproductive.

José Montalvo y Castillo, owner of ingenios in two areas in the western part of the island, considered that "excessive restraints on slavery are just as bad as excessive tolerance. A man forced to work all day and then put under lock and key all night cannot live contentedly. It is necessary to loosen the chains of slavery."[36] He asked for permission to devise his own system, rather than constructing barracks. His philosophy was shared by other hacendados, who made their thoughts known to the governor. Montalvo y Castillo also objected to the additional expense and to diverting workers from planting in order to carry out the mandated construction. According to Montalvo y Castillo,

> The only respite for the African is his hut, his family, and the pleasure he takes in his freedom and independence in the early evening. His animals, his garden plot, his simple chores, are at the very heart and soul of his existence. His very nature dictates the manner in which he should be governed and he who enjoys certain freedoms never chafes under the yoke of slavery. We must destroy the twin obstacles of oppression and desperation and never allow them to bring people together in their grievances. In my humble opinion, such a situation serves to promote clandestine gatherings of discontented people. On the contrary, it is better to divide them in order to better govern them.

The Marquis de Campo Florido agreed with Montalvo and indicated that he maintained strict watch on his farms without interfering with the comings and goings of his slaves. They were accustomed to living as families "and with the godchildren" in huts that they love like "an inviolable property, where they have all of their possessions legitimately acquired through their own work, done so willingly on their own time."[37] He concluded that any forcible enclosure would not prevent uprisings and perhaps would even encourage them, because "everyday as they lay down to go to sleep, upon hearing the door being bolted, the greatest, or perhaps the only one of their privations, can awaken or enliven in them the desire" to escape from slavery.

Avarice, attempts to economize, or the conviction that the barracks represented greater risks than the former system, all informed the planter class's firm opposition to the colonial directive. Some ten years later, in

March 1852, the lieutenant governor of Cárdenas reported that of the 221 ingenios in his jurisdiction, only 98 had barracks, and, of those barracks, only 73 were made of brick.[38]

Nevertheless, where night confinement was practiced, it made the slaves' former relative freedom of movement and exploits after sundown more difficult, but it did not eliminate them altogether. There were constant complaints about slaves who were spotted outside plantation perimeters and about their escapades in nearby taverns where they drank whisky or peddled their own wares or dealt in stolen goods.

The objective of preventing gatherings of local slaves and of eliminating the possibility of unauthorized forays never met with complete success. Whatever the wishes of colonial authorities and property owners, plantations simply could not exist in isolation from each other or be entirely cut off from neighboring towns or markets. Through many different mechanisms, rural slaves maintained regular contact with other farms, with sectors of the free population of color, and even with whites.

Plantations and Commerce

The specific nature of sugar and coffee production on plantations promoted a very close-knit relationship with the surrounding vicinity and with the means of transporting the harvest to market, such as railroads and major ports. Marketing those agricultural products, even with the widespread construction of railroads in the western part of the island, depended heavily on cart drivers who, except for the occasional white supervisor or freedman, were plantation slaves. It was no coincidence that those cart drivers almost invariably were implicated in conspiracies and aided in organizing them by acting as messengers. They paid keen attention to gossip and incidental rumors and duly passed them along.

Two other figures on the plantation provided similar services: the master's errand boy and his carriage driver. Both kept plantation slaves in touch with the immediate vicinity and with their contacts in town. Their frequent forays outside the plantation and, especially in the case of the carriage drivers, their opportunity to eavesdrop on conversations between the master and his friends provided those slaves with valuable opportunities to gather information, and they did not hesitate to take full advantage of such occasions. These apparently innocuous means of communication between plantation slaves and the outside world complemented other similarly licit points of contact between the two.

The neighborhood tavern held an attraction that few mayorals were able to counter. Typically, such establishments were located on the outskirts of the plantation or at a nearby crossroads. Despite being explicitly forbidden by masters, permission to visit these taverns frequently was granted on Sundays or holidays and sometimes even on workdays. Those establishments not only were visited by slaves but also were frequented by the racially and socially diverse masses that made up the surrounding rural population. There was gambling, drinking, and conversation about the earthly and the divine. No wonder the planters were hostile to all taverns in areas where there were large slave populations. They waged war on them, under the pretext that the slaves stole in order to satisfy the twin vices of liquor and tobacco. The colonial government, likewise, was openly unfriendly toward those taverns. Knives, machetes, ammunition, and even rifles all were sold there — no questions asked — to anyone with cold hard cash in hand.

Campaigns to limit the number of rural taverns or to force them to relocate to remote areas far from plantations appeared over and over again in the years before abolition. Such establishments were damned as enemies of the people, exercising their nefarious influence over blacks. A similar campaign was waged against the ubiquitous traveling peddler, a venerable entrenched institution, insinuating himself into every nook and cranny of colonial society. Not even the barracks system thwarted his visits, according to the testimony of Julia Ward Howe, who discovered a trader in the very heart of the barracks peddling white bread, bright cotton handkerchiefs, and other merchandise to the slaves. According to the statement by the salesman himself, he visited the plantation every Sunday and could take in up to twenty-five dollars a week.[39] As if this were not bad enough, a considerable number of those traveling peddlers were free coloreds and understandably added to the anxiety of colonial officials and masters.

There were repeated and ineffectual attempts to forbid any contact between those salesmen and muleteers, especially those who were freedmen or mulattoes, with the farms. The prohibitions were unsuccessful, as the constant references to those types of encounters demonstrate.

The slaves benefited from contact, whether licit or simply tolerated, with the hired help on the plantation, as they did from any commercial contacts afforded by the sale of any of the goods slaves produced on their own small plots. Produce and livestock from those small holdings provided the pretext for slaves to visit taverns and haggle with peddlers. Providing slaves with some small plot of land for cultivation during their free time or holidays and granting permission to raise chickens and pigs were both part of Spanish legislation dating from the sixteenth century. Similar practices were observed in other colonies such as Jamaica, Saint-Domingue, and the thirteen British colonies in North America.[40]

One of the main functions of those small holdings was to provide additional food in order to supplement the limited diet of plantation slaves. While the parcels were surely important for such an end in Cuba, a phenomenon duly noted in many travelers' accounts, the other most commonly cited purposes for peddling their goods was to obtain clothes and to accumulate cash toward manumission.[41] Both the slaves themselves and colonial legislation emphasized the importance of the sale of products from their small holdings as a means to attain their own freedom or that of family members. Article 13 of the Regulation of 1842 established the time-honored practices of assigning plots and working independently in an occupation for the purpose of "acquiring their own assets and attaining freedom." The advantage for slaves in making efforts to that end — instead of opting for freedom through violent means — was emphasized by the board of the Real Consulado de Agricultura y Comercio (Royal Consulate for Agriculture and Commerce) in 1799 as a fair and especially effective solution to prevent unwanted strife.[42]

Nevertheless, the assignment of small holdings required the mobilization of the slaves themselves during the first two decades of the nineteenth century. Some of the documents produced here were representative in this respect, with many landowners wanting nothing to do with legislation that allowed slaves the right to accumulate private assets. Even by 1842, when the Regulation of Valdés had not yet been promulgated, the Marqués de Arcos explained: "With respect to the so-called small holdings and the raising of pigs and poultry, I must say to Your Excellency that these are concessions that I already grant my slaves, although I consider this to be overly generous and somewhat coerced. If compelled to do so, I cannot begin to calculate the extent to which the slaves [will] be disposed to go in order to enforce its observance, nor the eventual consequences if we formalize this right."[43]

Many masters held the view that it was better to reserve discretionary power over such concessions for themselves, so that they could bestow them as a form of benevolent dispensation, effectively becoming yet another of the many manipulative weapons in the masters' disciplinary arsenal. Because of that, the slaves' struggles played an important part in the formal recognition of their rights and in their gradual extension over the entire island. That dissemination reinforced the tendency to see the garden plots as the most rapid and secure means for slaves to obtain money to buy their freedom.

The connection between rural slaves and commerce was significant, both in the midst of the plantation slave communities and in the outside world. At times, that connection took the form of barter, as was the case in Guamacaro in 1844 between slaves on the cafetal Marqueti and those on the ingenio La Merced. Francisco Lucumí, in recounting the terms of the agreement, noted that "those from the ingenio g[a]ve sugar to those of the cafetal, and those from the cafetal g[a]ve the equivalent amount in plantains," although in this case the sugar obviously was obtained illicitly.[44]

On the other hand, the documents also furnished evidence of transactions between slaves that were paid in cash. The sale of pigs was common, as a way not only to pay for the nuclear family's necessities but also to provide food for frequent entertaining and get-togethers. Some landowners, such as the master of the cafetal Angerona, were familiar with and encouraged this practice. Abiel Abbot recalled professing the maxim that "blacks must have money and should *spend* it." For that very reason, he created a company store on the plantation and sold fabric, dresses, crockery, crucifixes, and the like.[45] Alejo Gangá told how Velasco, a free Congolese, came to him expecting him to sell one of his pigs on credit, to which he indignantly retorted that "slaves did not sell without money," a standard backed up by many similar transactions.

Recent arrivals, the bozals, were rapidly incorporated into such trafficking agreements, and this was one of the factors behind work stoppages or outright rebellions to demand small holdings. José Luciano Franco even documented exchanges between plantation slaves and bands of runaways and palenque communities.[46] Pancho Mina, captain of the runaways in Cayajabos, described in lavish detail an exchange of wax for truck between the cimarrones and the slaves from the cafetal Landot and the payment the runaways owed for their lunch and any whisky the cafetal slaves provided.[47]

All such testimonials showed the degree to which slaves created their own channels of communication and commerce between themselves and the peddlers and other merchants who came to the plantations. The image of a plantation slave community totally isolated and under lockdown existed only as an ideal type. Whether or not such contact was permitted, the slaves themselves constantly pushed such an ideal type to the limit. Under capitalism, concern with the worker was limited to the quantitative management of maximizing labor during the workday. A slave system had to look out for its slaves not only during their working hours but during slaves' downtime and days off as well. That necessitated the constant supervision of the economic and extraeconomic aspects of its workers' lives. The documents in this book illustrate the complexity of such a system, of relations that were much richer and more profound than commonly believed. Because of that, and despite strict security, which was never lifted or eased, the slaves created specific mechanisms in order to maintain family bonds, ties with fellow slaves, and links with the free population. They collectively formed a social framework of far greater significance than previously thought.

Those networks extended to provincial cities and, often, all the way to Cuba's colonial capital. Some of the documents testified to the fact that those relations were maintained over long periods of time. A relative living in the next town over or in a city provided a very important means to achieve manumission and to seek protection in the face of excesses committed by masters or mayorals. The proximity to the seats of local or colonial power allowed, without a doubt, recourse to the legal system that conferred certain rights to slaves and established mechanisms to channel their grievances, within acceptable limits permitted in the slave system. Both options sustained the very real prospect, however minimal, for slaves to take the initiative toward reaching their goals.

Slaves in the City

As one might expect, urban slaves had a much wider range of resources and possibilities at their disposal than their rural counterparts on plantations. Because slavery was widespread in Cuban cities over almost all sectors, that circumstance favored the diffusion of slave labor at agreed-upon rates of payment. While leased slaves had constituted a social type since the colony's very beginnings, their significance grew steadily throughout the nineteenth century. Urban slaves became ubiquitous, whether in manufacturing, small business, or working at any of myriad tasks associated with a busy port.

Families, whether fairly well off or living in a state of genteel poverty, widows, soldiers, and even the occasional manual laborer, who might own a few slaves with no immediate tasks to keep them occupied, rented them out in order to avail themselves of a little extra income. It was impossible not to take notice of the relatively large numbers of those slave laborers in Cuba's cities and towns. Even local Cuban elites were not above hiring out their slaves as journeymen. The documents include multiple cases of local syndics intervening on slaves' behalf in negotiating their daily wage for having worked on holidays.

The practice of farming out slaves as urban day laborers was profitable enough to remain in place even during those times when the plantation system was expanding and slaves were in great demand. Urban slave journeymen continued to represent a significant percentage of the overall numbers of slaves on the island. In Havana, urban slaves made up nearly 30 percent of the capital's population in 1810.[48] According to the census of 1828, their relative numbers declined slightly, but urban slaves still made up a little more than 21 percent of Havana's residents. Those numbers steadily increased over time, and by 1841 urban slaves constituted just over 29 percent of Havana's population. An identical trend was seen in other urban areas, such as Matanzas and Santiago de Cuba.

By late 1857 the number of slaves residing in cities and towns accounted for a little more than 17 percent of all servile labor on the island (table 8). Only a small segment of those slaves were seeking freedom through the system of *arriendo* (rental/lease). Others worked directly for their own masters, and yet others were domestic laborers. Documentary evidence revealed that rented slaves made up a very special sector, whether they were *coartado* (slaves already appraised and their price set as part of the system of coartación) or whether they were, in contemporary parlance, full slaves.

In fact, leased slaves enjoyed a series of prerogatives simply out of the question for other categories of slaves. It was common for them to live independently rather than in lodgings provided by their owners. They entered into contracts on their own behalf, without the mediation of their masters. This leasing system made it legally possible for slaves to keep for themselves any hard-earned money they would have made on Sundays and holidays.

Slaves who were coartado were fully within their rights in retaining any payment in excess of the fixed amount to be paid to their masters. Given that "to enter into a coartación agreement entails fixing a slave's price, proportionally reducing the balance owed,"[49] these successive reductions granted the slave the right to hand over nothing more than the previously agreed-upon fixed sum to the master and to freely dispose of the rest. This opportunity was acknowledged universally as an important avenue to obtain one's own manumission and that of one's family members.

Despite the widespread nature of such a practice, the recognition of that

TABLE 8. Rural and Urban Slaves in Cuba, 1857

Residence	Men	Women	Total
Urban areas	30,081	34,771	64,852
Rural areas	192,426	115, 232	307,658
TOTAL	222,507	150,003	372,510

Source: ANC, *Gobierno Superior Civil*, 949/33547.

and other rights for slaves was only partially protected under Spanish colonial law. In actuality, those practices came about through slaves' determined resistance in which they exercised an intelligent and tenacious exploitation of those judicial channels that were readily available to them. The few cases of such instances referring to the captain general reprinted here were an eloquent example of this struggle. Some widely accepted observances, such as the practice of slaves pocketing any wages in excess of the set amount destined for the master, were the outcome of years of pressure dating from the early nineteenth century. Little by little, this practice gained acceptance among local officials who, already in the 1850s and 1860s, recognized that slaves were entitled to their own money. One of these officials, José Morales Lemus, commented that "he who has made a down payment on his freedom and as such has power over his own being"[50] was deserving of judicial treatment commensurate with that status.

Perhaps the developments that best reflected this new awareness of slaves' rights were controversies over a masters' power to transfer ownership of their slaves. Authority in that area began to be contested already in the 1830s. Using their status as coartados, those slaves openly contested the right of property owners to send them away, usually out into the rural countryside. No legislation supported that particular interpretation of the constellation of rights associated with being coartado. That being the case, both government institutions and local syndics almost universally rejected this category of slave complaint. Nevertheless, the unrelenting flow of grievances, on the one hand, and the proliferation of abolitionist and humanitarian ideas in general, on the other, created a favorable climate for the slow but sure recognition of the validity of such claims. The combination of favorable public opinion and the slaves' constant clamor encouraged a favorable resolution of such grievances sometime in the 1860s.

That tendency to extend rights to slaves, coartado or not, did not preclude the persistence of long-standing notions likening a servitor to a source of profit and of slaves as dehumanized entities, whether during a particular period of government or during the tenure of a particular syndic. But the historical evolution of the island worked toward modifying the circumstances under which juridical norms had to be applied. The initiative of the slaves themselves significantly contributed to such a transformation. In cases included here, it was impossible not to be impressed by both the eloquence with which slaves defended their aspirations and the slaves' apparent ability to exploit whatever influence and loopholes in the regulations and existing legislation that worked in their own favor.

The documents revealed an aspect of urban slavery usually only alluded to: the sordidness, the cruelty, and the routine violence often associated only with plantation slavery. Those cases, first and foremost, contradicted whatever hasty judgments one perhaps entertained about the possibility of the transformation of slavery from within. Those existing mechanisms allowing slaves to adapt themselves to the system, to exploit any flaws or gaps in order to reassert themselves as human beings, and even to expand their rights within certain limits did nothing to eradicate the inexorable nature of servitude and its attendant consequences. Whether magnanimously manumitted or purchasing their own freedom outright, those means constituted one path to liberation, but the individuals it actually touched and benefited were very few. The number of those manumitted in a year's time never exceeded two thousand, although that number is subject to confirmation by future generations of scholars.[51] That figure, compared to the total number of slaves on the island during the first half of the nineteenth century, puts the issue in its proper context.

Two institutions in Cuban civic life mitigated the excesses of the slave system: the civic syndic and cabildos for African slaves or slaves born in Cuba. The documents supported this assertion, especially after the 1830s. But very specific limits working to maintain a slave regimen remained and were impossible to surmount. The fact that since 1799 the aristocratic planter class continued to insist that coartación and manumission were adequate safety valves demonstrates that these limited mechanisms in no way jeopardized the continuity of slave society.

Slave Rebellions

Coping strategies such as adaptation and struggle from within the system were in stark contrast with frank defiance and occasional violent insubordination. Slaves, just like other subaltern classes, chose their confrontational tactics as demanded by their immediate circumstances, not as dictated by ethnic or cultural traits. The premise that those slaves coming from a particular African "nation" exhibited more of a tendency for cimarronería and rebellion lacks, in our opinion, historical corroboration. Case studies indicate that these movements arose from specific societal conditions and that their forms responded to factors operating within such frameworks.

A similar misinterpretation emerges from the assumption that Cuban-born slaves were more easily subdued and less likely to participate in revolts and uprisings than recent arrivals. The Cuban data did not support any such conclusion. Those actively conspiring and organizing rebellions included Cuban-born slaves as well as slaves only recently arrived from any of various American countries.

Stereotypes of this nature all too frequently distort analysis of slave systems. As new historical sources become available, the perspective of social scientists surely will come to include a more exact appreciation of historical reality and assign a more active role to slaves themselves. Nothing requires such a multifaceted point of view more than protest movements, in which the opposition of historic subjects determines the course and eventual result of their actions. Failure to observe these methodological norms has led to serious misrepresentations in which conflict, dynamic by its very nature, undergoes a radical change, where a sole actor performs in the midst of the almost complete absence of social context.[52]

Such a phenomenon especially is typical of histories of rebel slave movements. We now have an ample bibliography of the types and forms — individual and collective — of slave protests and struggles at our disposal. What we lack is a wider perspective, a point of view that correlates the latter with the local situation within which it takes place and to which it responds. At times, the data do not support an exact correlation between slave actions and other events in the given social and political order because of the lack of relevant information. Nevertheless, only an analysis of this sort will allow us to evaluate the real significance of protest movements and palenque communities, those hotbeds of chronic protest.

Runaway slaves, a regrettable and unfortunate by-product endemic to all slave societies, seem to be especially subject to definite fluctuations incapable of being explained away by punitive measures. Recent studies allow us to describe variations of the phenomenon over time and place, but the confirmation of figures requires investigations that isolate local factors that predominate in one or another region over a specific period of time.[53] A broad array of motives and incentives prompts escape attempts, requiring further study in order to grasp their probable connection to more general trends in the population at large.

Deschamps demonstrated that there were significant numbers of runaway slaves in urban areas and that a complex pattern of solidarity worked to safeguard escapees.[54] Runaway slaves had been considered a rural problem for a long time and only a secondary phenomenon in urban settings. However, a more exact analysis of the origins of fugitive slaves demonstrated that, among escapees and palenque dwellers, the presence of urban slaves was far from negligible and even sizable. Subsequent research will determine whether the case of El Cedro was a rare exception or an accurate reflection of business as usual in colonial society.[55] What is certain is that, according to those who apprehended fugitive slaves and to the accounts of the slaves themselves, escape attempts — whether short-lived or permanent —were regular occurrences within certain slave populations, taking into account their proportional weight within the larger servile population.

The case of Dámaso Criollo and his successful flight to Mexico — where any slave, whether from the United States or Cuba, who set foot on the mainland was considered free — opens up a whole new area scarcely touched on in research on runaways.[56] The fact that Cuba is an island and that its many ports enjoy brisk maritime traffic actually invites escapes. In fact, it is not at all unusual from among the vast array of surviving police documents to find records of arrests of these self-proclaimed stowaways. Even teenagers figure among their numbers, such as the fourteen-year-old Cuban-born slave José Bibián, hailing from an ingenio in the district of Aguacate, located relatively far from Havana.[57]

The circumstances surrounding these escapes revealed the existence of a wide collaborative network that made them possible. At one end, undoubtedly, were port workers, both slave and free, acting in collusion with some foreign crews, who created a support system enabling the escapees to elude port security. At the other, in destinations sympathetic to the plight of fugitive slaves, were black communities of a certain import and local populations willing to give shelter to and assist the fugitives as they settled into their new homes.

Mexico was the destination of choice, especially the Vera Cruz area. Beginning in the early nineteenth century, a significant number of political émigrés chose Mexico as their new home, their new homeland. New Orleans played an identical role, escapees blending effortlessly into the local immigrant population. Both destinations were centers of early agitation for independence and abolition on the part of both the white and black populations. The effort was reinforced by massive deportations ordered around 1844, as a result of the prosecution of those involved in the conspiracy of La Escalera.[58]

The struggle of Cuba's free black population, both on and off the island, organically integrated into the colony's political evolution, has yet to be chronicled. Nevertheless, what little is known emphasizes both the continuity as well as the depth of democratic thought as it permeated wide sectors of society. Efforts to enlist slaves in the struggle were successful initially, with the conspiracy of José Antonio Aponte in 1812, among others. In reality, the movement was an ongoing process marked by conspiracies, riots, and rebellions before, during, and after the decisive movement of 1844 and was fiercely repressed by the colonial government.

Some instances of slaves and their free advocates who collaborated in the planning and execution of rebellions are partially transcribed in this volume. From the great revolt of Sumidero in 1825 to the final movement in 1864, which was discovered and prematurely aborted, colonial society was periodically wracked by the tumult by slaves' relentless struggles for freedom. The most illustrative testimonies accurately reflecting the objectives and sentiments of those who choose this arduous path are reproduced over the following pages, without disregarding evidence that also demonstrates the limitations, duplicity, and even treachery on the part of some protagonists.

This array of documents has been selected specifically because it demonstrates the complexity of the slave system and the pronounced contradictory tendencies coexisting within the very heart of that system. Should the effect of this book prove to inspire research in new directions, especially concerning the slave as a historical subject, it will have fulfilled its purpose.

1. Slavery and Its Legal Regulation
The Slave Code

⚜ ROYAL DECREE AND INSTRUCTIONAL CIRCULAR FOR THE INDIES ON THE EDUCATION, TREATMENT, AND WORK REGIMEN OF SLAVES

May 31, 1789

The King. In the code of laws of the Partidas[1] and other bodies of legislation for these realms, in the Collection of Laws of the Kingdom of the Indies, in both general and limited decrees conveyed to my American dominions since the time of their discovery, and in the ordinances, examined by my Council of the Indies, which have merited my royal approval, the system for training slaves in useful endeavors has been established, observed, and consistently followed, and the appropriate measures for their instruction, treatment, and occupation provided, as their owners are obliged, in accordance with the principles and rules dictated by religion, humanity, and the well-being of the State, compatible with slavery and public tranquillity: nonetheless, as it is not feasible for my American vassals who possess slaves to acquaint themselves sufficiently with all the areas stipulated by law inserted into said compilations, and much less those found in the general and limited decrees, and in municipal ordinances approved for various provinces; and keeping in mind that for this reason, notwithstanding those measures ordered by my august predecessors concerning the instruction, treatment, and occupation of slaves, that over the course of time, slaveholders and their *mayordomos* [chief stewards] have introduced certain abuses inconsistent with and even in violation of the legislative system and other general and limited measures taken in this particular matter. For the purpose of remedying such breaches, and taking into account that with the free trade in slaves, which I have conceded to my vassals in Article 1 of the Royal Decree of February 28 last, the number of slaves in both Americas will increase considerably, meriting my attention to this category of individuals of the human race, during the time that, in the general code being formulated for the Indies, the laws concerning this important purpose are established and promulgated: I resolve that, for the present, all slave owners and slaveholders in those dominions faithfully observe the following directive:

Chapter I. Instruction. All slaveholders, of whatever class and condition, will be obligated to instruct their slaves in the tenets of the Catholic religion and in its necessary truths in order that they can be baptized within one year of their residence in my dominions, ensuring that they are properly instructed in Christian doctrine on all religious holidays, on which they will be neither obliged nor permitted to work for themselves nor for their owners, excepting harvesttime, when it is customary to grant special dispensations to work on holidays. On these days and all the others on which Church law calls for hearing mass, hacienda owners will bear the cost of a priest to celebrate mass for their slaves on these or other holidays, instruct slaves in Christian doctrine on religious holidays, and administer the sacred sacraments to them, likewise with other seasonal Church observances; taking heed that, every workday, at the conclusion of the day's toil, slaves pray the rosary in their owners' or their stewards' presence, with the utmost serenity and devotion.

Chapter II. Food and garb. Slave owners have a continuing obligation to feed and clothe their slaves and the wives and children of these slaves, whether such dependents be slave or free, until such time as they themselves can earn their keep, presumably by the age of twelve for females and fourteen for males. As it is not possible to dictate fixed standards providing for the quantity and quality of slaves' food and the type of garb that owners must provide, owing to the wide array of provinces, climates, temperament, and other specific factors, [the king] orders that, as far as these matters are concerned, municipal officials in the hacienda district, in accordance with the town council and the office of the syndic procurator, in his capacity as an advocate for the slaves, make known and determine the quantity and quality of food and attire that, proportionally, according to their relative ages and sex, slave owners must furnish their slaves with daily, in keeping with the reigning customs of the country, and consistent with what is commonly provided day laborers and clothing used by free workers. These regulations, after being approved by the district court, will be affixed every month to the doors of the town council building and churches of each town, and to those of hacienda oratories or hermitages, in order that these notices reach everyone and that no one can allege ignorance in this matter.

Chapter III. Slave occupations. Slaves' primary and foremost occupation must be that of agriculture and other rural labors, and not the trades associated with sedentary life; and, thus, in order that both slave owners and the State realize the profit due them from the slaves' work and that slaves carry out those labors as they should, municipal officials, in the same manner as the foregoing chapter, will determine the daily allocation of tasks for slaves, consistent with their age, strength, and individual vigor. As all work must commence and conclude between sunup and sundown. Slaves will be allotted two hours during the course of the day to devote to production of manufactures or to other tasks that result in the slaves' own personal gain and profit. Owners or mayordomos cannot oblige individuals over sixty years old, nor minors younger than seventeen, nor female slaves to work under "portareas" [a type of quota system], nor may they assign these same women to work at tasks incompatible with their sex, or engage in any toil obligating them to consort with men, nor compel them to work as day laborers. The owners of those slaves in domestic service will pay an additional tax of two pesos a month, as stipulated in Chapter VIII of the Royal Decree of February 28 last, cited above.

Chapter IV. Recreation. On religious holidays, on which owners can neither compel nor allow slaves to work, after slaves have heard mass and received instruction in Christian doctrine, the masters and, if they are not available, their mayordomos will see to it that the slaves on their haciendas amuse themselves in simple and harmless pursuits, just as long as they not mingle with slaves from other haciendas, and are segregated according to sex. These same owners or mayordomos must be in attendance, making certain that slaves not drink in excess and ensuring that these diversions conclude before the bell tolls for evening prayers.

Chapter V. Housing and infirmary. All slave owners must provide housing that segregates unmarried slaves according to their sex, and that is comfortable and sufficient to shelter them from inclement weather, providing raised beds, blankets or other necessary linens, with one person to a bed, minimal provisions for privacy, and no more than two to a room. Owners must designate another separate, sheltered, and comfortable room or quarters for anyone who is ill, and they are obliged to tend to their every need. In the event that owners wish to consign a slave to a hospital, whether because a hacienda's size does not justify one [a hospital of its own] or because a hacienda is located close to town, owners must pay for a slave's hospital confinement there, paying the customary daily rate as determined by the court, in the manner and form provided in Chapter II. Likewise, slave owners are obligated to pay funeral expenses of any slave who passes away.

Chapter VI. Concerning old age and chronic illness. Slave owners must see to it that any slaves who, due to their advanced age or infirmity, are not fit to work, and, also, any children and minors of either sex are all properly fed. Slave owners must not grant slaves their freedom in order to be rid of them, unless slave owners provide this class of individuals with funds adequate to maintain themselves with no need for additional assistance, as determined by the court in consultation with the office of the syndic procurator.

Chapter VII. Slaves and marriage. Slave owners must work to forestall illicit behavior between the sexes, encouraging marriage, and doing nothing to thwart marriages between slaves belonging to different owners. In the latter case, if the respective haciendas are so far apart that the consorts cannot live as husband and wife, the woman will follow her husband, the husband's owner buying her for a fair price as established by appraisers agreeable to both parties or, in the case of a dispute, by an impartial third party designated by the court. If the husband's owner does not agree to these terms, the wife's owner will have the same option [to purchase her husband according to these same provisions].

Chapter VIII. The obligations of slaves and disciplinary measures. While slave owners are obligated to support, instruct, and employ slaves in fruitful labors in keeping with their individual strength, age, and sex, and may not forsake minors, the aged, or the infirm, a reciprocal obligation likewise attaches to slaves, who are compelled to obey and revere their owners and mayordomos, to carry out those tasks and chores assigned to them as their individual strength allows, and to venerate them as they would their own parents; and, thus, any who fails to fulfill any of these obligations will and must be subject to corrective punishment for any excesses they commit, whether administered by hacienda owners or their mayordomos, according to the nature of the particular deficiency or offense, including imprisonment, shackles, chains, mace, or stocks, exempting the head, or no more than twenty-five lashes lightly laid on, that do not cause serious contusions or excessive bleeding, the administration of such disciplinary measures being restricted to slave owners or mayordomos.

Chapter IX. Imposition of harsher disciplinary measures. When slaves are guilty of wrongdoing, exhibit shortcomings, or commit offenses against their masters, their wives, or their children, mayordomos, or any other person for which the corrective penalties and punishments cited in the preceding chapter may be insufficient, the culprit apprehended by the hacienda owners or their mayordomos or whosoever witnesses the commission of the offense, the injured party or their representative must inform the court in order that in a hearing with the slave owner, assuming that the slave is not forsaken by his owner before responding to the suit and is not implicated in the accusation, and in all cases with the syndic procurator in his capacity as an advocate for the slaves in attendance, the proceedings follow the dictates of law, the procedures of indictment and sentencing, and the imposition of the corresponding sentence, according to the gravity and exact circumstances surrounding the offense, observing in every respect the same legal process that attaches to offenders who are free. And when the owner does not forsake the slave and the slave is sentenced consistent with the damages and injury done to a third party, the owner must be responsible for satisfying these, in addition to administering any corporal punishment, always in keeping with the gravity of the offense, that the slave perpetrator will undergo once [the penalty] is approved by the district court, if it is a case of the death sentence or a punishment calling for mutilation of limbs.

Chapter X. Wrongdoing or excesses committed by owners or mayordomos. Slave owners or their hacienda mayordomos who do not comply with measures set out in the preceding chapters of this instructional circular pertaining to slaves' instruction, nourishment, garb, supervision of appropriate work and chores, engagement in wholesome forms of amusement, guidelines for housing and infirmaries, or the abandonment of minors, the aged, or the infirm will incur a fine of fifty pesos for a first offense, one hundred for a second, and two hundred for a third, which must be paid by the slave owner, even in the case in which the mayordomo alone is guilty but lacks the means to pay himself, remitting payment in thirds, a third going to the accuser, another third to the judge, and the final third into a public fine fund, to be dealt with later. In the case that the aforementioned fines do not produce the desired effect, and a repeat offense is substantiated, additional larger penalties will be levied on the guilty party for disobeying my royal orders, and I will be duly and properly informed in order to take the appropriate measures.

When wrongdoing on the part of slave owners or mayordomos consists of administering excessive corrective penalties, causing slaves serious contusions, excessive bleeding, or mutilation of limbs, besides suffering the pecuniary fines cited above, the syndic procurator will press criminal charges against the slave owner or mayordomo, substantiating the grounds according to law, and imposing the appropriate sentence for the offense committed, just as if the injured party were free. In addition, the syndic procurator will confiscate the slave, in order that the slave be sold to another owner if he is fit to work, applying the purchase price to the public fine fund. Any slave deemed unfit for sale will not be returned to the former owner or mayordomo who is overzealous in their punishment. Rather, the owner must pay daily allotments for the slave's maintenance and apparel, as determined by the court, for the rest of the slave's natural life, paying it in thirds and in advance.

Chapter XI. Concerning those who do harm to slaves. As only slave owners and mayordomos can administer corrective punishment to slaves, while exercising the restraints outlined above, no other person who is not the owner or mayordomo can inflict bodily injury, punish, wound, or slay a slave without incurring penalties, as established by law, pertaining to those who commit such excesses or offenses against a person who is free, prosecuting, trying [a case], and making a ruling at the request of the owner of any slave who may have been so injured, punished, or slain; or, in his absence, officially by the syndic procurator in his capacity as protector of the slaves, who as such protector also will have a role in the first instance, even if there be an accuser.

Chapter XII. Slave rosters. Slave owners must present an annual roster signed and sworn to before the municipal court in whose jurisdiction their haciendas are situated, of all the slaves contained thereon, distinguishing them individually by sex and age, in order that the town council's notary public make an official entry to that effect in a special tome designated for this purpose and preserved in that same town council building, with lists submitted by slave owners. Should a slave later perish or quit a hacienda, the slave owner must inform the court within three days in order that, by virtue of a summons issued by the syndic procurator, it may be duly noted in that same aforementioned tome for the purpose of avoiding any implication that the slave may have been dealt a violent death. Any slave owner who fails to meet this condition will be obliged to account fully either for the slave's absence or his natural death. Should he fail to do so, at the request of the syndic procurator, the appropriate charges will be filed.

Chapter XIII. Means of determining wrongdoing on the part of owners or mayordomos. Given the extended distances between haciendas and towns, plus certain difficulties that ensue if, under the pretext of lodging a complaint, slaves are allowed to leave an establishment without the owners' or mayordomo's written permission stating the express purpose of their excursion, and the just laws prohibiting fugitive slaves from being aided, abetted, or concealed, it is necessary to develop the means to address all these circumstances, in order that it is possible to acquire information concerning the treatment of slaves on the haciendas. One of these means is the clerics who traverse haciendas for the purpose of expounding religious doctrine to slaves and celebrating mass. They can observe for themselves and hear firsthand from slaves concerning how owners and mayordomos proceed and how they comply with the content of this instructional circular. By giving secret and confidential information to the syndic procurator of the respective city or town, [he will] in this manner assist the person who inquires into whether or not the masters or mayordomos are lacking in all or in part of their respective obligations, with the ecclesiastic bearing no responsibility for charges found to be baseless, or a denunciation kept confidential by the ecclesiastic due to his ministry, or due to slave grievances. Any information they may provide should serve only as a basis for the syndic procurator to promote and request before the court that a member of the town council or another person of impeccable conduct be appointed to carry out an inquiry; this person submitting the appropriate indictment, and turning it over to a court of law, in order to substantiate and determine the grounds according to law, listening to the syndic procurator, and taking into account any legal precedent and instances cited in this instructional circular, to the district court and allow the possibility of appeal in those cases where a point of law is raised.

Besides this means, it will be advisable for municipal officials, in accordance with the town council and the assistance of the syndic procurator, to appoint a person or persons of good character and conduct, who are to visit haciendas three times a year and closely examine them, and duly report if the conditions singled out in this instructional circular are being implemented, making note of what they observe so that, upon presenting a competent defense [to the court], the matter be rectified through a hearing by the syndic procurator. Also, popular action can denounce the deficiencies or lack of compliance with one or all of the previous chapters, and, in the understanding that the name of the accuser will be forever kept confidential, and the designated portion of the fine will be applied, [the accuser will remain] exempt from liability except when the charge or accusation should prove to be notoriously and overwhelmingly slanderous.

Lastly, it is also declared that the residence trials[2] of municipal officials and procurators, syndics in their capacity as protectors of the slaves, will seek out any deficiencies of omission or commission they may have incurred by failing to use all necessary means in order to fulfill my royal purpose, as stipulated in this instructional [...].

In order that all the rulings prescribed in this instructional circular be duly and scrupulously observed, I hereby repeal any existing laws, decrees, royal orders, applications, and practices contrary to them.

Fernando Ortiz, *Los negros esclavos* (Havana: Editorial de Ciencas Sociales, 1975), pp. 408–15.

2. Slaveholders and the Slave Code

STATEMENT FROM HAVANA'S INGENIO OWNERS TO THE KING

Havana, January 19, 1790

Sire:

Hacendados from this city who own sugar-producing ingenios, advised of the royal decree issued in Aranjuez on May 31 last, which provides for the regulation of the education, treatment, and occupations of slaves in these dominions, submit this reverent representation to Your Majesty. We in no way intend to contest these regulations, nor will we attempt to recur to that economic authority which legally authorizes us to govern our establishments as we see fit. We recognize in Your Majesty the full and complete embodiment of the highest sovereignty. We have willingly obeyed Your Majesty as an expression of our love and devotion. Our love only makes Your Majesty's precepts all the more pleasing to us and our devotion compels us to observe them as sacred. We only wish to make known to Your Majesty the very grave problems that the implementation of some of the chapters of this same royal decree implies and how others are actually carried out in practice.

We know that, in the establishment of these laws, Your Majesty is prompted solely by a sense of justice and love for your vassals. Your Majesty's august father, whom we will never forget, provided us with many proven instances of that truth, and, assured in our conviction that anything departing whatsoever from that purpose is opposed to Your Majesty's sovereign intentions, we are inspired to direct our appeal to you. We predict that there will be dismal consequences for our economic interests. We already foresee our haciendas lying in ruin, our families wretched, and unimaginable arrearages for Your Majesty's treasury. Tithe rents destroyed, port commerce annihilated, our fields abandoned, agriculture devastated, the island subject to one calamity after another, and our slaves, in open revolt, without [. . .][1] leaves us with the disastrous spectacle of the bloodshed that will be necessary to contain them. These damages are exactly what will result from Law 24, Title 1, Book 2 of the compilation of these realms unless the observance of royal decrees and their provisions are suspended. We are being absolutely truthful, subjecting our observations to the closest scrutiny. We vow that Your Majesty will be pleased.

We ask that, as sovereign, you grant us the audience that we implore and that, in your paternal role, you kindly remedy the imminent ruin that menaces us. In any event, our obedience will be as natural as it is submissive, and no other interest will intrude to sway our beliefs or to lessen our devotion or our love.

Regarding Chapter I of the Royal Decree. It is the widespread custom of all ingenios to pray the rosary every day and to instruct the slaves in Christian doctrine, without the harvest affecting such a practice. This instruction is accomplished efficiently by using the time-honored practice of entrusting the religious education of the catechumens to their fellow slaves, who are established Christians. These slaves acting as catechists are deemed the baptismal sponsors of their charges, and many of the catechumens are baptized before a year is out. However, this is not the case with everyone, because those catechumens who are uncouth and slothful will take longer than others who are adept and energetic.

We never use slaves for the [. . .] of our services[2] on religious holidays, whose [. . .][3] observance of which we never have requested special allowances, nor the [. . .][4] are accustomed to incite it. But those servitors, in full view of bishops and parish priests, have from time immemorial worked on their own behalf. It is not incumbent upon us to examine the fairness of this practice, nor whether or not the opinion of those moralists who agree with this practice is good or dissolute, their position based on the gospel. It [the answer] can be derived from the priceless freedom that such [remunerative] work brings about (a cause that is far more important to them than their owners' good harvest, which the royal decree qualifies as a legitimate basis for special allowances). It possibly stems from [the fact that] the masters tolerated it [slaves working on their own behalf] in the past in order to thwart the drunkenness, robbery, and other wickedness on holidays, as opposed to behaviors sanctifying them. What is certain is that taking that resource [slaves working for themselves on Sundays and holidays] away from the slaves now, something that they rely on to emerge from slavery, will be a surefire basis for their resentment, they will once again observe holidays with lewdness and criminal behavior. The results will be momentous, and the majority of them will embrace whatever other alternative that presents itself to shake off the yoke of slavery, a burden that they already will have deemed perpetual for a lack of other means with which to aspire to the freedom they so long for.

All those ingenios that are profitable and are able to maintain a chaplain have one (if they find him) to celebrate mass on holidays and teach Christian doctrine to the slaves. But there are others that, either because they are but recently established or because they lack sufficient funds, cannot suffer such an expense. And there are yet others that, although able to pay, cannot locate a chaplain. Nevertheless, the masters of all of these see to it that their servile work force somehow hears mass, either on nearby ingenios or in rural chapels before allowing them to engage in any work whatsoever.

The latest rolls carried out on the rural properties in this jurisdiction document that there are 193 sugar-producing ingenios. On the entire island, there are only five hundred presbyters among the secular and regular clergy. These must serve the parishes in the cities, towns, and villages. They carry out religious observances and obligations in convents and monesteries. They provide instruction and administer educational programs. They minister in urban oratories, chapels; private hospitals and churches; jails, castles, and fortresses. With so few clergy, how is it possible to provide a chaplain to every ingenio in this jurisdiction and, how [. . .][5], to reach out to the rest of the island and others [. . .][6] in the rural countryside? How will it be feasible for tobacco operations, small farms, and estancias to pay for such an expense? And how will any master be able to comply with this portion of Chapter I of the Royal Decree, or especially to evade the unwarranted complaints from slaves, or other dire effects that ensue?

Regarding Chapter II. In Chapter II, Your Majesty deigns to order the creation of regulations governing food and clothing that must be provided for all slaves of both sexes in keeping with local custom and consistent with those given to day laborers and free workers. This law, Sire, in and of itself, is extremely just. But, once the slaves come to understand it, they will rise up against their masters. Owners will suffer unwarranted insults from their slaves on a daily basis. Undeservedly, masters will be required to constantly demonstrate their compliance and accountability. So it is that their slaves will become insubordinate, they will throw off the shackles of servitude, and no one will be able to restrain their arrogance.

It behooves owners to treat their slaves well, given that the masters' own sustenance and the very advancement of their haciendas is linked to the labor of those same slaves. Not only does a basic sense of human decency favor such a course, but owners' own economic self-interest does as well. For this reason, the best law is that law in which each party has a vested interest.

As a general rule, each slave will be outfitted with hemp clothing twice a year and be given a baize greatcoat . . . if this is not sufficient, just like those used by the hired help, and a half a pound of beef jerky that, made into a stew, is made into an individual portion that is almost more than they will be able to eat, a proportional amount of corn flour, as many plantains as they desire, without scrimping on the sweet potatoes, squash, and other root crops, nor shortchanging them on rice, when called for. No free day laborer eats as well or is better dressed. The slaves themselves give evidence of this, as once they are free, they continue to work on the ingenio as salaried help, and no one from these haciendas ever, once their ownership is transferred, wants to toil in any other fields than those of their former hacienda, renouncing any other offers for work. The masters who do not follow this general rule are but few. The government will deal with these individuals by keeping them under strict supervision, specifying the meat, root crops, and clothing that they must give to their slaves, without consulting them, akin to the way a magistrate deals with a father who abandons his children or with a husband who does not feed or clothe his wife, without recurring to a general regulation that, directed at ignorant and uncouth people, would take advantage of it to inflame feelings against their master.

Regarding Chapter III. It is impossible that officials in cities and towns determine the tasks that comprise the daily work of slaves, according to their age, strength, and stamina, because the changes and variation that these [. . .][7] undergo are continuous. The slave who today can bear a competent [. . .][8] tomorrow weakens and is incapable of tolerating it. There are [. . .][9] those who are feeble by nature and to whom death will be more sweet than completing even a simple task, than to those who are active and agile. There are those slaves in their forties who are constantly laid up, more frequently than those slaves in their sixties. And in this matter, none can better dictate the rules than the very master who manages them and who primarily benefits from the humanitarian treatment of his slaves, so that his prudent husbandry of slaves leads to the very profits to which he aspires. And so, if municipal officials become involved in this matter, either the masters will be adversely affected or their wretched servitors will be overworked.

It is well known that men are of different physical strengths and that the frail and fainthearted will be overwhelmed if, goaded by punishment or threats, they attempt to do the work of those who are by nature robust and especially hardworking.

It is common to give the slaves in our sugar refineries two extra hours of free time, in addition to the time allotted for eating lunch. But they spend that time eating, relaxing, and resting, with the exception of a few who use the time for their own work, and it will be impossible to force everyone to use the time wisely in producing their own goods or doing other tasks for their own benefit, as is borne out in practice.

If the daily work is necessarily from sunup to sundown, at harvesttime the ingenios cannot, Sire, respect such a schedule and it will be necessary to completely abandon [. . .][10] that industry and efficiency insist upon. For six months of the year, our slaves do not work at night, except for some light chores requiring a little over an hour, such as toting firewood, tending livestock, and other light domestic chores (which we will speak of later). During the other six months, at harvesttime, there is night work, which is divided into two or three shifts with corresponding crews. If there are only two shifts, then the first crew works from the first quarter of the night until twelve o'clock, and the second crew from twelve until dawn. If there are three shifts, the hours are adjusted accordingly. While those from one shift work, the others sleep, so that, even during this grueling time, slaves are able to sleep for seven or eight hours. This schedule is suspended once the harvest is over. And during the rest of the year, slaves are able to rest so much that they are able to get ahead in the work for their own financial benefit, on goods they produce themselves, and on animal by-products from their own livestock, the profit from which they put toward obtaining their freedom. The sugar presses come to life at midnight, grinding the cane, extracting its juice to make into *guarapo* [cane juice]. Depending upon how it comes out, it is collected through a series of pipes into *pailas* [huge copper cauldrons], where it is processed. The remaining operations proceed and, at ten o'clock the next morning, the sugar from this first batch of guarapo is ready.

The same process is repeated over and over, ending at nightfall. Work is always done from sunup to sundown, being necessary to suspend the [. . .][11] of sugar, until the first batch comes out, and [. . .][12] sequence to not grind more sugarcane than can be emp[. . .][13] in it, otherwise it is not possible to complete the entire process during daylight hours, nor is it possible simply to resume work on the guarapo or *meladura* [treacle, sugarhouse molasses] the next morning, because such interruptions cause the mixture to ferment and go sour on the spot, spoiling the entire batch and making it impossible to process into sugar.

Everyone familiar with operations on an ingenio is aware of this indisputable fact. If the process for producing guarapo is interrupted, and the unfinished mixture is held overnight, then it is certain to be completely ruined. Another hard and fast rule is that from the month of January, when the harvest typically begins, until May or the beginning of June, the latest possible date for the harvest (because not even the rains permit further delay nor can the length of the growing season for the new crop of cane be put at risk), the sun appears shortly after seven in the morning, or shortly after six, and even earlier, just after five. So, if the cane is ground beginning at midnight, then the first batch of sugar is ready at ten o'clock the next morning. If work is begun at five, six, or seven in the morning, whenever the sun comes up, work will be over at five, four, or three in the afternoon, and it is necessary for operations to come to an end. With sunset within a few short hours, there is no time to begin making another batch of guarapo that will be ready for processing into sugar and each sugar refinery observing this abbreviated schedule [. . .][14] will be able to produce only one-fourth of the sugar that they produced before. For this reason, foreign sugar producers do not prohibit night work. This is why those who have written about the subject specify the timetable, and any other method not respecting such a timetable bears out this useful and recommended agricultural practice.

All the huge farm expenses simply cannot be met with the profits from sugar. Even when the length of the harvests is abbreviated due to the depleted overworked soil and working at night as is the custom, we suffer financial distress and are deeply in debt. [Further regulation] will make it necessary for us to abandon our ingenios, and Your Majesty's royal treasury will suffer a significant lack of revenue from a major source. Income from tithes, previously sufficient to decently maintain two dioceses, will scarcely sustain their churches in an abject fashion, their cathedral chapters lacking endowments. Commerce that previously flourished due to sugar will be in ruins. Agriculture will be destroyed. The population will decrease, and formerly resplendent families will suffer hardship and want.

If it were not a digression, using this same evidence, we would pause to demonstrate to Your Majesty the probable ruin of small estancias dedicated to breeding and raising livestock [. . .][15] and that, indubitably, the branch of ta[. . .]¹⁶ will perish (one of the most precious sources of income of Your Majesty's treasury). The proper husbandry of both types of establishments requires night work. It is crucial that the tobacco worker irrigate the transplanted plants at night, because, if it is done during the day the sun destroys them. When pestilence threatens, field hands must eradicate worms that typically plague tobacco plants, commonly known as *rosguilla* and *cachuzudo*, or they will devour the entire tobacco field in short order. This type of eradication cannot be done during the day, because, with the light of dawn, these insects bore down into the soil and do not return to the surface until evening. The crop must be harvested late in the day, so that the sun evaporates the night dew and dries the moisture-laden leaves, so that they can be handled without breaking them and gathered into piles. It is necessary immediately to hang the leaves from sheltered wooden rods or *cujes*, so that they do not become scorched [by the sun]. These operations must necessarily be done at night, or one risks losing the crop. This aside only serves to demonstrate to Your Majesty the very grave and impending financial ruin threatening his royal treasury, and so by informing Your Majesty, you may deign to intervene before we are subject to [economic] havoc.

So that Your Majesty may have a more perfect understanding of what we have presented here, we will provide a brief summary [. . .]¹⁷ considering the work on our ingenios at [. . .]¹⁸ harvesttime, because during the rest of the year there is nothing that is [. . .]¹⁹ a common agriculture, with the exception of the cutting of firewood that is done for the sugarcane harvest, and we are left with very limited chores, and almost half of these [chores] are performed by salaried freedmen.

Late Sunday night, all the slaves gather at the building housing the machinery or the *trapiche*, and, after praying the rosary, the first shift goes to work while the remaining slaves go to bed. Already at this early hour, the sugarcane is piled high at the foot of the machinery. Two or three slaves pitch the sugarcane to two others, who load it into the *trapiche*, and another two remove it on the other side. Each team of oxen powering the machinery has its own drover. The *suco* [sugarcane sap] or *guarapo* that is produced is poured into the *pailas*, where it is cooked, and *meladura* is made. This is taken in short order to the *tachos* (boilers in which molasses is brought to the consistency necessary to convert it into sugar), where the process is completed. If there are eight boilers, ten slaves are required: four stationed at the *pailas*, two to slowly feed and tend the fire, and four working at the tachos, skimming off the foam that the meladura produces. They can sleep for at least three hours while the substance is more finely processed, at which point the assistance of the *tacheros* is once again required.

When the sun comes up the next morning, everyone is summoned, calling out those who have slept as well as those who have worked. This is the time of day that it is always done, even when it is not harvesttime. Some are assigned to the *casa de purga* [curing house or purging house] to work adding clay to the sugar, the clay purifying and whitening it. Others are assigned to the *secadero* [drying shed] to separate the white sugar from the brown sugar, others transport it in carts [. . .][20] from the fields to the trapiche, others clean the building, remove [. . .][21] and similar simple manual domestic labor. The morning is spent in [. . .][22] until nearly nine o'clock, at which time they eat their morning meal, and, later, those hands assigned to fieldwork go out to cut more cane. Each slave has to cut one cartful of cane, although free salaried workers are expected to harvest twice that amount. At midday, they return home, eat, and relax for two hours. Afterward, they return to the fields and, finishing much of their work by five o'clock or before, they go to rest in their huts, which are comfortable and agreeable.

This is the harvesttime regime. In the summer, the off-season, it is necessary to cart firewood in the early evening, otherwise the harsh sun is so unbearable that the oxen are overcome with fatigue. The carters transporting sugar also do it at this time of day for their own comfort. The annual overhaul of the foundries is a long and arduous process that must be conducted in an uninterrupted fashion, resembling a long and painful operation that cannot be interrupted, and it, too, necessarily requires night work of the slaves. Because of this standard, except at the time of the sugarcane harvest, slaves only work at night when it is absolutely necessary or when working at night makes the tasks more comfortable and faster for the slaves.

These details, invariable and accurate, will enable Your Majesty to appreciate that the work is extremely reasonable and well tolerated. Far from exhausting the slaves during milling time, the cane and guarapo make them more robust, healthy, and active.

If you would deign, Your Majesty, to allow us, as a result of your steadfast goodness, to lament our misfortune made even greater by the long distances separating us, taking us far from Your Majesty's royal personage, making it difficult for us to demonstrate to you how the reports against our conduct may have been misinterpreted. No abuses opposed to the system of legislation, or religious maxims, or humanity will be found in our sugar refineries. We beseech Your Majesty to carry out the most assiduous inquiry of our case. Your Majesty should corroborate a calumny which some overzealous indiscretion or some unchristian envy causes you to hold us in contempt, then Sire, we will be forced to draw attention to comparisons between the night work prohibited our slaves and the widespread practice of night work among miners in the realms of Peru and Mexico, or among agricultural workers reaping olives and other types of agricultural crops on the Iberian Peninsula, or the night work of sailors, bakery workers, and the like. None of those artisans are exempted from working at their trade at night. Miners divide their workers into two shifts, one day and one night. Sailors work different shifts, so that while some sleep, others keep watch. Troops safeguarding fortified port cities also work in shifts. All of these workers are free. Our slaves are not. Slaves only work night shifts for six months of the year. Miners, sailors, and soldiers do night work all year long. Any fatigue suffered by miners is indisputably greater than that endured by workers in our sugar refineries. Slaves there do not work on holidays, as the abovementioned free workers do. Oh, Sire, how can we make Your Majesty appreciate that our steadfast hearts are wracked with pain! Your Majesty forming, as a result of those reports, such a low opinion of our religious devotion and our conduct, Your Majesty does not grant us what he [. . .][23] other vassals, to some the treasure of his benevolent acts, exempt from taxes [. . .][24] work of their salaried workers until making them happy. At the same time, the work of our slaves is so limited by conditions that we will not be able to maintain our haciendas. We live only for the hope that, when Your Majesty hears evidence in this matter, our sentiments will be justified and Your Majesty will rule favorably on our case and deem us innocent.

Making use of abundant evidence, we would be able to prove to Your Majesty the humane treatment our slaves receive, without losing sight of the welfare of the State, public tranquillity, and the system of legislation, if we were not trying to limit knowledge of the regulation; but we will provide Your Majesty with one or more reflections that will prove that we speak the truth.

If our slaves were not well fed and clothed, if we treated them inhumanely, if we encroached on their rest periods, and if we did not allow them ample time to attend to their own affairs, then vast numbers of them would not be gaining their freedom. Your Majesty himself has two battalions consisting of this type of freedmen, and more than enough to form yet another. Most of them free their women first, and many their children as well. Each head, that is, adult slave, pays out at least three hundred pesos for his or her freedom and for those slaves who are sugar masters or ply another trade, that amount is higher yet. How could they not spend money to support themselves? And how would they acquire it if they had been granted no free time and suffered mightily from undue affliction?

Because foreigners fomented the idea that the black man without physical strength serves no purpose, and they use everyone they consider necessary in their service, when the British seized this town, a large part of our slaves retreated to the interior of the island, persuaded that the English inevitably would dominate them. Once Your Majesty's august father was restored, the slaves themselves sought us out on their own, under no undue influence or persuasion (fugitives, criminals, and the wicked excepted). Would they do this if we killed them out of necessity, if we treated them inhumanely, if we treated them with the same rigor as the British? Would they not seek, in that case, to change owners and to better their circumstances?

Meanwhile, a great many black slaves who obtain their freedom, as already indicated, continue working on the very same ingenios where they have been slaves or on others at a limited salary. They would not maintain this affection for the hacienda had it been the theater of their calamities, nor would it be normal for them to wish to remain on the employ of their former owners if those very same owners had been such tyrants. There is no doubt about this, and should Your Majesty ever choose to investigate this matter, our version will be wholly proven.

A careful reckoning of the bozals who come ashore at this port, taking into account the respective dates of disembarkation, shows that the number that survives is excessive when compared to ages of men in normal population profiles. This should not be, given the differences in climate and food or their susceptibility to smallpox and other illnesses.

There can be no greater proof that our slaves are not mistreated or subject to the harsh punishments more typical of the English and the French, under whose care we can assure Your Majesty the reckoning will not be the same, nor lead to the same conclusion. The slaves can never forget the kindness with which we treat them. Masters typically feign harshness and rigor with their slaves so that fear may induce them to swallow their natural pride and the threat of severe punishment may reduce them to doing their duty. They appreciate that we care for them as the [. . .][25] of our assets. The ingenios with considerable capital, maintain salaried [. . .][26] surgeons for the healing of their afflictions, and other [. . .][27] bear this expense jointly. They observe that when an illness is serious and the slaves cannot go out into the fields, we take them into the city and nurse them back to health in our own homes, our wives visiting them, and nurses [whom] we pay taking care of them. It is no secret to the slaves that our instructions are very clear: at the appearance of the most minor symptoms of any affliction threatening their health, they are to be relieved from their work, with no further inquiry into whether the infliction is feigned or real. Likewise, the slaves are quite aware that the mayorals have standing orders to remove slaves from night work whenever they are too sleepy on the job in order to head off a possible tragedy with the trapiche or the boilers. Sire, we ask you, could a father do more for his own child?

Before ending our commentary on this chapter, we advise Your Majesty to consider the compassion and charity with which we treat the female slaves on our ingenios. We pity them, and we always arrange for them to be assigned to jobs that are compatible with their sex. We ensure that the mixing of sexes, when necessary, presents no risk whatsoever to their virtue. We encourage marriage, and we have thought about increasing the number of females on our establishments in order to foment licit propagation, thus avoiding loathsome and wicked transgressions. Thus, we conserve the capital paid for our initial acquisitions, and the servitude continues with the love inspired by one's place of birth, replacing those who die with those who are born, thus not suffering the expense of purchasing more Africans, and depriving the foreigners who deal in slaves of profit.

Regarding Chapter IV. The entertainments blacks most prefer are the barbarous dances of their homelands. They dance to the strain of kettledrums (which are hollowed out tree trunks with dried cow leather stretched over one end), to small flutes fashioned from wild cane, and to marimbas made from several different types of wood joined together, played with wood implements in harmony. We never forbid dancing on holidays, during their rest periods, or at work. They dance just as much as they like. The mayorals are on the lookout to see that nothing else happens, spending the night at these feasts, guarding against any threat to the morrow's obligations. When both black men and black women attend, they also are vigilant that modesty and proper conduct prevail. With these requirements, the bishops and synods have permitted both sexes to attend the same dances that are held at their own cabildos on holidays. And the truth is that if they are denied these activities, it will cause them unbearable anguish and there could be serious consequences. The conscientiousness and discretion of the owner, the mayoral, or capatazes makes this possible, and those responsible for watching over the event never let their guard down.

Regarding Chapter VIII. In the eighth chapter, we are prohibited from punishing the immoderation of our slaves with more than twenty-five lashes, administered by means that do not cause serious bruising or bleeding. We especially are vigilant in protecting our investment by ensuring that these punishments are of a moderate nature, as severe punishments can incapacitate slaves for many days, causing them to miss work. Only in cases when the offense is extraordinarily serious, or when it behooves us to make an example of a slave for the benefit of others, do we deem additional lashes necessary, but the [. . .][28] of this law and the fixed idea that the slaves have that [. . .][29] can we impose more severe punishment on them, it absolutely will make them lose any fear they have of us, they will feign ignorance of the due obedience owed their masters and mayorals, there will be complaints lodged against us with the government if we compel them to do their duty, they will abandon the haciendas, and there will be other tragic, irreversible consequences.

In order that Your Majesty understand the gravity of this truth, it is necessary to define who these black bozals are, and to take pause to explain something of their temperament, nature, and conditions. They are barbarians, audacious and ungrateful for any advantages bestowed upon them. They never abandon the detestable practices associated with heathenism. If they are well treated, they become insolent. They are, by their very nature, hardened and austere. Many of them never forget the horror of the *pitegórica*[30] transmigration, growing up forever mindful of these vivid memories. They dread that horrid legacy far more than they fear being murdered by their fellows. They are prone to desperation, to mayhem, to robbery, to drunkenness, to perfidy, are easily inflamed, and are susceptible to all classes of vice.

In order to prove the validity of our argument, we could support our case with authentic documents detailing the appalling crimes the slaves so shockingly perpetrate in the countryside any time their masters subject them to less rigor or treat them too leniently. We are constrained in this by our desire to forestall the diffusion of such information.

On one occasion, blacks removed the heart of he who governed them and roasted it, using their rage to concoct a most flavorful dish. United, they avoided being brought to justice, preferring death to surrender. They established palenques or *rancherías* [shantytowns] in the most remote scrubland. From this base of operations, they sallied forth to rustle cattle, assault wayfarers and rural dwellings, robbing one and all, and forcing themselves upon any women they happen upon. Fed up, they have mutinied in the ingenios, killing, wounding, and laying waste to whatever they found. On occasion, it was necessary for the government to come to the rescue, armed and spilling a great deal of blood in order to contain them, at times ordering the rebellion's ringleaders summarily lynched. After heaping vengeance on their masters or overseers, they were wont to hang themselves, drown themselves, or commit suicide by some other means. They fired houses and newly sown fields, as recently witnessed on the ingenio belonging to Don José Ignacio de Orta, whose people were assaulted by a gang of maroons. It was necessary to contain the violence using weapons and, at the same time, to extinguish the raging fires, the combat lasting for quite some time at the cost of several casualties, including serious injuries and loss of limbs. And, just recently, there was an uprising in Guarico, a neighboring French colony, which badly frightened one and all and caused extra precautions to be put in place. Nevertheless, harsh treatment and fear usually had the desired effect of restraining slaves' behavior, so that when masters governed their slaves with apparent rigor, without being tyrannical, such tragedies were far less frequent.

One Holy Thursday, the first Count of Casa Bayona, wishing to display the proper degree of humility that is part of the day's ceremonies, washed the feet of twelve slaves from his ingenio and administered Holy Communion to them. Whether because he did not do the same for other wretches or because he believed that it was more humbling for him to serve his own slaves and better commended him in the eyes of the Church, the exercise backfired. The slaves, abusing their master's benefaction and charity, afterward refused to work. When leniency and persuasion were to no avail, it was necessary to use force. Their pride swollen with arrogance, they summoned others to join the mayhem, they rose up and affronted that ingenio and neighboring establishments as well. It became necessary for the government to restore order forcibly, at the cost of several lives and great carnage.

Given the nature, temperament, and condition of slaves [. . .][31] should they become aware that none of their excesses will be punished by a penalty of more than twenty-five lashes lightly laid on with respect to [. . .];[32] according to their severity must be legally [. . .],[33] forsaking work on the ingenios as set out in Chapter IX. A protector is appointed to defend them; masters and their mayorals are fined for the least transgression as set out in the Chapter X, and they are threatened with criminal charges, with the confiscation of the servitor, and with transfer of ownership to another master; a slave is presumed murdered unless his master reports his death or escape within three days according to Chapter XII. Chaplains are charged with the inquiry and confidential denunciation of disturbances, and this type of allegation becomes a citizen's arrest, according to Chapter XIII, and establishes a syndic procurator based on residence to carry out the defense of the slaves. At once, overwhelming pride will cause the slaves to rebel, they will attempt to defy the orders of their owners, who will be unable to restrain them. In the form of a disorderly horde, they will pursue the auspices of a protector. It goes without saying that the ingenios will suffer irreparable damage from this interruption of work. Once convinced those resources are inadequate, the slaves will go into the heavily wooded backlands. From there, they will harass everyone in the vicinity, and armed force will be necessary in order to eradicate them, killing many and ruining their masters. That is, unless the fugitives are able to establish palenques in the remote scrub, as inaccessible as those erected and still operating in Jamaica, which not even the exploits and perseverance of the English have yet been able to eliminate.

These will be the least disastrous consequences. The more likely scenario is one in which the slaves, spared that fate, instead mount a rebellion against the owners and mayorals on their own ingenios, killing them and reducing the farms to ashes. No one will be able to travel the roads safely. Certainly none will be willing to expose themselves to certain abuse by working as a mayoral. This will be the case from now on with the publication of the Royal Decree. Before, the proper subordination of slaves was ensured as they endured severe and rigorous treatment, fearful of their masters who doled out punishments consistent with the seriousness of their offense, suitably administered with the attendant authority, and excluding torture, banishment, or mutilation of limbs. Now, slaves can go confidently to their haciendas and the mayorals who govern them, understanding all the while that any authority their owners may have had serves for naught, with the full knowledge that twenty-five lashes will be the maximum penalty they will suffer for any infraction they may commit. They understand that any deviation from this limit will cause, at the very least, their owners to be deluged with paperwork, and exempt the slave in question from work while an investigation takes place. Turmoil and upheaval, uproar, disobedience, and blood will prevail.

The slaves who, because they detest their masters, are prone to callously mutilate their hands or render their arms useless in order to avoid serving their masters, will endeavor to provoke their superiors solely for the pleasure of seeing them taken prisoner and treated as common criminals. They will commit horrendous crimes that will ensure their arrest and necessitate their removal from the ingenio. The result will be countless criminal cases pending, and almost all the field hands will be removed to the courts, to the jails, and to the woods.

This demonstrates, Sire, the recognition of the immense difference between our scrupulously humane treatment of our slaves and that treatment which is provided for by law, although it is one and the same. The latter approach causes slaves to become insolent, rousing and inciting them against their masters, and the former approach requires them to look upon that same master as a beneficiary of their labor. They consider one a legal obligation that authorizes slaves to make demands of their masters, and the other is deemed a boon owing to their masters' innate sense of fairness. One rewards them for humbling themselves, and the other encourages them to become haughty.

Law 13, Title 5, Book 7 of the Collection of Laws of these realms wisely explains how to govern slaves in but a few clauses. It charges those who govern to be zealous in the proceedings concerning slaves, exercising the utmost care. It ensures that they are instilled with a sense of caution and wariness, and charges them to adroitly forestall any disorderly conduct that may disturb the public order and tranquillity, in which they must be very well instructed and judicious. The sovereign legislator knew very well that the governance of slaves was no ordinary matter, but rather one requiring a great deal of vigilance, counsel, caution, wariness, and circumspection. In order to ensure that the slaves not become insolent, it is necessary to administer any punishment with dispatch and to keep from them any explanation of the unqualified protection they enjoy. Inhumane treatment is not to be tolerated, but neither are slaves to be informed of the benefits and immunities that are their due. Slave owners are forbidden from engaging in any acts of cruelty against slaves, and they will be appropriately chastised for any such transgression, but all must be carried out in such a way that the proscription of such treatment does not unleash any impudence on the part of the slaves. All of this conscientious order provided for by the law is not compatible with what is laid out in the chapters of the royal decree, and, therefore, the results of their implementation likewise will be various and regrettable.

We would contemplate that, as far as our own slaves are concerned, we must conduct ourselves as would a good father, and that, in imitation of this, we have the ability to give to them, just as we might to one of our own children, twelve or twenty lashes for a slight infraction, twenty-five or thirty for a more serious or a repeat offense, and additional lashes administered with a riding crop if they appear incorrigible. We never have believed that someone who displays less serious, natural human frailties necessarily should be punished, such as someone who is cohabitating, who pilfers, who blasphemes, or who quarrels with his brothers or sisters or with his fellow servitors. We considered ourselves authorized to mete out the penalties for excesses without resorting to a judge, with the exception of severe punishments calling for banishment, mutilation of limbs, or the death penalty. Only these latter punishments, in our opinion, lay outside the sphere of the prudent legal authority on the part of a father or a master, while the former less serious punishments would come under the authority of a good head of household.

Concerning all of Title I, Tratado 5 on penalties for maritime personnel who commit offenses in their respective cases. Many of the punishments are quite serious, long, and unpleasant, as demonstrated by those imposed in Articles 46, 47, 51, 52, 53, and 55. Among these are floggings administered while tied to a cannon, a diet of bread and water, shackles, and dunkings from the highest yardarm. The captain of the vessel can do virtually anything he chooses, without due process or the din of court. In Article 50, punishment is left to the captain's discretion, such wise laws having as their sole purpose the maintenance of the proper subordination of people on sea voyages and to assure that there are no disturbances aboard the vessel. Nothing will be accomplished on our haciendas if our prudent judgment is compromised, while that of the slaves is extended and subject to immunity.

Law 21, Title 5, Book 7 of that same collection imposes a sentence of fifty lashes on any slave at large for four days, one hundred lashes if at large more than eight days, and two hundred lashes for remaining at large for four months. Law 26 proposes dismissing charges against this category of persons. While we never resort to such serious punishment, it is extremely useful that the slaves at least consider the possibility that such penalties are within our discretionary powers, without resorting to a magistrate, in order that a fear of reckoning compels them to do their duty, without actually carrying [the punishment] out. No grounds protect them from that penalty, nor from more serious penalties that their crimes may merit, because we see older free Spanish Christian sailors not being exempted in this way. Soldiers suffer penalties for relatively minor crimes, as related in Title 10, Tratado 8, Volume 3 of your Royal Ordinance, similar to those committed by our slaves on the ingenios.

We would be less than truthful if we were to deny that one or another ingenio master ever gets carried away in the administration of punishments, and even that they treat their slaves inhumanely. But it is not fair that the coercion applied to those few individuals applies indiscriminately to this entire group of hacendados, most of whom have never had occasion to resort to such cruelty. The penalties must be limited to the offenders. This concerns the survival of a branch that sustains commerce, which constitutes the very [economic] lifeblood of this island. It is crucial to foment and encourage this branch by removing any hindrances and shackles it may suffer, by making the arduous hardships of tilling the soil more remunerative by broadening privileges and exemptions. Everything must work toward the greater good. If the freedom of the cultivator is compromised, the ends work against the means and cause serious upheaval. For this reason, Your Majesty's glorious predecessors bestowed special privileges upon agriculture, deeming it one of the three principle sources of wealth. The tillers of the soil were protected from legal disputes and conflicts during harvesttime. Their creditors were kept at bay, exempting their equipment from sale or embargo. Your Majesty's august father ordered the enclosure of farmland in those dominions in order to make them more productive. Your Majesty, once he assumed the throne, observed a frank dedication to these wise maxims. Your Majesty ordered that the access to game reserves be restricted, in order that game animals not have an adverse effect on the neighboring farmland. The people always know which ingenio owners are bad managers. Any lowly plebian decries it. Such scandalous news resonates throughout the entire Republic. The government is on the lookout to correct, contain, and punish this class of inhumane men, and to make certain that their actions not taint all agriculture. The penalty that they deserve does not affect the others. May they suffer in isolation and not bring universal ruin to all.

Concerning Chapters XII and XIII. It is extremely difficult or impossible for hacendados located eighty leagues from this city to notify the syndic or government of fugitive or deceased slaves within three days, unless officials defray the cost of a postal relay to convey such correspondence. This is not in the public interest, as escape attempts are continual and it will be necessary for the postal system to make repeated dispatches and deliveries. Authorizing any person whatsoever to make accusations brings pernicious consequences in its stead. Such power undoubtedly will appeal to the greediness of countless slackers, moving them to infiltrate our haciendas, corrupt our slaves, and ignite slanderous charges, plotting among themselves how to split up the fines as they basely denounce us at their pleasure. All of this will distract us from running our haciendas. In the end, the haciendas will fall victim to the legal proceedings, which is why it is best to exempt the farm laborers from these [regulations], deciding things for them in a simple, instructive way, and without the din of the law.

The ingenios make up a type of hacienda whose construction costs are ever rising, even not taking into account the cost of the lands on which they are established. Their construction consumes more than fifty thousand or sixty thousand pesos, and so exhausts the founders' ready money. They must surmount the immense annual operating costs just to break even, and only then go on to contemplate the unpredictable and unfortunate consequences of weather-related events, of the death of slaves, and the vagaries of war, such as we had to confront with the last two conflicts inflicted upon us by the English. As if this were not enough, now the crown declares royal protections for our slaves in such a way that we are subject to grievous insults, our ruin is indisputable, and the free trade of blacks with the English is now absolutely impossible. And if after the immense annual outlays spent in their own maintenance, the expense due to the unpredictability of inclement weather, to the death of slaves, and to the irreparable harm and delays inflicted upon us by the last two wars against the English, royal protection of our servitors is declared in such a way as to insult us. Our ruin is all but certain, and free trade in slaves with them is absolutely unprofitable. Haciendas cannot survive such a fate, and ultimately they will lay in ruin. With this, the acquisition of slaves will be to no purpose, and we likely will tend to suppress the numbers of what will come to constitute notorious enemies, whom we are unable to rule.

We must not, Sire, sacrifice these matters to silence nor to modesty. It is praiseworthy to inform Your Majesty freely, in honor of the public good. Neither fear nor weakness of spirit must silence any tiller of the soil, something that is damaging for both society and the State. We are encouraged in this, and we believe that Your Majesty, treating your vassals with such love, will find these maxims to your royal pleasure, and Your Majesty will mercifully take our observations under consideration as useful in forming a more complete and exact idea of the ingenios, of the slaves thereon, and of the benevolent management of this island. Agrarian laws always are established with an eye to the nature of the country, the quality of the lands, the range of climates, to which each region adapts and withstands, and our exposition being conducive to just such a purpose as this.

It never was our intention to challenge Your Majesty's supreme and unerring judgment. We limit our endeavor to enlightening Your Majesty concerning those uses and practices on our ingenios that inform our management of them and to the hope that Your Majesty's greater familiarity with this general set of circumstances may lead to the lucrative ends that Your Majesty ever desires concerning the economic benefit of his subjects.

Finally, we reverently entreat Your Majesty to deign to subject the government of this city to the most scrupulous investigation concerning all that we have put forth, including the customs and practices on our haciendas, the nature and character of the slaves there, and our treatment of them. We charge Your Majesty to rectify and forthrightly reform any abuses involving one or more hacendados, forever doing away with any impediments and obstacles to the progress of agriculture. May Your Majesty observe the utmost conscientiousness, caution, prudence, and care in such an important matter. Agriculture is this island's sole means of support, so it is imperative that farmers not be ruined in the observance of certain general laws that do not accommodate the circumstances specific to this country or its practices and customs.

Should Your Majesty not deign to fully attend to our official request and prefer to dictate general laws on the education and treatment of this island's slaves, we implore Your Majesty to make such laws applicable at the municipal level, and their establishment in keeping with the uses and customs particular to this country, in consonance with this region and those things found unacceptable therein. May such laws foment population growth, the agricultural advances on which it depends, and encourage trade to thrive. May the government commit itself to the formation of regulations through means of municipal hearings, of deputies named by hacendados, along with those members of other bodies. Thus, Your Majesty's devout wishes will be carried out, and our establishments will grow, and towns will be maintained in justice and splendor. There will be no affront to the public welfare. Tranquillity will reign in the midst of an unalterable peace. We will continue submitting our vow that God lavishes Your Majesty with His blessings, that the realms of your most immense empire prosper, and that Your Majesty's precious life be prolonged forever glorious, forever triumphant, and always happy.

Havana, January 19, 1790.

Note in the original: Don Miguel de Moya drew up this statement and submitted it to the king, signed by almost all ingenio owners in this jurisdiction.

Expediente instructivo para suavizar la suerte de los esclavos negros. Archivo Nacional de Cuba (ANC), *Junta de Fomento,* 150/7405.

3. Toward a New Slave Code

3.1. SURVEY BY CAPTAIN GENERAL GERÓNIMO VALDÉS

Havana, February 23, 1842

For the purpose of devising an effective system that I find acceptable for the health and well-being of those slave populations destined for service on rural farms, compatible with their proper management and growth, and that takes into consideration the servitors' health and reproduction while performing a fair day's work for their masters, I require the benefit of your enlightened knowledge and established practices in order to acquaint me with the details of matters I address below. I hope that, consistent with the noble disinterest so characteristic of you, with the humanitarian sentiments of an honorable patrician, and as just reward for the trust in you that is my due, you will carry out this responsibility by expressing your opinions in a clear and unambiguous fashion. You may rest assured that I will personally appreciate your contribution, just as posterity will be grateful for any benefits produced by your report.

Issues to be resolved are the following:

1st. Whether or not the health and nutrition of slaves is better served by the current practice of issuing unprepared rations or by issuing food that already has been prepared and is ready to eat at predetermined times.

2nd. In either of these cases, it is necessary to determine the type and quantity of viands and meat that must be provided to slaves and the seasons of the year that it is appropriate to discontinue the use of dried corn, which commonly causes dysentery.

3rd. The determination of the type of clothing that must be provided to slaves, the number of changes of clothing issued per year, the type of nightclothes and outerwear, and the length of time each item is expected to last.

4th. Determination of the work schedule, specifying those fixed times to arise and to retire, as too those periods reserved for rest and meals, taking into account seasonal considerations and the varied chores specific to particular times of year, whether these be associated with planting or with the harvest.

5th. Determination of the most appropriate infirmary system, recommended both by considerations of compassion and of profit. This includes specific dimensions of the place so designated for this purpose, its floor plan, the number of personnel, the provisioning of the dispensary, nursing and doctor care, the type of beds and nourishment, all of which should be conducive to the relief of the afflicted. Determinations as to whether or not the building should be situated in an isolated location, and the security measures necessary to prevent contact between outsiders and patients, both to prevent contagion of diseases of the skin and to discourage malingering in the infirmary, and are to be included in this report.

6th. Determination of the most suitable system to normalize the customs and morals of married slaves. This includes decisions as to whether they are to live as families in individual huts, any possible deleterious effects for owner's interests, and the appropriate age for children to come under their parents' immediate supervision.

7th. Determination of suitable practices concerning pregnant slaves, the type of work they should do, and the number of hours a day they should work. Likewise, once the baby is born, determination of subsequent arrangements once the initial forty-day maternity period has expired, including the diet and care of mothers and infants, and mothers' participation in breast feeding their children at regularly scheduled feeding times and intervals is called for. It also is necessary to establish the most appropriate floor plan for nurseries where competent individuals meticulously care for the infants in order to prevent any misfortunes resulting from mothers' lack of practical experience [caring for infants].

8th. I desire a definitive explanation of the widespread practice of providing slaves with a plot of land, a small holding, in order for them to sow crops and earn money from the sale of this produce, similarly with respect to raising pigs and other permissible livestock. As every living being responds to the profit motive, and possesses an innate desire to own property, this practice [of giving slaves a garden plot] necessarily contributes to slaves' moral development, to their ties to their place of residence, and to persuade slaves to conceive of their masters' haciendas in terms of economic benefit, in that their own gain is a direct product of the hacienda's [prosperity].

Using ingenios and cafetals as archetypes, you will be able to make note of some clarifications concerning other types of farms common to this island. You are requested to complete the report as soon as possible.¹

3.2. THE HACENDADO JACINTO GONZÁLEZ LARRINAGA EXPLAINS HIS METHODS

San Antonio de los Baños, April 14, 1842

First issue: I consider it most fitting, and it is a most common practice on all ingenios, to provide crews with previously prepared rations at midday, and unprepared rations in the evening. On Sundays, both rations are unprepared. Three messes must be prepared daily: one especially prepared for those patients able to eat, in addition to those with limited diets consisting of *puchero* [stew] or *atole* [maize-based beverage], another for new mothers and their infants, and yet another, larger meal for those slaves who are in good health and working. It would be detrimental and inadvisable to issue unprepared midday rations, because slaves would have to spend the greater part of their rest period in preparing them, and [in their haste] they would prepare the food poorly, given that this is the time they use to care for their livestock and for their own rest.

It is fitting that the Sunday ration be unprepared because, as they have ample time, they can prepare it and season it according to their own preferences, supplementing it with produce from their small holdings, and typically saving part of their dinner for lunch the following day. However, Sunday rations are and must be prepared for those who are ill, the young, and new mothers.

Second. The meal ration consists of six ounces or more of good beef jerky and half a dozen plantains or their equivalent of yucca, starchy root crops, sweet potatoes, and other foods or finely ground corn flour without the hull and flavored with salt and butter or pork. When there is an abundance of other foods, corn flour, which is healthy and nutritious, is not provided. The dinner food allotment is distributed unprepared. On Sundays, along with the unprepared rations, a corresponding amount of salt is dispensed. On an occasional Sunday, for the sake of variety, it is advisable to give out some eight ounces of codfish. During sugarcane milling season, they are given cane liquor. When milling is over, it is advisable to dispense some pleasing infusion, such as diluted lemon extract sweetened with brown sugar and a little cane liquor in the morning before beginning work. Likewise, it is advisable to administer this same infusion of spirits when slaves are soaked [by the rains].

Third. In December and June, typically cold and rainy months, slaves are given a change of clothes made of good nankeen, with an everyday bandana and cap. They also are given a blanket one year and a shirt made from lightweight, economical fabric or baize the next. Special categories of slaves and tradesmen receive a better quality of clothing, including a straw hat, deer leather shoes, and a short jacket made of lightweight economical fabric or baize.

Fourth. They should arise an hour before daylight, then and there drinking a previously prepared infusion. At first light, they proceed to work in the fields and in the processing area. The bell tolls at eight o'clock in the morning, and work is suspended. They eat their morning meal, and half an hour later the bell tolls again, signaling the resumption of work. At eleven o'clock, another bell summons them home, where they attend to personal business. If it is milling time, they drop off the sugarcane at the casa de purga, and the *bagazo* [bagasse, part of the sugarcane left after the juice has been extracted] at the *fornalla* [lower part of a furnace, from where ash is collected and cleaned out] house. Once they have completed these tasks, they receive their noon meal ration on earthenware plates made right there on the farm, retiring to their huts [to eat]. At two in the afternoon, the bell tolls, and they go out to work until after sunset, when they retreat to their quarters. As darkness falls, a bell tolls, and everyone lines up inside the ingenio's big house, where they say their prayers, the credo, and a blessing. After reciting the Ten Commandments, they receive their unprepared evening meal ration, and retire to their huts. At nine o'clock, the bell signals lights out, and they go to bed.

During milling time, after prayers, the slaves are divided into shifts. The first shift lasts until midnight, when another shift relieves those workers. On many farms, it is customary to have yet a third shift, its crew sleeping all night in order to get up and work the next shift. In this way, no crew works more than four shifts over the six-day workweek. Expectant and new mothers, anyone who is ill, and small children all are excluded from this work [regimen]. On Sundays, first thing in the morning they all arise to pray the Hail, Mary!, they tidy up the ingenio and boiler house and do other light chores until eight o'clock, they pray the rosary, and rations are distributed. There is no sentry unless it is sugar season. At five o'clock in the afternoon, the bell tolls, and everyone reports, neat and clean, their clothes tidy and mended, the slaves having been issued needle and thread for this very purpose. Then the milling starts up, the furnaces are fed with the bagazo, and so on. In the off-season, security on Sundays is minimal, and everyone goes out to work on their small holdings, care for their livestock, attend to their personal needs, cook, mind their children, and so forth.

Fifth. Infirmaries must be at least one hundred feet long and sixty feet wide, although many are larger. They are partitioned into separate areas for men and women. Each of these is subdivided further into four sections comprised of a ward, a salon, and two exam rooms. This is more than sufficient because a growing slave population, treated as I have specified here, cannot have many patients. The beds are continuous raised platforms, and can be set up and broken down, with straw pallets, canvas sheets, and blankets. The doctor, who usually calls every other day and daily when necessary, has a well-stocked dispensary at his disposal, with everything that he requests and deems necessary. The mayordomo scrupulously inspects the area daily and is charged with the management of the three or four quite knowledgeable, sensible nurses who work on each farm. The kitchen and latrine are in close proximity to the infirmary but detached from it. The food for both those who are suffering from fever and those who are gravely ill is prepared according to doctor's orders, and consists of jerky, rice, and fresh chicken, beef, or pork broth. The infirmary should be located within the main manufacturing complex and, where appropriate, isolated [from the other buildings].

Sixth. It is appropriate and reasonable that the slaves live with their families in their own huts. This is preferable to confining them to locked barracks. Children can live with their parents in houses or huts once they have reached seven years of age.

Seventh. Only after daybreak do pregnant slaves go out and work at light chores. They stop work an hour before the rest of the slaves, they return to work in the afternoon long after the regular field hands, and they come in before the sun has set. They do not work in shifts or do other heavy labor until they are no longer breastfeeding. They are given chicken broth during labor and, afterward, *ajiaco* [dish made with boiled meat and vegetables], completely hearty, flavorful, and plentiful for lunch and their regular supper in the evening. The items included in the layette are of quite high quality. Infants are fed bread crumbs or balls of rice flour cooked in well-seasoned cow's milk, and are nursed by their mother, or, if the mother is unable to nurse or otherwise is unwell, by a wet nurse. The nursery should be sufficiently large . . . staffed with one or more wet nurses, who busy themselves breast-feeding infants and looking after children younger than seven years old. Single slave women who prefer the nursery to the huts can live there. The nursery can be of the same dimensions as the infirmary. Beds consist of hard, low platforms. Beds for adults and single women are collapsible to facilitate cleaning.

Eighth. Families on the ingenio customarily receive a parcel of land that they can cultivate and pass down in usufruct. . . . They sow it with maize, which they harvest twice a year and sell at will, each separate harvest yielding about eight bushels, and in a good year even more. They also harvest rice, which they sell in the hull by the *arroba* [twenty-four to thirty-six pounds], in addition to tobacco, okra, pumpkins, and other foods that they reserve for their own personal use and for any livestock they raise. Both swine and poultry are permitted. Swine must be housed in enclosed pigsties. They raise poultry for their own personal consumption and to sell.

The management of coffee plantations is identical to that of ingenios in terms of food, garb, lodging, and infirmaries, but not in terms of labor. The work on coffee plantations is lighter than on ingenios. Cafetal slave crews enjoy uninterrupted nights' rest and sleep, which contributes a great deal to the improved procreation, vigor, and health of this category of slave.

These are the methods that I have established and practice on my farms, with very few departures from what I have written Your Excellency, above. And I must express, with the objectivity for which I am known, that, in my opinion, any departures that are attempted in these time-honored practices, observed for more than a century with such gratifying results, that go counter to the precise fulfillment of same are and will be extremely counterproductive for owners of all categories of farms, those very individuals these practices are intended to benefit, and, consequently, for the royal treasury, because [disregarding the above methods] would necessarily result in insubordination and discouragement; failing to observe the above methods guarantees that no one enjoys the intended outcome, and ownership rights over slaves, respected by civic and cannon law, likewise become illusory.

Inquiry carried out by order of the superior court to reform the regulation of the hygiene, morality, and diet of servitors engaged in agriculture, 1842.

ANC, Gobierno Superior Civil, 941/33186.

3.3. EXCERPTS FROM THE SLAVE CODE

November 14, 1842

Article 1. Every slave owner must instruct their slaves in the principles of the Apostolic Roman Catholic religion in order that they may be baptized if they have not yet . . .

Article 2. The religious instruction referred to in the prior article must be conducted in the evening, upon the conclusion of the workday, and immediately thereafter they shall be made to pray the rosary or some other devotional prayers.

Article 3. On Sundays and religious holidays, after fulfilling their religious observances, the owners or officials in charge of farms may use their slaves in order to tidy up houses and offices for no more than two hours. Slaves may not be used for hacienda work, unless it is harvest season or they are needed for pressing tasks that cannot wait, because in these cases they will work as they do on normal workdays.

[Article 4. Missing.]

Article 5. Owners will use the greatest possible care and diligence in making slaves understand the obedience that they owe the constituted authorities, their obligation to revere priests, to respect whites, to exercise good conduct toward people of color, and to live in good harmony with their fellow slaves.

Article 6. Masters will provide precisely two or three meals per day to their field hands, whatever they deem best, which will be sufficient to maintain and invigorate them, it being understood that a sufficient and necessary daily diet for each individual consists of six to eight plantains or their equivalent in sweet potatoes, yams, yuccas, and other nutritious edible roots; eight ounces of meat or codfish; and four ounces of flour, rice, or some other mixed vegetable stew.

Article 7. Owners also must distribute clothing to slaves twice a year, in the months of December and May, each issue consisting of a shirt and underwear of nankeen or *rusia* [coarse fabric used for hammocks and slave clothing], a cap or hat, and a handkerchief; and, in addition, in the month of December, a baize shirt or jacket one year, and a blanket to keep them warm during the winter the next.

Article 8. Newborns or infants, whose mothers go out to work on the farm, will be fed very light fare, such as soup, atole, milk, or other similar liquids, until they are no longer breast-fed and have teeth.

Article 9. While mothers are at work, all small children will remain in a house or room required on all ingenios and cafetals, under the care of one or more black women. The master or mayordomo determines the number of caretakers according to the number of children to be cared for.

Article 10. If infants become ill before they are weaned, then they must suckle at the breast of their own mothers, the affected woman being reassigned from fieldwork to domestic labor.

Article 11. Until children reach three years of age, they must wear striped undershirts; those children from three to six years old can wear undershirts of nankeen; girls from six to twelve years old will be given skirts or long shirts; and boys from six to twelve years old also will be provided with breeches. Anyone older than this will use the same clothes as the rest of the adults.

Article 12. Under ordinary circumstances, slaves will work from nine to ten hours a day, the master scheduling those hours in whatever manner he deems best. On ingenios during harvest season, slaves will work sixteen hours, these allocated in such a way that slaves enjoy a two-hour rest period during the day and sleep six hours at night.

Article 13. On Sundays, religious holidays, and during rest periods on regular workdays, slaves will be allowed to work on the farm in occupations or in producing goods that result in their personal profit and gain, in order to be able to acquire privately held personal earnings and to buy their own freedom.

Article 14. Neither slaves over sixty or under seventeen years old nor female slaves will be required to work por tareas. Likewise, these same categories of slaves will not be assigned work that is not in keeping with their gender, age, vigor, and stamina.

Article 15. Owners of those slaves who, because of their advanced age or illness, are not fit to work must provide them with food and are prohibited from giving those slaves their freedom in order to shirk their responsibility toward them, unless they provide them with sufficient income as approved by law . . .

Article 16. On every farm there will be a secure room set aside for the storage of tools, the key to which will never be entrusted to any slave.

Article 17. On going out to work, each slave will be given the implement required for that day's tasks, and, as soon as the slave returns, that same implement will be collected and locked in the storeroom.

Article 18. No slaves will leave the hacienda with any implement in hand, much less with a weapon of any type, unless they are escorted by their masters or mayordomos or the mayordomos' families, in which case they will be allowed to take their machetes and nothing else.

Article 19. Slaves belonging to one farm will not be permitted to visit slaves on another farm without the express consent of the masters or mayordomos of both establishments; and when they must go to another farm or depart from their own farm, they will carry written permission from their own master or mayordomo stating the slave's physical description; the day, month, and year; the destination; and the length of time for which the permission is valid.

Article 20. Any person, regardless of social class, race, and social standing, is authorized to detain any slave found outside the confines of their masters' dwellings or property if this slave does not present the written permission slaves are required to carry, or if, upon presenting the document, it is evident that the slave has markedly strayed from the course or address of their stated destination, or if the time period for which the trip is authorized has expired.

[Article 21. Missing.]

[Article 22. Missing.]

Article 23. Masters will permit their slaves to engage in respectable entertainments and recreation on holidays, once they have completed their religious observations, provided that the slaves do not leave the farm or associate with slaves from other farms; that those activities take place in an open area and within the purview of those same masters, mayordomos, or capatazes; and that such activities last only until sunset, when the bell tolls for evening prayers, and no later.

Article 24. Owners and mayordomos are charged very especially to exercise the utmost vigilance in order to prevent excessive drinking [of alcoholic beverages], and to guard against the presence of both slaves from other farms and free men of color at the entertainments.

Article 25. Masters will carefully see to the construction of spacious rooms for unmarried slaves in a dry and well-ventilated place, segregating the sexes, enclosed, and under lock and key, with a light that will burn throughout the night. Where the means permit, separate rooms for each married couple will be provided.

Article 26. At bedtime (which will be eight o'clock on long fall and winter nights, and nine o'clock on short spring and summer nights), roll will be taken, so that no one but sentries remain outside their rooms. One sentry will be assigned to maintain silence and to notify the mayordomo immediately of anything out of the ordinary concerning his fellow slaves, of the arrival of outsiders, or of the occurrence of any other incident of interest.

Article 27. Also, on each farm there will be a secure locked room with separate spaces for males and females, and two others besides for cases of contagious diseases, where physicians will attend any slaves who fall gravely ill, and nurses will care for those with less serious ailments requiring only home remedies.

Article 28. Patients, whenever possible, will be placed in separate beds, made up with pallets, ticks or bedrolls, bolster pillows, blankets, and sheets, or on a platform that provides sufficient relief for treatment . . . but always elevated . . .

Article 29. Slave owners must forestall any illicit conduct between the sexes by encouraging marriage. There will be no impediment to marriage between slaves belonging to different owners, and the couple will be afforded the opportunity to live under the same roof.

[Article 30. Missing.]

Article 31. When the master of the husband purchases the wife, he also must purchase any of her children who are less than three years old, because, according to law, the mother must suckle them and raise them until they reach that age.

Article 32. Masters can be compelled by law to sell any slave whom they humiliate, woefully mistreat, or cause to suffer excesses that are contrary to humanity and to the rational manner with which they should be treated.

[Article 33. Missing.]

Article 34. No master will be allowed to refuse to permit their slave to enter into an agreement of coartación, once that slave has made a down payment of at least fifty pesos toward his purchase price.

Article 35. Coartado slaves cannot be sold for an amount exceeding that price fixed at their most recent appraisal, and this same condition will prevail as they pass from one buyer to another.

Nevertheless, if the slave desires to be sold against his master's will without just cause, or if a slave's bad conduct gives his master cause for the transferring ownership, the owner will be allowed to raise the slave's coartación price by an amount that includes any excise taxes and the costs of the deed required for the sale.

[Article 36. Missing.]
[Article 37. Missing.]

Article 38. Any slave who discovers a conspiracy to disturb the public tranquillity plotted by fellow slaves or freedmen will be granted his freedom and receive a prize of five hundred pesos . . .

[Article 39. Missing.]

Article 40. Slaves also will acquire their freedom when it is so granted in a will or by any other legally justified means and as a result of an honest or praiseworthy purpose.

Article 41. Slaves are obligated to obey and respect their masters, mayordomos, mayorals, and other superiors as they would their own parents, and to carry out tasks and work as instructed. Any slave who fails in any of these obligations will be subject to and must suffer disciplinary measures administered by the farm boss, and, according to the severity of the shortcoming or excess, including prison time, shackles, chains, mace, stocks (feet only, never the head), or lashes, not to exceed twenty-five in number.

Article 42. Slaves who commit more serious offenses or some crime for which the above disciplinary measures or penalties are insufficient punishment will be restrained and turned over to the court.

Article 43. Only owners, mayodomos, or mayorals will be permitted to impose disciplinary measures on slaves, exercising restraint in administering the punishments described above . . .

Article 44. Any owner, supervisor, or farm employee who does not comply with or infringes upon any regulations in this directive will incur a fine of between twenty to fifty pesos for a first offense, a fine of between forty to one hundred pesos for a second offense, and a fine of eighty to two hundred pesos for a third offense, according to the greater or lesser degree of the violation of the particular article.

[Article 45. Missing.]

Article 46. If the offenses committed by owners or supervisors charged with administering slavery on the farms were due to excesses in administering disciplinary measures, causing serious bruising, wounds, or mutilation of limbs, or any other major injury, then, in addition to the aforementioned monetary fines, criminal charges will be filed against the person who inflicted the injury . . . and the owner will be obligated to sell that slave if he is able to work, or, if he is unable to work, then to set the slave free and pay a daily stipend as determined by law for the slave's maintenance and clothing as long as the slave lives, payment due one month in advance.

Fernando Ortiz, *Los negros esclavos* (Havana: Editorial de Ciencias Sociales, 1975), pp. 442–49.

4. Slavery and Family Life

4.1. EXCERPTS FROM THE PROCEEDINGS AGAINST ILDEFONSO CARABALÍ, SLAVE OWNED BY DON DIEGO FRANCISCO DE UNZAGA, FOR ATTEMPTED SUICIDE

Havana, September 11, 1807

A. Statement of Don José Mieres, twenty-two years old, single, salaried worker in Unzaga's workshop.

... Prompted by a complaint from a neighbor woman ... that his slave Ildefonso had molested her little black *chinita* [diminutive form of *china*, young light-skinned black woman], and made her fear ... dire consequences, Don Diego resolved to apprehend his slave and forcibly detain him with the help of some of his other slaves. They struggled with Ildefonso, who was brandishing the sharp tool he had been using to dress deer leather. In the meantime, the master became apprehensive lest some other calamity come to pass. He urged everyone to remain calm while awaiting the arrival of the sentry from Puerta de Tierra, whose commander had been alerted as to the situation. Before help could arrive, Ildefonso emerged from the common room, wounded.

B. Statement of Don Diego Francisco de Unzaga, native of Vizcaya, thirty-two years old, single, merchant.

... [After the neighbor woman complained] he decided then and there to shackle Idelfonso in order to get the truth out of him, and, at the same time, prevent him from getting away through the tiled roof, as he had on other occasions in the past ...

C. Statement of Carlos Prieto, native of Guinea, twenty-two years old, single.

... [upon being forewarned] he came upon a brawl [in the workshop, and found Ildefonso] vowing that if they did not give him his papers so that he could sell himself [to a new master], he would have to kill himself or execute his master. In the midst of this ordeal, the master ordered that the sentry from Puerta de Tierra be sent for. That was when Ildefonso first stabbed himself and, upon entering the common room, he endeavored to stab himself again. Everyone went to his assistance as he threw himself out of the patio. They only were able to overpower him once he fainted due to the loss of blood . . .

D. Statement of the slave Josefa Hernández, native of Havana, seventeen years old, single, owned by Doña Josefa Molina.

. . . she had only heard about the slave Ildefonso's stab wound secondhand, because her mistress, Doña Josefa Molina, had her locked in the room during all the commotion at Don Francisco de Unzaga's house between his relatives and his household staff. . . . [She told] the aforementioned Unzaga that the slave Ildefonso had gotten her pregnant. . . . [The events that transpired] induced the slave to resist being put into shackles as a punishment for having made her [the deponent] go missing from her mistress's house and prompted him to stab himself [illegible] provided that he had been the perpetrator, because he was with the deponent almost every night . . .

E. Statement of Ildefonso Carabalí, thirty years old, single, states that he is not Catholic for he has not been baptized.

. . . he was ill and dressed in bandages due to a self-inflicted [stab] wound in an attempt to take his own life and seek some respite from his master's abuse. He was working in the shop, dressing deer leather, when he saw them attempting to restrain him by shackling his neck and feet, with a chain connecting the irons. He made up his mind to kill himself, using the very implement he held in his hands. He took leave of his fellow slaves and went into the common room. Once he was alone, he stabbed himself in the neck . . . [he was going to be punished] because of the complaint that Doña Josefa Rubio had lodged against him, charging that he had gotten the china she owned pregnant. . . . His friendship with Josefa was chaste, a relation as innocent as that he had with the rest of the members of the household. Therefore, it was untrue that he had carnal relations with her, or that he had given his word to put her in the family way. He considered himself blameless even as his master resolved to punish him. . . . Then he stabbed himself with the implement, just as he said, going out onto the patio covered with blood. That is when the rest of his fellow slaves and his master came out in order to help him and forestall any further incidents.[1]

ANC, *Miscelánea de Expedientes*, 224/Z.

4.2. THE TRAGIC FATE OF RITA GANGÁ: EXCERPTS FROM THE CASE AGAINST JUAN GUALBERTO TOLEDO FOR THEFT OF THE SLAVE WOMAN

Remedios, June 25, 1835

A. Statement of Juan Gualberto Toledo, native of Pipián, inhabitant of Macurijes, twenty-two years old, single, farmer, carpenter.

. . . [He was in jai] because a commissioner of the Royal Court of Justice found him in the environs of the village [of Remedios] on the afternoon of the twenty-third of this month making his way to town in the company of a slave woman, and with a mind to continue on to his final destination of Santiago de Cuba, where he intended to establish himself. . . . He departed from his parents' house on the seventeenth of this month. . . . He had been working for nearly two years now on the ingenio Jesús María, owned by Don Diego López de Villavicencio and Santiago Ramón Sánchez. . . . His salary, which had topped out at 287 pesos, two and a half reals, discouraged him greatly. Over that same period of time, he carried on a love affair with the servant in question. . . . Once convinced that he was the father of her unborn child, he came up with the idea of paying for her with wages he was owed for work he had already completed, removing her from the farm, and bringing her along with him and freeing her. Returning to her owner, he would collect whatever money he was owed for his back wages and apply that amount against her value until she was completely paid for. In his estimate, her balance could not amount to very much more, as she was a field hand. It was with this idea in mind that he removed her from the farm in the first place and hid her in the cane fields on that very farm, where she had been since last February 3 . . .

B. Statement of Rita Gangá

. . . she is a slave belonging to Don Santiago Ramón Sánchez, living under his auspices in the jurisdiction of Matanzas, where Don Diego López Villavicencio also lives. [They are the co-owners of the ingenio where Juan works and she lives.]

Don Diego mistreated her, and for this reason she ran away, abandoning his service. She hid for some days in the cane fields on that very farm, until one day the man who brought her there came along down the road. He told her that if she wanted to see her master Sánchez, who was up ahead nearby, that he would take her to him. Because she consented, he proposed that they go together. He met her last year, when he was working as a carpenter on the ingenio. He fell in love with her, and made her pregnant . . .[2]

ANC, *Gobierno Superior Civil*, 938/33097, and *Miscelánea de Expedientes*, 166/H.

4.3. CARLOTA MORENO, MORENA,[3] BRINGS SUIT AGAINST HER SISTER

Havana, March 8, 1836

Carlota Moreno, with the utmost respect, appears before Your Excellency and declares:

Last year, in 1825, she found herself reduced to servitude and held captive as the property of Dionisia Respeto, morena, for a mere 150 pesos. Dolores Díaz, who was her biological sister, was free, and possessed of a modest fortune. Rather than granting her sister's freedom outright, and heedless of any appeal dictated by ties of both nature and consanguinity, she heartlessly purchased her sister, conferring upon her the same [lowly] position and status as that bestowed by her sister's former mistress.

Shortly after this acquisition, the petitioner paid five ounces of gold toward the balance of her purchase price, leaving an outstanding balance of sixty-five pesos. She steadily paid down this amount by applying the wages of three-fourths of a real a day from her work as a journeywoman, which by any standard of measure constituted insufferable usury. Nevertheless, she scrupulously continued to make payments and satisfy the proper paperwork. Then, one day, the women's brother, José Claro, fell ill. He, just like Carlota Moreno, was a slave owned by his very own sister. She [the petitioner] spent much in excess of two hundred pesos nursing him and sitting in constant vigil during the seven months of his recuperation. With this, she believed that she not only had amply compensated her mistress for her remaining balance, but, after soliciting her [the petitioner's] certificate of manumission, she found that her former mistress [and sister Dolores Díaz] was in the position of owing her [the petitioner] the difference.

Besides this, once the petitioner left for the countryside with her mistress's blessing, she [the former mistress] left her belongings as a deposit [on the debt owed the petitioner] and a great deal of clothing belonging to a third party, their total in-kind value being something in excess of 150 pesos, for all of which she [the petitioner] had ample documentation.

Several years have gone by. The petitioner's sister and former mistress refused to settle the debt, despite the petitioner's demands. In this circumstance, she [the petitioner] has been shocked by some further actions that have filled her with great consternation and bitterness.

The fact was that she was unable to gain access to the interior room where she lived, in the house of the moreno Tomás Gangá. Lieutenant Don Prudencio Baldés Álvarez went and removed her chickens and some of her furniture on the order of, so they say, the petitioner's sister and mistress, forbidding the homeowner from allowing anything else to be removed.

The petitioner is free, by virtue of both law and deed, for having paid off her purchase price, and because her sister and former mistress owes the petitioner amounts exceeding her balance, a thing soon to be rectified (as she asks for legal intervention in the matter) . . .[4]

ANC, *Gobierno Superior Civil*, 938/33092.

4.4. JOSÉ AGUSTÍN CEPERO PETITIONS FOR THE FREEDOM OF HIS DAUGHTER JUANA

Havana, July 12, 1836

The slave José Agustín Cepero, moreno, authorized by his owner, Don Joaquín de Cepero, to claim the freedom of his daughter Juana, a slave belonging to Don Antonio García, appears before Your Excellency and respectfully states:

In the middle of last month, he appeared before Your Excellency to demand freedom for his aforementioned daughter, Juana, offered by her owner, Don Antonio García. Since that time, Don Joaquín de Cepero has been legally responsible for her, and communicated as much to her owner, the aforementioned García, in a timely fashion. The petitioner knew that this gentleman had proceeded legally against Don Joaquín de Cepero, demanding that he return the slave, Juana, in addition to her wages. García disregarded the lawsuit that had been filed against him. With her in his power once and for all, he would use his authority to completely overwhelm her, oblige her to abandon her rightful claim, and transport her to the rural countryside from where it would be impossible for her to raise her voice in protest in a court of law.

The petitioner recurs once more to Your Excellency to request that he assert his authority in order to thwart Don Antonio García's cunning and safeguard the rights owing his daughter as privileges of her freedom . . .[5]

ANC, *Gobierno Superior Civil*, 938/33089.

4.5. PETITION FILED BY MARÍA DE LOS DOLORES FRÍAS, NATIVE OF AFRICA AND RESIDENT OF BARRIO DE GUADALUPE, REQUESTING THAT HER DAUGHTER BE ALLOWED TO CHANGE MASTERS

Havana, September 11, 1837

. . . She says that, some fifteen days ago, her daughter Ana María, a slave belonging to Don Marcos Padrón, appeared before Your Excellency and accused her master of mistreatment, requesting the intervention of the syndic in order to seek out a new master. Your Excellency assented and ordered the aforementioned Padrón to hand her over within three days.

Excellency, the petitioner's daughter tarried but little in her purpose, and by the end of the second day she had located a buyer. But Don Marcos Padrón was determined to seek vengeance on his unfortunate and wretched slave for lodging her just charge against him. He told the buyer that she was a runaway . . . and was otherwise defective, in order to dissuade the new owner . . . and proved so successful in his endeavor that the sale fell through.

His scheme realized, and without waiting for the expiration of the short and limited time period granted for said slave to locate a buyer, he proceeded to take her to his farm, in the town or district of Alquízar, where he subjected her to precisely the same abuse of which she had complained.

Excellency, the petitioner is the mother of that wretched slave. She finds herself very distressed by the harsh treatment of her daughter, who has been coartado at 350 pesos . . . [For this reason she is requesting to be transported to the city in order to locate a new master there] . . .[6]

ANC, *Gobierno Superior Civil*, 938/33099.

4.6. OFFICIAL REQUEST BY THE FREEDMAN ROMUALDO GARCÍA TO FREE HIS WIFE

Havana, October 17, 1837

The freedman Romualdo García, formerly a slave on the ingenio Santa Lutgarda (also known as La Iberia), owned by Don Joaquín and Manuel González Arando, appears before Your Excellency and states:

As a result of losing his sight, he can no longer work on the ingenio. This has prompted his masters to grant him his freedom and provide him with a total of two hundred pesos. With his impaired vision, such a crucial faculty, he finds himself in the unenviable position of living off the charity of compassionate souls. This circumstance and [the fact that] he has no one to care for him and console him in these trying times, have prompted some individuals to come to his aide by providing the money necessary to obtain the freedom of his wife Damiana, a slave on the aforementioned ingenio. The money has been deposited in care of the syndic . . .[7]

ANC, *Gobierno Superior Civil*, 938/33092.

4.7. OFFICIAL REQUEST BY JUAN PABLO SOBRADO SEEKING AUTHORIZATION TO REDEEM AN UNBORN CHILD

Havana, April 7, 1853

. . . He says that the black woman Águeda, a slave belonging to Don Pedro Esteban, finds herself pregnant and has asked the petitioner to act as godfather to the infant to whom she will give birth. The petitioner not only has demonstrated his willingness to do so but also has offered Águeda the twenty-five pesos required in order to redeem the unborn child. However, the slave's owner, declining to state his reasons, has refused to accept that amount. Águeda, an aggrieved mother, frustrated in her attempts to arrange for her child's freedom, has recurred to the syndic Don Francisco Goyri, requesting his intervention in obtaining the documents allowing her to seek out a new owner. However, the syndic has sent her home without attending to her requests, and, as of this date, she finds herself confined to the farm . . . (The petitioner asks that his twenty-five pesos to redeem the unborn child be received, and that the mother be allowed to locate a new master.)[8]

ANC, *Gobierno Superior Civil*, 948/33492.

4.8. COMPLAINT FILED BY DOMINGA GANGÁ, SLAVE OWNED BY DON PEDRO MACÍAS, SEEKING VISITATION WITH HER CHILDREN

Havana, April 14, 1853

. . . [The complainant] previously was a slave belonging to Don Juan Antonio Alemán, resident of Casa Blanca. Her former master fathered her four children, who remain in his custody in the town of Casa Blanca. She went to visit the children there on the twelfth, at about four in the afternoon. She carried with her the permit issued by her current master, enabling her to hire herself out as a day laborer but otherwise be free to spend the night wherever she chose. However, the aforementioned Don Juan Antonio, bitter because the complainant refused to continue with their illicit cohabitation and because she demanded freedom for her children, would not allow her to see them. This prompted him to have the warder in Casa Blanca capture her as a runaway slave. The warder was not sufficiently satisfied with examining her permit, which she most humbly submitted for his inspection. . . . They put her into the stocks, and the following day they made her direct them to the home of her current master, who was fined five pesos, which he paid her attendant.

May Don Juan Antonio Alemán be compelled to recognize the complainant's maternal rights to see her children and involve herself in all matters concerning their well-being.[9]

ANC, *Gobierno Superior Civil*, 948/33490.

4.9. OFFICIAL REQUEST BY MARÍA BELÉN MEDINA TO FREE HER SON SIMÓN

Havana, July 25, 1853

María Belén Medina . . . asserts that it was a mother's wish to see her son, Simón, spared from slavery. She approached his master, Don Agustín Medina, about redeeming his freedom, and he asked for the sum of four hundred pesos. She paid him, and he demanded an additional one hundred pesos. She made immense sacrifices in order to acquire the requested extra one hundred pesos required of her! These she also paid to him.

The aforementioned Medina is unwilling to accept the five hundred pesos, and he insists, in his own words, "that tomorrow it will be seven hundred, eight hundred, or a thousand pesos," and that neither the syndic nor the law holds any sway with him . . .[10]

ANC, *Gobierno Superior Civil*, 948/33487.

4.10. PETITION OF MIGUEL MORENO, SLAVE OWNED BY DOÑA MERCED POLO, TO FREE HIS DAUGHTER TOMASA

Havana, August 6, 1853

. . . His proprietress and mistress, as attested to by the permit issued for this purpose and accompanying this petition, authorized him [the petitioner] to appeal to Colonel Don Miguel de Cárdenas y Chávez, to deal with His

Honor concerning the freedom for the petitioner's daughter, an eleven-year-old morena named Tomasa. His Honor agreed to her emancipation for the sum of six hundred pesos. This was an excessive amount, especially as it was [supposedly] granted as a special consideration and, as such, constituted an impediment to her freedom. In the midst of this situation, he humbly sought out the syndic procurator to intercede on his behalf. Such forethought was in vain, because the girl's master, the colonel, despite having been ordered [to appear in court] in observance of the proper formalities, disregarded the dutiful summons.

It seems that this difficulty cannot be resolved without [the benefit of] Your Excellency's most exalted authority . . .

[The permit, dated July 23, says, word for word:] Permit for my slave Miguel to free his daughter, Tomasa, eleven and a half years old, slave belonging to Colonel Don Miguel de Cárdenas y Chávez, this act expressly obligating me to maintain and raise her for as long as he [the father] remains my slave.[11]

ANC, *Gobierno Superior Civil*, 948/33487.

4.11. ANTONIO CUESTA, FREE MORENO, PURCHASES THE FREEDOM OF HIS SON, A SLAVE ON THE INGENIO SANTIAGO

Havana, January 18, 1854

The freedman Antonio Cuesta, moreno, affirms before Your Excellency that the price for the freedom of his son Isidro, slave belonging to Don Bonifacio Cuesta, was fixed in the amount of eight hundred pesos. Subsequently, the seller refused to transport him from the ingenio Santiago, where he held him, to this city, unless he was paid an additional one hundred pesos . . . [On February 15, Antonio once again appeared before the captain general, informing him that the master] demanded seven hundred pesos to that end, and would only then have his son fetched from the rural countryside. The petitioner produced the funds in cash. Now, sixteen days have passed, and his son's whereabouts still have not been confirmed . . .

He implores that you command the syndic to compel the former owner to produce his son in court as soon as possible, and that his son be freed . . .[12]

ANC, *Gobierno Superior Civil*, 949/33552.

4.12. LUCIANO GUTIERREZ PETITIONS TO PURCHASE HIS DAUGHTER'S FREEDOM AGAINST HER MASTER'S WISHES

Havana, January 28, 1854

The free moreno Luciano Gutiérrez appears before Your Excellency and states:

Long before the black woman Sabina, a Cuban-born slave belonging to Don Juan Pedro Veguerí, gave birth to the pickaninny Margarita, daughter of the petitioner, Excellency, he attempted to free the unborn child. He observed the utmost privations and foreswore even the most basic necessities in order to raise the sum of twenty-five pesos, which was the stipulated amount necessary to redeem the freedom of the unborn child of any slave.

To this effect, he met several times with the aforementioned Mr. Veguerí, but their negotiations came to naught. In the meantime, the slave woman gave birth, and thus the petitioner's financial sacrifice was immediately doubled. Nevertheless, and inspired by the noble purpose of freeing his daughter, he raised fifty pesos, the fixed amount for freeing any baptized infant . . .

. . . the petitioner has been frustrated in this second attempt [to free his daughter], as it has been seven months since the slave woman Sabina gave birth to his daughter, the infant has yet to be baptized, and, what is more, remains a slave . . .[13]

ANC, *Gobierno Superior Civil*, 949/33573.

4.13. CANUTO HOUSSIN WANTS TO FREE JULIANA AND THEN MARRY HER

Havana, February 14, 1854

Canuto Houssin, free moreno, native African, and resident of the town El Cerro, respectfully appears before Your Excellency and states:

He had in his possession the cash money to purchase the freedom of the morena slave Juliana, resident of the aforementioned town El Cerro, owned by Don Norberto Galarrage, whose master was absent. He intended to marry Juliana, the woman in question, and appeared before the syndic procurator general, because he had been advised that the property of the aforementioned Don Norberto Galarrage was under an injunction and that the purchase of the slave woman's freedom could not move forward without judicial intervention. To this purpose, the syndic procurator general issued an order for Don Francisco Galarrage, under whose authority the servant girl found herself, to appear in court to explain whatever he knew concerning the details surrounding said injunction. The aforementioned Don Francisco effectively confirmed that such a general injunction did apply to the aforementioned property . . . the proceedings in this matter being passed on through regular administrative channels to the lieutenant general of the municipal court of Cárdenas.

This state of affairs disqualified the syndic procurator general from ruling on the matter in question, and he had no alternative but to direct the petitioner to the aforementioned town of Cárdenas to submit his petition there.

The petitioner, Most Excellent Sir, finds himself ill and without the necessary means to embark upon a journey to Cárdenas, and the slave woman bemoans the harsh burden of slavery and continues to serve her master . . . (for which he requests expediting the proceeding in order to settle the matter) . . .[14]

ANC, *Gobierno Superior Civil*, 949/33573.

4.14. PETITION BY ANTONIO ABAD PALOMINO REQUESTING THAT HIS DAUGHTER OFFICIALLY BE GRANTED HER FREEDOM

Havana, May 26, 1854

Antonio Abad Palomino appears before Your Excellency with the utmost respect and states:

According to the terms and conditions of Doña Josefa de León's last will and testament, executed on February 3, 1844, the Cuban-born pickaninny, María Rufina, daughter of the petitioner, was granted her freedom. By virtue of the aforesaid testamentary provision, he obtained his daughter's certificate of manumission from the executor of the will, Don Benito González González, on October 27, 1848, as established by the enclosed document.

However, as of the present time, the provision is effectively null and void, given that the petitioner's daughter finds herself serving the lieutenant governor of the city of Santiago de las Vegas. To this day, the mother of the aforementioned freed child has been unable to gain custody of the child, frustrated in her endeavor by the powers that be. The petitioner does not hesitate to recur to Your Excellency's superior and beneficent protection, entreating that you deign to order the authorities in the aforementioned locality to relinquish the freed slave girl María Rufina, daughter of the petitioner, without further delay, unto her mother. It is this act of mercy that the petitioner hopes to merit as an instance of Your Excellency's noble righteousness.

(Required by the highest authorities to give an account of the case, the lieutenant governor of Santiago de las Vegas responds:)

Eleven months ago, I brought the Cuban-born Negro woman María Rufina into my wife's service. She had resided in the hamlet of Corralillo in a state of the most abject poverty since 1844, in the company of María Francisca Abreu, another of her same class. She was utterly abandoned by her mother and completely unaware of the identity of her father, because not even baptismal documents, copies of which I have the pleasure to enclose, were able to attest to paternity.

Some six months ago, Petrona, a Cuban-born Negro woman, appeared at my door, stating that she had come to take her daughter away. The daughter, awash in tears, pleaded with me not to forsake her, for she did not know whether or not that woman truly was her mother, as she did not recognize her, given that her real mother had abandoned her some ten years earlier. Pitying the poor little thing, I told the mother that she should leave her be, because her design was to place the child elsewhere (so she said) and that the child was earning as gainfully in my service as she could elsewhere.

Things remained unchanged until two months ago, when Petrona revisited her scheme. On the surface, this seemed peculiar but actually was entirely consistent with her despicable selfishness. When her daughter served no purpose, she abandoned her. She only laid claim to her when she could engage the child in the obscene trade in which she herself was caught up. According to what she herself told me, she never lived with Rufina's father and, currently, was living with the moreno slave Domingo Díaz.

The morena Rufina knows that she is free, and she has worked in that capacity as a nursemaid. The very person who has utterly neglected the child for ten years cannot deem the child's freedom illusory . . .[15]

Santiago de las Vegas, June 6, 1854.

ANC, *Gobierno Superior Civil*, 949/33543.

4.15. JUANA EVANGELISTA SUAZO REQUESTS THAT HER SISTER CHANGE MASTERS

Havana, September 3, 1860

Juana Evangelista Suazo, free morena, states before Your Excellency:

For many years, the value of her sister, María Cayetana, has been set at 350 pesos. Currently, she works as a slave belonging to Juan Ignacio Rendón, from whom she does not receive the treatment commensurate with her good service and disposition. For this reason, she has called upon the petitioner to seek out a new master for her, as permitted by law.

[In her own words] In early June of this year, I arranged for my sister to be purchased by Mrs. María Teresa Lima de Elosua, the sale to be finalized within eight days, as requested by the master. This deadline expired, as did other subsequent deadlines sought by the respective buyers. Finally, on July 7, I filed suit with the syndic, Don José Bruzón, who, on *motu propio* [on his own impulse] and to my sister's detriment, granted postponements of one new deadline after another up until the present time, exempting himself from the lawsuit in order to avoid an open conflict with the owner, according to what he has told me . . . (for which she requests resolution) . . .[16]

ANC, *Gobierno Superior Civil*, 954/33667.

4.16. ANTONIO SÁNCHEZ DEMANDS FREEDOM FOR HIS WIFE LUCÍA CARABALÍ

Havana, March 21, 1862

Antonio Sánchez, freedman, states that he left his wife, Lucía Carabalí, behind on his former master's cafetal when he became free. Observing the utmost economy in order to raise money, the petitioner saved three hundred pesos, which he considered an amount sufficient with which to free her. He gave the money to Don José Valdés, a minor official from the chief syndic's office, and was issued a receipt. This individual informed the petitioner where he could find Lucía, whom he had not seen for seventeen years, and the petitioner made the arrangements with said syndic for his wife's freedom. He made payment on November 26 of last year. Ever since, he frequented the syndic's office to monitor developments, but he had been able to ascertain only that Lucía lived on the ingenio Destino, belonging to the Compañía Territorial Cubana, and that the money continued to be held by the syndic's bailiff.

The petitioner entreats Your Excellency to take the appropriate action.[17]

ANC, *Gobierno Superior Civil*, 954/33689.

4.17. JUANA SÁNCHEZ Y SÁNCHEZ DEMANDS FREEDOM FOR HERSELF AND FOR HER SON

Havana, August 12, 1862

Juana Sánchez y Sánchez, native-born Cuban, and slave belonging to Don Gregorio Marsá, lieutenant in the militia and also resident of this city, most humbly and respectfully states:

She is able to establish that her daughter Ángela is also the lawful daughter of the aforementioned Mr. Marsá, and she believes that for this reason she [should be able to] secure her freedom . . . (so requesting it).

[The matter was turned over to the syndic Don Nicolás Azcarate for review,[18] who stated that] the mulatto[19] woman sustained that her owner had seduced her and that he was the father of her infant daughter, who appeared in court along with her, although it was clear that she lacked any hard evidence to substantiate her claim. The owner, for his part, roundly denied the charges. In the interest of avoiding a scandalous legal dispute, he agreed that it was best to free the child and set the mother's value at seven hundred pesos, although he had purchased her for more than one thousand.

ANC, *Gobierno Superior Civil*, 954/33696.

4.18. BENIGNA RENDÓN REQUESTS A REVISED COARTACIÓN OF HER SON FÉLIX CANTALICIO LINARES

Havana, March 27, 1863

Benigna Rendón, free morena, and mother of Félix Linares, pardo[20] . . . states:

Last September she bore witness in Superior Court, notifying the authorities that her son's owners were attempting to demand the exorbitant amount of nine hundred pesos from the petitioner for the freedom of her son Félix, when his worth was no more than five hundred pesos. The petitioner also documented that the five hundred pesos had been deposited in the syndic's office in Guanajay long before September . . .

More than half a year has gone by, Excellency, and the pardo Félix still does not enjoy the sacred right of freedom. His aging mother finds herself suffering from the greatest anguish, ignorant of the outcome of her complaint . . .[21]

ANC, *Gobierno Superior Civil*, 954/33693.

4.19. JUANA VALENZUELA FILES A COMPLAINT AGAINST HER MASTER AND HUSBAND

Havana, October 6, 1864

Your Excellency Sir Captain General:

[In her own words] With due respect and humility, tearfully, I come to ask for justice. My master says that should I go to the syndic he will punish me without cause. My claim amounts to nothing more than what he already has offered me in writing, before witnesses, and what I deserve by virtue of my labor and my good service.

Pardon me, Your Excellency, for speaking in such a frank manner, but I must tell the truth. Your Excellency acts as God on earth, and I come to seek my rights, concealing nothing. I have been married to my master since I was fourteen years old. I have a son with him, and he has offered me my freedom. I have helped him build a house using my wages; I have given him my lottery winnings, which he now keeps from me; I have made candles for him to sell in his chandlery; because he has money, I have sacrificed myself for him, nursed him when he has been ill, lived, pardon me, Your Excellency, as a wife with her husband, and always trusting in his promise to set me free. And now, because he has married another, he has given me my permit to sell myself, the first for four hundred pesos and the certificate of manumission for five hundred and fifty pesos, and the excise tax, when I cost him but twelve ounces of gold. Taking into account nothing more than [the value of] my labor and my lottery winnings, I have [amply] repaid him. Thus, I hope that, in the interest of charity and justice, Your Excellency grant me my freedom, for which God will reward you.[22]

ANC, *Gobierno Superior Civil*, 1056/37631.

4.20. MANUEL VALERIO, CONGOLESE, AGREES TO CHANGE OWNERS, PROVIDING THAT HE IS PERMITTED TO SEE HIS CHILDREN

Havana, June 13, 1864

Manuel Valerio, native African, Congolese, and slave belonging to Don Juan Bautista Núñez, resident of the city of Santa María del Rosario, across the street from the church, comes before Your Excellency and states that:

He was sold this year to the aforementioned Núñez on two conditions: that once a month he receive a pass to travel to the capital to see his children, and that the moment he became dissatisfied in his service he would be granted an authorization to seek another master. Neither of these conditions was met, and on several different occasions he protested his master's lack of compliance with the above stipulations, desperately wishing for his master to abide by the terms of the agreement. In light of such distressing circumstances, he resolved to run away, and effectively did so on June 8. [This he did only] in order to plead his case before Your Excellency by means of the account in the report submitted in support of his petition, and to learn if by virtue of your intervention his owner could be compelled to issue the permit necessary to seek out another master. This was the only remaining solace for this wretched slave in compensation for his suffering and by virtue of all that had befallen him.

I beseech Your Excellency, should he consider it reasonable, to summon the above-named Don Juan Bautista Núñez to appear before Your Excellency in court and to compel him [Núñez] either to comply or to enforce the above-stated conditions. In the meanwhile, he [the petitioner] will go wherever Your Excellency may deign to send him as a surety, trusting that, as an act of your renowned benevolence and justice, you will bestow such a boon upon him.[23]

ANC, *Gobierno Superior Civil*, 1056/37611.

4.21. EMILIO PIÑEIRO DEMANDS HIS MONEY OR HIS FREEDOM

Havana, December 1864

Emilio Piñeiro, Congolese, slave belonging to Manuel Piñeiro, owner of a former canteen on the Plaza del Cristo, and, as the latter's servant, appears before Your Excellency and states:

A little more than three years ago, his concubine had the good fortune to win the lottery, and she bestowed fifteen ounces of gold upon him in order to begin the process of coartación. He accepted the money, and gave it to his master for this purpose. His master, [the very individual who] was responsible for his petition, told him [the petitioner] that he did not want to own a coartado slave. The petitioner left, intending to tell the person who had so generously given him such a large amount of money [for his coartación]. The moment his master saw him leave, he ordered the petitioner seized, as he effectively was. He was taken back to his master, who, very discomfited, had those same men who had seized the petitioner take him to a gentleman named Francisco El Largo, resident of the third district,

43 San Miguel Street, to a place where coffee is roasted. On his master's orders, the petitioner was given a thrashing he would never forget, beating him twice, first as he was lashed to a ladder, and then once again when he was not bound. Besides the punishment, upon disrobing, they made off with the fifteen ounces of gold that he carried concealed in his waistband. To this day, the gold has not been returned, as it obviously should be.

[The petitioner] brought suit against his master. The entire story came out there in the offices of the syndic, who at that time was Don Pepe Martín Rivero, resident of San Nicolás Street, as well as in the office of the *alcalde* [mayor], Mr. De Pellijero. It was evident that a black slave named Carlos, an Arará who still belongs to Don Francisco, made off with the petitioner's fifteen ounces of gold. Moreover, the petitioner had a witness who would attest to the truth of the matter, a gentleman known as Captain Don Matías Aguado . . . (he requests that his money be returned to him) . . .[24]

ANC, *Gobierno Superior Civil*, 961/34046.

4.22. DOLORES ROCA'S ORDEAL TO HAVE HER DAUGHTER TERESA APPRAISED

Havana, August 30, 1866

Dolores Roca, free morena, native-born African, residing at 54 Suárez, states that Bernardo Montenegro, resident of Corral Falso, has refused to allow the appraisal of her daughter, Teresa. Your Excellency already is familiar with the circumstances. Such behavior is inexcusable, even in the context of all the hardships that might be visited upon this wretched slave woman. It is rumored that her master has sold her to Don Rafael Pozo Hernández, from the same neighborhood. It is advisable, Excellency, should Your Excellency deign it just, that the aforementioned slave be assessed in this city by professional appraisers . . .

(A note in the file said that the black woman went to the syndic Antonio María de Zayas, of Corral Falso, and deposited fifty-one pesos with him in person, in order to guarantee her claim, and he even so much as had her daughter's master summoned to appear before a judge in order to fix her price. Four months went by, according to Dolores, without the summons ever being served. Obliged to remain in that town [at her own expense], her expenditures having mounted to eighty-five pesos, and weary of abiding there to no purpose other than incurring even more expense, she decided to file a claim with the syndic for the aforementioned amount of money in order to plead her case before Your Excellency, requesting that the appropriate party appraise her daughter and set her purchase price.)

(The syndic in Colón denied that Roca's expenses could have been so high. He explained that) the black woman Dolores Roca, far from expending the sum of eighty-five pesos as she claimed, had earned enough money while there to cover her travel expenses, and even enough to clothe herself, and that she had received free room and board. She slept and often ate at the home of the free black woman, Teresa Abadía, at no cost, and, alternatively, she frequently worked as a washerwoman while dwelling in the home of other women of like circumstances, Regina González and Agustina Peñalver, who paid her six reals a day, plus board. If she had free room and board at Teresa's house, and if she had a paying situation as a journeywoman at Regina's and Agustina's house, then it was clear that the expenses that Dolores claimed were misleading...[25]

ANC, *Gobierno Superior Civil*, 967/34139.

4.23. CARLOTA POLO DEFENDS THE RIGHTS OF HER STEPDAUGHTER AND DEMANDS FREEDOM FOR HER STEPDAUGHTER'S SON

Havana, October 5, 1866

Carlota Polo, freeborn morena, seamstress, residing at 35 San Miguel, in the name of and representing Asunción Meireles, morena, slave belonging to Don Ramón Meireles, and the petitioner's stepdaughter... states that:

Asunción [the petitioner's stepdaughter], appraised in the amount of 450 pesos, found herself pregnant and notified her master. She loaned her stepdaughter the money she desired in order to set the unborn child free.

[In her own words] Three times, Excellency, I went to the home of my stepdaughter's masters with the money, and three times they refused to accept it and issue a receipt for the freedom of the unborn child! Without this receipt, the money forever would be vulnerable to seizure. This obliged me to turn the money over to the office of the deputy syndic of this city, according to the receipt I have in my possession.

The syndic summoned [her stepdaughter's] master to appear in court on several occasions. When he finally did appear, he accepted the payment, but not before the deponent revealed that gentleman's true intentions to the deputy syndic.

[In her own words] In conversations between my stepdaughter's master and myself, he stated that if I took the money to the office of the syndic, he would be compelled to accept it. However, he threatened to send my stepdaughter, Asunción, to the ingenio to give birth there and to enslave the newborn child, claiming that the infant had died. It did not take long, Excellency, for him to put his nefarious plan in motion. I had the receipt for the redemption of the unborn child, dated September 6. On September 13, at noon, the porter forcibly removed my stepdaughter from the house where she had been lodging, not even allowing her to pack her clothing. She was dragged along by virtue of brute force, all according to Mr. Meireles's instructions, and sent out into the rural countryside the following day, to the ingenio, where he intended to carry out his despicable plot. Precisely which ingenio and where it was located, I still do not know . . . (She requests that her stepdaughter's owner be compelled to produce her stepdaughter in court.) . . .[26]

ANC, *Gobierno Superior Civil*, 968/34232.

🌳 4.24. JUANA SOCARRÁS CHARGES THAT HER MOTHER AND SON ARE UNJUSTLY ENSLAVED

Havana, November 6, 1866

(The lieutenant governor of Remedios forwards to Your Excellency the official request submitted to him by the free morena Juana Socarrás, in which she denounces certain events pertaining to the unjust enslavement of herself, her mother Tomasa, and the continuing enslavement of her son José de la Luz, whose owners currently are attempting to transfer his ownership.)

The aforementioned morena states that in 1812 her mother Tomasa Federia signed on as a cook aboard the Portuguese brigantine *General Silveira*, along with eight other moreno crew members, all of them free. They set sail from Río de Janeiro, making for Havana. While not far off the coast of this island, a privateer out of Cartagena de Indias [captured the ship and] took them prisoner. The pirates headed for Remedios with their [illicit] cargo and handed the prisoners off to a man from Catalonia, now deceased, named Francisco Romeu, known as Pancho Avemaría. Serious charges warranting prison time and a fine of seven thousand pesos were filed against him, and records of those proceedings must exist somewhere in the files . . . and therein lies the proof that all the captured morenos were found to be free.

The petitioner's ill-fated mother had the misfortune of falling into the hands of Don José Oliva, Doña Micaela Naranjo's son-in-law, who sold her several times, but always was obliged to take her back, for lack of a formal bill of sale. Finally, she had to pay one hundred pesos for her freedom, freedom that she never should have lost, as confirmed by a document executed on February 27, 1856, filed in the office of the scrivener José Jiménez.

The petitioner was born during her mother's forced and illegal captivity. She was baptized as free in the parish of Jesús María de la Habana. She was taken to Remedios by Oliva, and sold to Don Felipe Socarrás, who in turn paid seven hundred pesos to reinstate her freedom, as attested to in the document executed on April 30, 1862, also filed in the aforementioned scrivener's office. . . . And a son, José de la Luz, also was born while his mother was enslaved, and she has been unable to obtain his freedom. She fears a painful separation if his reputed masters successfully transfer his ownership, as they intend. In the interests of the boy's freedom, and in due consideration of the quantities of money the mother and daughter already have paid out to recoup their freedom, as well as their wages over the period of time that they have been subject to unjust servitude, the parties associated with these respective debts must satisfy them . . .[27]

ANC, *Gobierno Superior Civil*, 967/34183.

4.25. THE DRAMATIC STRUGGLE OF DIMAS CHÁVEZ TO FREE HIS MOTHER

Havana, December 7, 1866

Dimas Chávez, native of Havana, residing at 53 Prado, states:

In October of this year, he deposited 306 pesos with the syndic Ramón Betancourt, originally for the purpose of freeing his mother, Lorenza Chávez, a slave owned by Pedro Acosta, who has concealed his mother on the ingenio Los Atrevidos, Colón. The syndic, in observance of his duty, sought out Chávez's mother, Lorenza, by virtue of issuing an edict and publishing a proclamation in the government publication *La Gaceta*, but he was unsuccessful in locating her.

As a result of due consideration, the petitioner now considers that, in view of such serious circumstances, [he must demand that her owner be compelled to produce his mother in court] . . .[28]

ANC, *Gobierno Superior Civil*, 968/34211.

5. The Plantation Social Network

5-1. Slaves and Mayorals

❧ 5.1. THE SLAVES ON THE CAFETAL CATALINA WALK OUT ON THEIR MAYORAL IN PROTEST AND RUN OFF INTO THE SCRUB (EXCERPTS FROM THE SUIT)

Guanajay, July 12, 1828

A. Statement of Francisco Martínez, native of Güira de Melena, thirty years old, married, illiterate, mayoral on the cafetal.

. . . he had been mayoral for two months, in charge of a work force of ninety-one slaves. . . . He gets the slaves up for work at daybreak, at the hour that morning prayers were already being said on other farms. Customarily, they rest for two hours after lunch and after dinner, which is late, with adequate time to rest, everyone going straightaway to their huts, under no obligation to do any other work. . . . The only thing that had occurred to him as a possible cause of such a mass exodus was that the previous mayoral apparently had accustomed the slaves to a lighter work load. But the deponent was new at his job and made them work a little harder, allowing little respite from the tasks at hand for the grass out in the fields was high now . . . (he believed that this was the cause for their insubordination) . . .

B. Statement of Feliciano Carabalí, appearing to be some forty-five years old, married.

More than a week ago, the deponent and his fellow slaves José Dolores, Gabriel, Manuel, Roque, Esteban, José Elías, Pablo, Fernando, Pedro, Rafael, Casimiro, and Ruperto were out in the scrubland. The deponent was in the infirmary weaving baskets when, at lunchtime, that is at twelve, everyone began to say that they were going off into the scrub, because they could no longer put up with the mayoral. No one in particular acted as the leader. They were going out there in the scrub to wait for their master, Don Matías Vildóstegui. They were going to tell him that the mayoral did not give them anything for lunch, how he did not allow them to smoke their pipes, how he did not allow them to talk, how he punished them if they got dirty, how at night that mayoral interrupted their conversations with their women and called for silence, and broke their earthenware vessels. At lights out, no talking was allowed, and doors to the huts had to be secured. Then he would patrol, listening at each hut to see if he could hear anyone talking. If he did, he ordered the door opened and made them be quiet. All of these things were behind their decision to go to the scrub to await their master, Don Matías. . . . He did not remember the exact day of the walkout to protest the mayoral, but it had nothing to do with their masters. As soon as they had their meat allotment in one hand, their flour ration in the other, they fled into the bush. They each grabbed a stick to defend themselves against the dogs.[1] They never intended to use them as weapons against any people.

They knew that the mayoral was rounding up a posse and dogs to go to look for them. A few days later, they all assembled at the edge of the thicket, sticks in hand. The deponent saw the mayoral coming their way, along with some white men and dogs. Before that party caught up to the slaves, the deponent said to the mayoral, "Don't sic no dogs on us, we not goed too fer into da thicket and, yessah, in our masser's [thicket], if our masser cum, we be goin' to where da masser be, that no, we not be goin' out der 'cuz we not want to work." When they realized that the mayoral and white men accompanying him were going to try to capture them by siccing the dogs on them, they fled to the big house there on the cafetel. Their other master, Don Antonio Toscano, was there. They knelt down before him and told him that the mayoral was very wicked, that he did not feed them anything for lunch, that he did not want them to smoke their pipes, that he did not want them to talk among themselves, along with all their other grievances. They told him that it was not necessary for the mayoral to go out looking for them; that their master's mere presence was enough for them to go back to work on the cafetal. The mayoral was very wicked. Then, their master, Toscano, told them to go get their rations, that everything was all taken care of. So, one by one, they set out for their huts. They were snacking on some tidbits when they heard a racket. They heard people approaching, saying, "Grab them! Cut them off!" At this, the deponent put his head out the door and saw that it was the mayoral and a lot of people with dogs. The deponent took flight once again, and seven slaves in all successfully escaped.

These days, they eat twice a day, once at twelve and once in the afternoon. Before, when their former master was alive, they ate three meals a day. They have a two-hour break after the first meal. On holidays, they are free after ten o'clock. They return to work at sunset.... Each and every one of them has their own garden plots, hogs, and chickens as well. When they have time off on holidays, they go to work on their plots and do their own chores until late afternoon, when they go back to work for their master. ... The deponent has never been punished, nor have any of them. Ever since these masters and the mayoral have been on the cafetal, they have never laid a hand on him. His fellow slaves have seen them give some floggings using a manatee whip, but nothing that can be deemed excessively harsh...

C. Statement of Casimiro, Mina, thirty years old, married.

... He has no complaint against the man who currently runs the estate, Don Antonio Toscano, that is. The mayoral is very harsh, punishing them severely. Although the mayoral has done no more than punish the deponent by shackling his wrists, he has been known to be harsh with the rest of the slaves. The slaves are looked after properly, provided with victuals, and given any other necessities, and they really have no grounds for complaint in that respect. They receive two rations a day, one at eleven o'clock in the morning and the other in the afternoon. When they are sick, they are attended to without delay with all that is necessary.

The slave Feliciano told everyone that in the old days, their owner Don Matías Vildóstegui would come to the estate every week to look around. They obeyed him because he had the law behind him. Once the new mayoral was hired, the master stopped coming to the estate every week, which is why Felicino himself told them that they should all go into the scrub to wait for Don Matías Vildóstegui. It was a long time before Don Matías showed up, and they intended to remain in the scrub until he arrived. When the slaves realized that [there was a search party] looking for them, they set out for the factory courtyard there on the estate and their huts instead, where Don Antonio Toscano met with them. He told them to calm down, that everything would be taken care of, and that they were forgiven. He told them that they should go home, and, with that, he distributed some rations. Shortly thereafter, several unfamiliar white men showed up at the quarters. They seized seven of the fourteen slaves, taking them off to the stocks. The rest of the slaves were quick to flee.

Taita Feliciano, the moreno working the fifth shift, Roque, and José Eleno Criollo met with Don Antonio Toscano, and right away they asked, by virtue of the pardon, that Pablo, José Dolores, Julián, and Ruperto be released from the stocks. Toscano agreed, giving them the key. They released their fellow slaves, set out to find Toscano, and thanked him for his actions. He replied that they should go to their huts to rest. A few moments later, a gang of white men materialized. They apprehended them and put them in the stocks. The seven who got away were Esteban, Manuel Bibí, Cristóbal, Roque, José Dolores, Gabriel, and Feliciano.... The only thing that Feliciano told them was that, when the whites went out in search of them, they should not do anything. If the dogs attacked them, then they could take action. Whites were whites. They could kill the dogs, but they should exercise great caution with the whites, they should not do anything to harm them...

They have barely had any time to rest since the current mayoral has come. They work incessantly in order to fulfill their duties without being punished. From the beginning, the entire crew has been dissatisfied with this mayoral because once they file out, he makes them run the rest of the way to the work site.... They have no complaint concerning the various chores they do. They do not work on holidays and they do not work overtime. They arise for morning prayers, they clean the factory courtyard, and, once this is done, they go out to work in the fields. Work stops at twelve o'clock, when they eat lunch, and they rest for two hours. Then, they return to work cutting grass until sunset. Later they go home and eat...

D. Statement of Fernando, Congolese, thirty-five years old, married.

... His fellow slave Feliciano told him, "Let's make for da brush. We work a lot, and dey don't give us no lunch, dey won't let us smoke our pipes, we can't talk to nobody out der in the fields. We not dun take off from the work 'cuz of our masser. Dis ain't like before. We be going to the scrub 'til Don Matías come, so dat he give in and hand over our lunch to eat. We not be leaving work 'cuz of our masser." That is what he told Feliciano that on Wednesday of last week, at two o'clock.... On holidays, they get off work at noon. They do not have any place to wash their clothes.

... If their fingers are injured or they have a stomachache, they tell the mayoral, and he immediately sends them to the infirmary where they are well looked after. The deponent has been sick on many occasions but has told the mayoral that he is all right anyway. The mayoral has replied that he still cannot go back to work. They have no complaint against this particular mayoral.... Their ideas of leaving and going into the countryside was so they would reduce the work they are doing...

E. Statement of Pedro Lucumí, forty-five years old, married.

... the one known as Feliciano said that they all were going to the thicket in protest, because he took away their lunch, he would not let them talk, he would not let them smoke their pipes, and he overworked them, and it was unbearable. Before there was none of this.

... Since this mayoral has been here, he only has punished the deponent twice, striking him a good number of times using a manatee leather whip. The only work they give them is weeding the fields and the rest of the chores that need be done on this estate. They do not work because they are threatened with harsh punishment. The mayoral punishes the deponent's fellow slaves when they deserve it.

F. Statement of Cristóbal Carabalí, thirty-five years old, single.

[Asked why he was in jail, he responded:] The reason was because he was fed up with being sick and he did not do the work that they ordered him to do because he knew how to avoid work. Once he fled to the thicket, he found thirteen of his fellow slaves there, and was talking with all of them. He confessed that he was slacker ...[2]

ANC, *Gobierno Superior Civil*, 936/33025.

5.2. SAVAD CARABALÍ BIBÍ ASSAULTS THE CARTER FROM THE INGENIO SAN JUAN BAUTISTA

Puerta de la Güira, July 1, 1831

A. Statement of Antonio Ribero, native of Guanabacoa, forty-two years old, married, illiterate, mayoral of the ingenio.

... he was at the ox herd's house when he heard a racket over by the carter's house ... he immediately ran to see what all the shouting was about. When he got to where it was coming from, that was the house of the aforementioned [sic] Quiqutis [sic] house, he found that the man had already been wounded. ... The aforementioned [sic] Savad did it because he was half crazed. This had to be because Quiqutis was ill at the time and merited compassion. Savad entered the latter's house, without so much as a by your leave and proceeded to slash him twice. (He believed that Savad was crazy) because over the last year that he had run the plantation, he had never seen Savad either interact with or speak to anyone. That slave never seemed to be able to make out what was said to him, and no one understood what he said. The deponent could not get Savad to live with the other slaves. Instead, since the beginning, Savad chose to live in the infirmary, and no one was capable of convincing him to do otherwise. The deponent was a softhearted person who treated everyone in a benign fashion, and simply could not bring himself to force Savad out. ... (After the attack)

Savad showed up in the middle of his parlor, wielding his machete. The mayoral used all the resources at his disposal to capture Savad alive and well, without casualties, but, finally, had to hit him over the head in order to temporarily stun him and take away the machete . . .

B. Statement of José Quiqutis, native of Guayabal, twenty-nine years old, carter, married, illiterate.

. . . the only thing to which he can attribute Savad's actions is that this big bozal has fallen in love with his wife, just like what happened with several other slaves on this estate. The aforementioned Savad may have believed that by killing the deponent, he could then take the woman as his consort. . . . She has told him that every time that Savad comes out of the infirmary, where he lives, or anywhere else that he sees her, he cannot take his eyes off of her. Whenever Savad needs something, he asks her for it. The other day he brings her a bundle of sugarcane, laying it in front of her house for her, instead of just giving it to her.

C. Statement of Luisa Pérez, native of Alquízar, twenty years old, married, illiterate, wife of the previous deponent.

. . . The slave Savad could not take his eyes off of her whenever he saw her, and would not stop gazing at her until she was out of sight. . . . That was the very same slave who brought her a bundle of sugarcane and then disappeared without saying a word. . . . One day, that very same Negro showed up, and, using gestures, he made it known that he wanted thread to sew on some buttons. She never heard that slave say even one word, because he was not in the habit of speaking to anyone . . .

D. Statement of Antonia Herrera, native of Guanajay, thirty-seven years old, the mayoral's wife, illiterate.

. . . (She asked Savad) what had happened, but he was unable to respond. He knelt down before the carter's wife, never saying a word, although she asked him several questions. The deponent called another slave named Félix to come and speak to him. Although he did it, Savad refused to answer, because he was speaking a language that no one understood . . .

E. Statement of Francisco Chil, native of Corralillo, thirty-two years old, married, ox herd.

. . . the reason Savad seems crazy instead of sane is because no one has been able to understand him, nor does he understand anyone, so he has been some sort of outcast here on the farm . . .

F. Statement of Savad Carabalí Bibí, with Adrián Bibí, a slave there on the ingenio, acting as interpreter.

[Asked if he is a Christian, he responded:] all he knew is that they sprinkled some water on his head . . .

. . . it was the carter himself who was flogging him the night before last. The deponent begged him to stop, saying that he was good. The carter refused and continued lashing him. He raised the machete that he had in his hand and gave it to the carter good. [Upon examining him and verifying that he did not show any outward signs of a beating, Savad responded] that when he was being whipped, he had on two shirts. . . . The carter flogged him at night in his quarters, when they came home from work, after vespers. The carter punished him because the deponent had not brought the carter the seed cane. . . . The deponent went to look for a little tobacco at the carter's house. Because he was met with a flogging, he attacked the carter with his machete.

Asked if he understood the whites' language, he said that he absolutely understood every word that the whites say. Asked if he knew the carter's wife, he said that he knew her . . . and, smiling, Savad said that he did not seduce black women, so how in the world would he be attracted to white women . . .

ANC, *Miscelánea de Expedientes*, 207/F.

5.3. GASPAR LUCUMÍ INJURES THE MAYORAL ON THE CAFETAL NUESTRA SEÑORA DEL ROSARIO

San Luis de la Ceiba, July 27, 1835

A. Statement of Antonio Morales, native of Santa Cruz de Tenerife, forty years old, married, mayoral on the cafetal.

. . . That morning, before he departed, he left orders with his field hands, thirty-four in number, including their contramayoral Simón Lucumí. Nine of the most ladinos were to work at removing coffee bush seedlings from the seedbed. The rest were to load the plants and sow them in the furrows that had been prepared for that purpose. Upon returning that afternoon, he went out to inspect the fields. He found that his orders to transplant the coffee seedlings to the seed plot that had been prepared for them had not been followed. Rather, they had removed the seedlings and transplanted them in another, different location. He summoned Simón Lucumí, the contramayoral, who asked to be forgiven. Simón told him that, in his [Antonio, the mayoral's] absence, he [Simón] went along with those removing the seedlings, who were working rapidly, to see how they sowed them. In the meanwhile, those who had been engaged in moving the seedlings had changed the site where the plants or, at any rate, some of them, were to be transplanted, putting them in another location. The mayoral [Antonio] whipped him [Simón] and another of the offenders named Gabino Gangá, dealing them six or eight lashes, because they had been too hasty in their work, instead of doing it little by little. He struck Gabino twice, Pascual Gangá twice, and Pedro José Lucumí twice. He struck Gaspar Lucumí once but, upon being beaten, the slave wounded the contramayoral on the forehead with his work machete. . . . He dragged him inside by his arms, and called out to the other slaves who were there, that is Pascual Gangá, Domingo Lucumí, Gabino Gangá, Cristóbal Lucumí, José Lucumí, and Pedro José Lucumí. They gathered round, not intending to harm anyone, but to restrain Gaspar Lucumí, which they were unable to do, because they were without machetes . . . and he ran off through a cornfield. The rest went out to work where the contramayoral was, with the exception of Gabino, who accompanied him to the courtyard and later went on to work . . .

B. Statement of Pascual Lucumí, not Gangá, like the mayoral said, thirty years old, widowed.

. . . Before his mayoral left yesterday morning, he told them to transplant the seedlings.[3] He and the "most ladino" of his field hands were to transplant [only] the smaller seedlings, because there had not been much rain and the larger ones were withering in the sunlight.[4] He showed them the section of the seedbed that they should remove them from, [where the soil was moist and the seedlings were easily dug up, with soil protecting the roots]. He warned them about those sections where the soil was compacted, making it impossible to remove these [seedlings] along with soil without damaging the roots.[5] When the mayoral came that afternoon, he saw that they had not continued to transplant the seedlings in the location he had indicated. He ordered the contramayoral to deal Gabino and Cristóbal six or eight lashes each. Then, when the contramayoral left with a different slave-crew with other seedlings to transplant, the mayoral was alone, grumbling about the situation. He dealt two lashes to the deponent, and he gave two lashes apiece to the seven or eight other hands who were there. When he came to the last slave, Gaspar, he was able to flog him only once, because there was a ruckus. Gaspar went up to the mayoral, clinched him, threw him to the ground, and attacked him with the machete. Then the mayoral called out to the deponent and Gabino, telling them not to let Gaspar kill him, and they came and restrained Gaspar and got him off the mayoral. The mayoral got up, and took out his *machete de hoja* [regular machete with a blade approximately one yard long], and struck Gaspar, cutting him on the arm. Gaspar showed them his wounds and told them, "Mayoral, dun cut me wid machete," violently shoving them and escaping. Just then, the mayoral's dog attacked Gaspar. The dog had latched onto his shirt and was hanging onto it. Gaspar had to get the dog to release his grip on his shirt. Then Gaspar had another opportunity to hurl the mayoral to the ground once again, and took off running and dove into a nearby cornfield . . .

[After several attempts to find Gaspar, a neighbor, Manuel López, stated:]

He was inspecting his cornfield, walking up and down the furrows, when he smelled a terrible odor, breathing in an unbearable stench. Following it up, he came upon the fugitive slave's remains hanging from a *guásima* tree [large native tree whose leaves and fruit serve as feed for hogs and cattle]. The body was so decomposed that the remains were almost completely skeletonized. He probably had been there for eight or nine days. Although he did not recognize him, he presumed that it was Gaspar Lucumí from the neighboring plantation. . . . Judging by what he saw, Gaspar was hung by the leather lash that the mayoral used as a whip . . .

ANC, *Miscelánea de Expedientes*, 33/A.

✿ 5.4. THE CONTRAMAYORAL BENIGNO LUCUMÍ LEADS A REVOLT AGAINST THE OX HERD FROM THE INGENIO INTRÉPIDO

Macurijes, August 14, 1835

A. Statement of Luis Piedra, native of El Cano, twenty-four years old, single, ingenio ox herd.

. . . on Wednesday of this week, he took away a sharp knife that Benigno, the black contramayoral, was carrying and put it in the mayoral's quarters. On Thursday, he saw Benigno with the same knife once more and took it away again, this time breaking off its sharp tip, and put it away. The witness believed that the attempted revolt was caused by this repeated dispossession of Benigno's knife. The witness was cutting a series of notches in several beams that he had removed from the scrubland bordering the cane fields, close to where the slaves were working. The witness was crouched down engaged in this task at hand when he was dealt a cowardly blow from behind on the back. Taken by surprise, the victim hit his assailant, Benigno, with the auger that he happened to be holding in his hand at the time of the attack, causing him to loosen his grip on his weapons, a blade and a knife. They tied the witness up by dint of force, dragged him to a stake that they had made ready, where they tied him fast and blindfolded him. Benigno said, "Let's kill him," to which someone else, he does not know who, responded that they should leave him alone for now. They began to ready another stake nearby for the mayoral, intending to kill them both at the same time by burning them at the stake. Once they had made this decision, they left. The witness had the unexpected good fortune of being able to loosen his bonds, break free of the stake, and return safely to the ingenio . . .

B. Statement of Benigno Lucumí, thirty years old, contramayoral.

. . . he said in the few days since the ox herd and the mayoral came here, they had been punishing them relentlessly in the cruelest manner, using a manatee leather whip. They no longer allowed them to rest a while at regular intervals, nor allowed them to drink as much water as they liked. In light of this excessive harshness, the rest of the field hands, Canuto, Gregorio, Eustanquio, Víctor Bibí, José Francisco, the bozals Francisco Mandinga and Pacho Gangá, Domingo Mandinga, and José de Jesús Gangá, approached the deponent, saying that they wanted to punish the ox herd, as, effectively, they did.

They asked the deponent how it was that his shirt was bloodstained. He said that on the morning of the very same day that the ox herd flogged him with the manatee leather whip that the ox herd found the deponent in the possession of a sharp knife. This was not unusual, for the deponent was the one who dressed the cattle and the hogs on that farm. He had asked the ox herd for the knife one day in order to kill a hog. The ox herd gave it to him and sharpened it. Later, the deponent's wife, who works in the mayoral's house, returned the knife to him, which is why it was sharpened . . .

. . . Although the deponent knew that they were going to carry out the attack, he did not participate in tying the ox herd up. Rather, along with other members of his work crew, he kept on weeding out in the fields. He responded to the cries for help, and they saw the ox herd tied to a stake. That is when the deponent called out to them and warned them not to go out into the scrub. Instead, they should follow him. Together they would go to Don Rafael Montalvo's farm. Two of them sought refuge in the scrub anyway. The deponent and the others went to that particular farm, looking for the mayoral, Vicente María Álvarez.[6] They told him that the ox herd on that ingenio had just been assaulted. They wanted the judge to come to take their statements and to install a new mayoral and ox herd until such time that their master returned. The two who fled into the scrub were José de Jesús Gangá and Domingo Mandinga. In the end, they confined them in the big house there, stripped them of their tools, and brought them to this farm.

C. Statement of José Francisco, slave of the [. . .] nation, twenty-eight years old, single.

. . . [they beat the employee] because, ever since the ox herd came to work on the ingenio, he flogged them incessantly using a manatee leather whip. He did not allow them to take breaks, nor did he allow them to go get water. They did not like that individual, because he thrashed them all the time, for no good reason . . .

D. Statement of José de la Torre, native of Calvario, forty-five years old, married, mayoral.

. . . on the ingenio in question, there were and remain . . . 153 slaves of both sexes and a variety of ages. . . . In effect, the ox herd inappropriately punished them severely with a manatee leather whip without the proper authorization . . .

E. Statement of Domingo Fernández, native of Asturias, over twenty-five years old, married, plantation mayordomo.

. . . He is certain that the ox herd treated the slaves very cruelly, constantly flogging them with a manatee leather whip . . .[7]

ANC, *Miscelánea de Expedientes*, 614/A.

5.5. SLAVES BELONGING TO SAN JUAN DE MANACAS FLOG THEIR MAYORAL

Guaminao, Santiago de Cuba, June 23, 1840

A. Statement of Bernardo Serrudo, thirty-seven years old, mayoral on the hacienda cafetal San Juan de Manacas owned by Gabriel Segundo Sorzano.

. . . On the twenty-third of this month, once the deponent had completed some chores that he had begun a little after five that morning, he ordered some slaves to remove the lids covering several piles of coffee beans. Once this was done, without any provocation whatsoever, as the witness was leaving the drying shed where all the other slaves were gathered, the slave Nicolás took him by surprise and violently overpowered him. The assailant bid the others to join him, and Francisco, the contramayoral, and Esperanza [a male slave] responded unreservedly and enthusiastically. All three of these slaves exercised great influence over their fellow slaves, even those who were older, stronger, and wiser, as well as the ladinos. They hurled threats to incite the rest of the bozalons to join in the attack . . . leading the witness to a ladder, and the slave Esperanza tied him to it, even as he was kicking him with his foot along with the black slave Nicolás. They both attacked the deponent with the same malevolent purpose. Francisco, the contramayoral, aided and abetted those two. He stationed himself at the foot of the ladder for that purpose, flogging the victim with the same long whip that Francisco had used on them when he was contramayoral. . . . The slave women María Belén, Rita, Felisa, Caridad, and Luisa hastened into the fray, encouraging the slaves to make the beating more and more ruthless and unrelenting, disregarding the will of God, the law, and the due respect servitors are obliged to observe toward those who rule them. As a result of repeated reflection . . . the witness reminded the main assailants that each and every individual must exercise compassion and live in fear of the law and that the more severe and inhumane their punishment of him, the greater would be the severity of the arm of the authorities who would be fully informed of the crimes they committed there. He managed to assuage their furor and daunt them to the extent that they loosened his restraints and helped him to stand up. Meanwhile, another slave made fast his arms, saying that they were going to escort him to the road so that he could be off. This, only on the condition that he never set foot on Manacas ever again. If he did, he would receive twice the punishment, so said the slaves who led him to the road, to his salvation. The witness presumed that, in lieu of this agreement, they would have taken him far away from the hacienda and killed him . . .

B. Statement of Francisco Carabalí, thirty-eight years old, single, contramayoral.

. . . At dawn, the mayoral . . . (left) the deponent in the first drying shed along with the women to uncover some mounds of coffee beans. The mayoral, with a work crew, went to remove the coffee beans from the warehouse and move them over to the last drying shed. Shortly thereafter, he heard them beating someone, but he could not determine who it was, because some of the drying sheds were higher than others. He did not think anything of it at first, because the mayoral was very harsh, constantly meting out severe punishments. When the women told him that it was the mayoral whom they were beating, he ran to help him . . .

C. Statement of Nicolás Gangá, forty-five years old, single.

... The mayoral ... who habitually bludgeoned the deponent, one day even knocking out two of his teeth, hit him with a stick while the slaves were finishing up some extra work after their normal workday. Aggravated, the respondent cinched the mayoral and knocked him to the ground, thinking that the incident would go no further. He had scarcely knocked the mayoral down when the slaves Ambrosio, Esperanza, Dionisio, and Fernando intervened and took over and, along with Damián, put him on a plank and flogged him with some *bejuco* [pliable reed or cane]. Francisco arrived shortly thereafter ... and he too beat the mayoral with a long horsewhip ...

D. Statement of Geraldo, native of Curazao, thirty-two years old, single.

The deponent asked Francisco, the slave contramayoral, how he could abide such an act. He replied that he abided it in exactly the same way that he tolerated the mayoral beating the slaves ...

E. Statement of Casimiro Carabalí, fifty years old, single.

... He ate their hens, he absconded with any produce they raised on their own garden plots to give to his hogs, and he beat them all the time ...

F. Statement of Damián, Congolese, eighteen years old, single.

... He treated them very cruelly, he took away any produce they raised on their own plots, ate their hens, and would not let them sleep as late as they were accustomed to ...

G. Statement of Carlos Carabalí, fifty years old, single.

He treated them very harshly, meting out severe punishments, giving them insufficient food rations, and not allowing them to sleep enough ...

H. Statement of Gabriel Segundo Sorzano, native of Nuevo Reino de Granada, over twenty-five years old, owner of the cafetal.

... The deponent was quite aware that Serrudo administered [the estate] with a degree of harsh punishment, even for minor infractions and at times recurred to the use of overtime, and he spoke with Serrudo about this matter. He excused him for this when the mayoral explained that they were behind schedule. The rainy season was near at hand, a time of year when the slaves did not have much work to do. As for now, it was impossible to let up during the day, and he had them work from four in the morning until nine or ten o'clock at night, with no breaks other than what was minimally necessary for meals. The slaves never had complained to the deponent ...[8]

ANC, *Miscelánea de Expedientes*, 235/H.

5.6. FERMÍN LUCUMÍ, A FORMER AFRICAN CHIEFTAIN, KILLS HIS MAYORAL ON THE INGENIO BALEAR

Rancho Veloz, July 31, 1840

A. Statement of Victor Gangá, age unknown, single, contramayoral.

. . . Yesterday, the mayoral sent the hands out to the fields, and he assigned the ladinos to a different chore. The mayoral left with the bozals. He ordered the deponent to go and look for a horse and tie it up out there in the field. He did as he was told, following the mayoral along with the bozals. . . . And as the deponent led the horse toward the mayoral and the bozals, he saw that the bozals were coming toward him very hurriedly, machetes in hand, as though to attack him. He saw that while the mayoral had left mounted, now that horse was roaming loose. He did not see the mayoral around anywhere. Hence, in order to escape the furor of the mutineers, he loosened the horse that he had been leading by the hand, and fled to find safe haven in the carpenter's quarters, with the assailants at his heals. At this, he called out to the carpenter and the doctor, alerting them as to the situation, and when he was sure that they [the mutineers] had gone, he left there and went on to notify his master . . .

Asked who was pursuing him, he said that, in reality, it was none other than Fermín, a Lucumí, who threatened him with his work machete. Although there were four or five others, they were quite a distance away from him, and he could not recognize them . . . he was not aware (of any possible grievances), but Lucumí bozals were full of brio, just like all of their compatriots. It was Fermín who, for the most part, tended to be most withdrawn and uncommunicative, even with his own countrymen . . . (the mayoral) not only did not punish them, but he actually preferred them to the ladinos, not unduly pressing them in their work, and allotting them special clothing . . .

B. Statement of Nicolás Lucumí, aided by an interpreter.

. . . The night before the incident took place, the slave Fermín climbed up into the loft that served as living quarters. As he was slow about it, the mayoral flogged him and in the process lashed a pustule that he [the deponent] had on his buttocks. Fermín became very angry, and said that he was going to kill the mayoral. The next morning, when Fermín left for work, instead of setting out for the sawyer's, where he was supposed to have worked, he armed himself with his machete and mixed in with those hands going out to work in the fields. Upon coming to the outer edge of the banana grove, he stayed behind in the gully, waiting for the mayoral to go by. He struck him from behind with his machete, stunned him, knocking him right off his horse, seriously injuring him. . . . He alone was the perpetrator, the others being some distance off. As soon as they saw him flee, they followed him. The deponent could do nothing less, because, just like those around him, he loved and respected Fermín a great deal because he was a leader back in their native land.

Asked if he knew that killing a white person, and especially the mayoral, was a crime, he responded that he knew it because it was the first thing that his countrymen told him when he arrived on the farm . . .

C. Statement of Pedro Lucumí, an old man, with the aid of an interpreter.

Asked if he knows that it was a crime to kill . . . he answered that he had not been in this land for very long, and that back there, in his homeland, killing was allowed . . .

D. Statement of Fermín Lucumí, through an interpreter

. . . He is called Malade in his homeland. Here, his master calls him Fermín. He is a Lucumí. . . . He alone was the killer. He was resentful over the flogging that the mayoral had given him the night before. It was then that he came up with the plan to use his weeding machete to take off the mayoral's head. He did not do it that very night because they slept under lock and key. No one else abetted him in his deed. He was asked why he had not informed his master after the mayoral punished him, rather than commit attempted murder. He replied that, in his land, when he killed someone in wartime, he did not have to inform anyone. . . . He only killed those who attacked him. . . . After they saw him flee some of them followed him, for back in their homeland he was their superior. Once out there in the scrubland, they scattered, going off in different directions . . .[9]

ANC, *Miscelánea de Expedientes*, 235/E.

5.7. THE MYSTERIOUS DEATH OF ALEJO CRIOLLO ON THE INGENIO SANTA TERESA

Bahía Honda, February 18, 1863

Report from the administrator to the lieutenant governor of this Jurisdiction:

. . . at the present time, eight o'clock in the evening, I was informed of the discovery of a black man hanging from one of the trees in the ingenio courtyard.... (Once the authorities arrived) they found a Negro hung by the neck from one of the branches of a sapodilla tree some three hundred paces north of the big house, dangling from a length of doubled leather greased with tallow and tied to a branch... some four and one-fourth yards off the ground.... The black man was five feet tall, according to Spanish units of measure, about thirty years old, very fat, dressed in pants and shirt made out of rusia in good condition, wearing crude leather sandals on his feet... and also confined by a new pair of shackles...

B. Statement of the administrator José Aguiar Mella, native of Santiago de Galicia, fifty-six years old, married.

... At about eleven thirty that day, the exalted Don Rafael de Toca, owner of the ingenio, was on the premises when the slave Alejo Criollo came before him, asking to have a word with his master. In this undertaking, he was accompanied by several black women and pickaninnies and also by the slaves Felipe, Pío, and Benigno. They were led into the far end of the shed adjacent to the big house, and there their master, owner of the ingenio, along with some other gentlemen who were in his company, were prepared to hear what the aforementioned Negro Alejo had to say. Alejo, speaking in a loud and resolute tone of voice, stated that they all were Cuban born, and they had come to complain about the administrator and the mayoral because they made them work a lot and punished them a great deal. Alejo's master was displeased by this affront, and he commanded them all to break it up and go back to work and ordered them to obey the administrator, who acted on his behalf on the ingenio.

The slave Alejo and those accompanying him were adamant in their endeavor, and all were talking. He [the master] forced them to disband, once he compelled them to remove their shirts and established for the record that none of them showed any indications of recent physical punishment. He exhorted them to behave themselves, so that their master would continue to reward them in the future, just as he had done the day before when he gave all the slaves their annual bonus. Without further delay, he ordered that the one o'clock bell be rung to call all the slaves into the factory courtyard. In front of everyone, the previously mentioned slaves were disciplined for the offenses they had committed, that is, for uniting for the purpose of making improper and unjust demands of their owner. In effect, they were summoned and punished at the designated time. Alejo, Pío, and Felipe received twenty-five lashes each on the buttocks and were shackled straightaway as an example to the others. Finally, at eight o'clock that evening, the mayoral reported that Alejo was missing. One of the contra-mayorals who had been searching for him found a black man suspended from a tree, and it turned out to be Alejo himself . . .

(The slaves were well treated, well fed, and well clad. They had their own garden plots, hogs, and hens. They received religious instruction, and were so well indoctrinated that slave marriages on this ingenio customarily were sanctioned by the Church. . . . Alejo always was rebellious and created disturbances. At times, he exhibited a certain lack of attentiveness, but the deponent does not know to what it could be attributed . . .)[10]

ANC, *Miscelánea de Expedientes*, 829/C.

5-II. Conflicts within the Plantation Slave Community

5.8. CEFERINO MANDINGA KILLS PANTALEÓN CARABALÍ IN AN ATTEMPT TO COLLECT A DEBT

Guanabo, November 25, 1823

Statement of Sabino Gangá, twenty years old, single, slave on the ingenio San Joaquín, owned by the Marqués of Prado Ameno.

. . . He saw that Ceferino Mandinga was responsible for the death of Pantaleón Carabalí. That happened today, at about one o'clock in the afternoon, in front of the door to his hut. The whole thing started when Pantaleón first came around looking for Ceferino Mandinga in order to collect one and a half reals that he [Pantaléon] said that he [Ceferino] owed him. They argued about it, and Pantaleón flogged him [Ceferino] a number of times with a leather whip. Then, he [Pantaleón] left him [Ceferino], and he [Pantaleón] went to the witness's hut. A short while later, Ceferino appeared at that hut, machete in hand. Pantaleón saw him with it, and asked him if he had brought the machete along in order to go ahead and kill him. Ceferino defiantly replied that he had come to see if Pantaleón dared to flog him with the whip again. His furor unloosed, Pantaleón flogged Ceferino. Ceferino hurled Pantaleón to the ground, and the battle was underway. Ceferino ended up falling down, and Pantaleón sat on top of him, and was pummeling him in the face and mouth, saying, "Go on, get up, go tell the mayoral." In the course of this mêlée, Ceferino spied a knife at Pantaleón's waist, snatched it, and used it to stab Pantaleón. Pantaleón keeled over, dead on the spot, and Ceferino fled, taking the knife with him. . . . The moment this brawl or row began, the witness also began to cry out for the mayoral, who did not hear anything, because he was too far off . . .[11]

ANC, *Miscelánea de Expedientes*, 1198/O.

5.9. THE CONTRAMAYORAL FRANCISCO DOES HIS DUTY AND IS MURDERED BY A FELLOW SLAVE FOR HIS TROUBLE

Aguacate, November 11, 1829

A. Statement of María Guadalupe Mandinga, thirty-five years old, married to the contramayoral Francisco, residing on the ingenio San Matías, owned by the heirs of Andrés Armenteros.

. . . at about five o'clock this afternoon, more or less, her husband Francisco arrived at the slave quarters, complaining of his fellow slave, José del Rosario. Shortly thereafter, the contramayoral Francisco set out to punish José del Rosario by putting him in the stocks for having sassed him. Straightaway, Francisco realized that José del Rosario had pulled out a dagger or knife that he had hidden at his waist. The witness got herself into the middle of the fracas, telling her husband to leave that slave alone, but he paid her no mind. Infuriated, José del Rosario stabbed the witness in the thigh, and went on to stab her husband Francisco, leaving him for dead. The witness could do nothing more than cry out and try to revive her husband . . .

B. Statement of Bárbara Gangá, twenty-five years old, single.

. . . the witness was in the kitchen of the big house at about five o'clock in the afternoon with her fellow slaves Dolores, Vicente, and José del Rosario. Vicente said to José, "Why don't you feed and water the horses? If Francisco comes back and discovers that they haven't been fed, you will be in big trouble." José del Rosario replied, "What do I care? The horses won't say anything." A little while later, Francisco arrived home, grumbling. José del Rosario left the kitchen and went over to Francisco's house, where the witness heard Francisco say to her fellow slave, "Let's go to the stocks, José del Rosario," and the latter answered, "I'm not going to the stocks, not even Facundo put me in the stocks, and neither will you." The witness stayed in the kitchen, but a few moments later she heard her fellow slave [María] Guadalupe [Francisco's wife, above] say, "Francisco, José del Rosario has killed me," and Francisco replied, " Ah, woman, I cannot help you, for he has killed me as well!" At this point, the witness hurriedly went out [of the kitchen] and found both of them covered in blood, with Francisco in the throes of death . . .

C. Statement of José del Rosario, native of Guatao, thirty-three years old, single. He said that he inflicted the wound that killed his fellow slave Chico [diminutive for Francisco][12] because he was going to punish the witness without cause. . . . (He wounded María Guadalupe) because she got mixed up in the middle of their scuffle imploring Chico not to punish the witness. When the witness stabbed Chico, he ended up wounding Chico's wife instead. . . . He said that he knew very well that he had committed a grievous offense and that therefore he must be punished, but that he killed his fellow slave Antonio [Francisco] because he was a very troublesome fellow. . . . The dispute arose because Francisco had sent him with the dogs to fetch a bull that had gotten into the paddock. The witness confessed that he had forgotten to do it. When the contramayoral Antonio [Francisco] came back in the afternoon and asked him why he had not completed his task, the witness responded that he had forgotten. That was when he punished him and wanted to put him into the stocks . . . [13]

ANC, *Miscelánea de Expedientes*, 1246/C

5-III. Fugitive Slaves Cannot Always Rely on Help from Their Fellow Slaves

5.10. CIRILO DIES AT THE HAND OF A RUNAWAY SLAVE

Bauta, March 4, 1831

A. Statement of Lorenzo Galbín, native of Cano, forty-one years old, married, mayoral of the ingenio San José owned by Diego Mayolí.

. . . at about nine forty-five in the evening, the black contramayoral Ramón, looking in the direction of the slave quarters, notified him that "it seems to me that the slave Cirilo is dead and that Boticario ['The Apothecary'] is his killer." . . . That would be Francisco de Paula, a Congolese. . . . The slave Francisco Congo (alias Boticario) was a fugitive and had gone to Cirilo's hut earlier to ask him to get him some warm cane liquor and some pipe tobacco. Cirilo alerted Ramón, the contramayoral, and Ramón said that he was going to conceal himself in Cirilo's hut, so that later, when Boticario came back, he would be able to grab him when he came in. This is exactly what happened. Ramón testified that the moment Boticario entered the hut, he seized him by the waistband of his breeches. As Boticario struggled to get away, Ramón told Cirilo to help him. Cirilo came and clinched Boticario, and then Cirilo fell to the ground, and there Boticario stabbed him . . .

B. Statement of Ramón, forty years old, single, Boticario's baptismal godfather, contramayoral.

(The moment Cirilo was wounded, he exclaimed:) "Hey! Taita Ramón, he is killing me!" He said it twice. . . . at that time he did not know that he [Boticario] had [the knife], but he [Botario] had carried it before on many occasions, and the witness had taken it from him and broken it and had disciplined him just as he would a godson . . .

C. Statement of the fugitive slave Francisco de Paulo Congo, alias Boticario, thirty years old, single, carter.

(He responded that he killed Cirilo) for no good reason. . . . He ran away because he was missing a leg iron that he had removed without permission. He had been in shackles for running away once before. One Sunday he removed it and hid it along with his weeding machete and some of his hemp clothing. When he went to look for it to put it on again and go back to work, he found that it had been stolen. Fearful of being punished even more, he fled, and that is why he had gone missing for eight days before the killing . . .[14]

ANC, *Miscelánea de Expedientes*, 207/D.

5.11. A SENTRY GAMBLES WITH HIS LIFE FENDING OFF FUGITIVE SLAVES

Guanabacoa, August 13, 1834

A. Statement of Claudio Carabalí, slave from the ingenio Jesús María owned by the widow the Countess San Fernando de Peñalver.

. . . His job on the plantation, for quite some time now, was to keep watch and guard the banana groves. Last night, right around midnight, he was patrolling the groves, because it was an opportune time for thieves to strike. He came upon three black men. One of them was loaded down with a sack of plantains, and the other two took off running. The witness seized the one with the plantains, intending to take them away from him. He was able to fling the man to the ground, in spite of the resistance he put up. The witness got on top of him, and the thief began to shout for his accomplices, who had fallen back. Unseen by the victim, they attacked him with a barrage of machete blows, which were impossible for him to dodge. The assailants incapacitated him, and the three ran off, he did not know in what direction. . . . It seemed to him, although he could not be sure, that they were slaves from La Chumba, an ingenio belonging to Mrs. Concepción del Manzano, but this was nothing more than conjecture . . .[15]

ANC, *Miscelánea de Expedientes*, 256/Q.

5.12. PEDRO CRIOLLO CONFESSES TO THE MURDER OF HIS SWEETHEART MARÍA DEL ROSARIO GANGÁ

Pipián, April 2, 1837

A. Confession of the pardo slave Pedro, native of Jibacoa, thirty to thirty-five years old, single, from the cafetal La Probidad owned by Rafael Hernández.

He killed María del Rosario Gangá, who was his sweetheart. They had not been getting along very well for several days. They had been quarreling, and he threatened that it would not go well for her if she did not change her ways. Rather than heeding him, she insulted and cursed him. On that fatal Sunday, chatting over a bit of coffee, María del Rosario told the deponent that she would rather give the coffee to the dogs than to him. This provoked an argument in the kitchen, and the deponent threatened her, saying that this very well could be her last day on earth. María del Rosario shamelessly taunted him. Then, it was as though the deponent was possessed by the devil himself. He went to his hut, he took a blade and a knife that he had concealed there, and he returned to the kitchen. María del Rosario was serving lunch to her masters and came back into the kitchen. They got into another quarrel, and then the deponent fell upon her, dealing her multiple machete blows. María del Rosario fled to her shanty and collapsed. He caught up to her there and continued stabbing her, first with the machete blade and then with a knife, wounding her on the back and on the neck. The Devil had him in such a blind rage that, momentarily reflecting on what he had just done, it occurred to him to kill himself rather than suffer the penalties he would receive both from his masters, who are such good people, and from the law . . .

(The incident) came about because he had been engaged to marry her with her master's blessing. He was deeply in love with her. The marriage had yet to take place, because the bride's baptismal certificate could not be located. They both had agreed that, until such time that the paperwork was in order, they would live in good and devoted harmony, as if they already were married. He fully supported her in every conceivable way, and even had a daughter with her named Felicia, who now would be a year old, and lived in their masters' big house. He even was happy to pay debts that she contracted, as her masters who collected the money from the confessant can attest.

Just before the murder attempt, the deponent was sent on his owner's order to punish the slave María del Rosario. He obeyed, although, as one might imagine, with a heavy heart. Shortly thereafter, his master sent him to administer the same punishment to the very same slave once again. Instead, a slave from his same farm, Valentín Congo, did it for him. The repetition of such acts was so extremely disagreeable for the confessant that he complained, and this came to the attention of his owners. They ordered him shackled as a punishment. He still had a shackle on his right foot and offered it as evidence to the prosecutor who interrogated him. Although he had asked his master to remove them on several occasions, his owner replied that it was necessary for him to pay him twenty reals in order for them to be removed. Otherwise, he would leave them on for twenty years.

He remained shackled, and continued to monitor his beloved's behavior. She, far from feeling compassion for him, ridiculed his misfortune. Even more painful for the deponent, she was shamelessly unfaithful to him. Any doubt about this was dispelled the night he found her in the arms of the Negro Fernando Lucumí, another slave on that estate. Caught in the act, rather than ask for his forgiveness, she insulted the confessant. She even so much as told him that if he did not want to witness such an act, that he should go away, and let her carry on, then hurling a number of particularly hurtful and undeserved affronts at a man worthy of more consideration. In the end, these were the reasons that motivated him to seek vengeance in the manner stated in his confession. His heart was rent by a struggle of conflicting passions and caused him to not be of sound mind.[16]

ANC, *Miscelánea de Expedientes*, 267/M.

5.13. CHINESE COLONOS MURDER A BLACK SLAVE

Matanzas, September 9, 1865

A. Statement of Gil, thirty-five years old, single, from the ingenio Santo Domingo de Domingo Aldama, native of Macao, China.

Asked where he was last Friday, the day of the Nativity of the Blessed

Virgin . . . he said that at around noon he went out to cut palm with his compeers Luis and Felino and the black slave Pascual Lucumí . . .

Asked who was in charge, he said that the slave Pascual was in charge of him and his compeers. After Pascual had cut [the palm], he made the deponent load a basket with palm, but the deponent objected to loading it, hurling it to the ground [instead]. Then the slave Pascual punched him in the face. This was why the deponent and his compeers Luis and Felino assaulted the black slave Pascual with their machetes, until he was left for dead. . . . They attempted to escape by hiding in a house, where they were captured . . .

B. Statement of Felino, twenty-five years old, single, native of Macao, China.

. . . He says that he threw down the baskets because they weighed a lot and then Pascual punched him in the shoulder, which is why those three together accosted Pascual bodily, striking him with machetes . . .[17]

ANC, *Miscelánea de Expediente*, 1319/P.

5-IV. Solidarity in the Face of Injustice

5.14. THE ADULT MEN DEFEND THE YOUTH NEPOMUCENO

Güira de Melena, October 23, 1827

A. Statement of Ramón Viera, native of Quivicán, over twenty-five years old, single, mayoral of the cafetal El Carmen belonging to Pablo Villegas.

. . . after quitting work at the usual time and going home, he called for the black cook Pomuceno to bring him his dinner. When the cook did not appear, he sent the slave who was guarding the factory courtyard out to look for him. Not finding him, he went over to the common area. He saw the black woman Celedonia come out, and he asked her about Pomuceno. She did not respond. He heard noises up in the office and asked who was up above. He went inside and approached the noise carrying a torch and saw that Pomuceno had climbed up there. He grabbed the youth by the leg and pulled him down. He noticed that he was drunk, smelling strongly of cane liquor. He took him to the *tendales* [hard surface for drying coffee beans in the sun], and the contramayoral ordered him to lay face down for a *bocabajo* [vicious face-down flogging]. The free moreno mason Francisco Ruiz drew near, volunteered to act as his sponsor, effectively getting him released. Ruiz then ordered Pomuceno to be off and to take the mayoral his dinner. Turning toward the house, Pomuceno went to the well and descended into it, by means of a rope attached to the bucket. The witness heard the noise, went out there to investigate, and saw that Pomuceno was down below. Then the witness went in search of a length of rope to try to get him out, calling out to the other slaves to give him a hand. The slaves gathered there all together began a clamor, some shouting and others crying out, and the commotion grew more and more serious. The witness heard them saying that he himself, as mayoral, should be the one to go down into the well to get Pomuceno out. The witness saw the throng's resolve as the slaves began drawing ever nearer, in order, it would seem, to accomplish their purpose. The witness drew his machete and assumed a defensive posture. He retreated, seeking safe haven in the big house. The mob pursued him, yelling, especially two of them, Ventura and Simón. They continued to harass him until he locked himself in a room. They attempt to force the door using their machetes and rocks. In desperate straits, the witness opened the door and attacked them with his machete, wounding the slave Juan Bautista. With this, they dispersed and left him alone. The clatter and clamor of the mob continued until the district lieutenant arrived with the others . . .

B. Statement of Celedonia Mandinga, no age given, married.

. . . It was all true, everything that took place on this farm between the mayoral and the slaves. It was also true that the slave Pomuceno threw himself into the well. She did not see him before, when he went into the common area, but she did hear the noise. It was very dark, and when she asked who was there, he [Pomuceno] replied that it was he. He smelled of cane liquor and said that he was hiding so that the mayoral would not find him. That was why he had not answered right away; also, because he wanted to polish off a bottle of cane liquor that he had. That was when the mayoral himself arrived, asking for him [Pomuceno]. The mayoral went into the commons with a torch and found Pomuceno. He got him outside and that is when the rest happened. The slave men were all worked up over Nepomuceno's fall into the well. Everyone except the sentry began shouting, "Let's grab the mayoral, let's lock him up, let's put him in the stocks, let's stone him." They even sounded the estate's signal bell. The witness was with the other slave women, standing near the tendals, ignorant of what the slave men were proposing. The main agitators behind the movement were the slaves Buenaventura, Simón, Manuel José, and Ignacio. The slave Juan Bautista, although he found himself caught up in the tumult, came to the mayoral's defense, gathering the little ones together, and telling his fellow slaves, "Do not attack the mayoral over the youth since he is not dead." It was just as though the lights had gone out. The aforementioned Juan Bautista set out to gather all the little ones together and calm down his fellow slaves. This is the reason why the mayoral came upon him and wounded him with the machete.... He was going to punish Nepomuceno for having drunk cane liquor and for allowing the entire dinner to burn.

All the men pursued the mayoral. The witness heard shouts of "Catch him and take him to the infirmary, and lock him in until the master arrives." She did not know who battered the door with stones and machetes...

C. Statement of Buenaventure (Ventura) Congo, over twenty-five years old, married.

... After having finished his chores, the witness went to his hut. He was with his wife eating maize porridge when he heard the mayoral lashing the cook, the boy Pomuceno, and vowing to give him a bocabajo later. The tumult and clamor of all his fellow slaves, young and old alike, began shortly thereafter. He went out to see what was going on, and they told him that Pomuceno had thrown himself into the well. There followed a great deal of ruckus and frustrated attempts to get him out. The witness spoke up and said that the only person who should go down below and get him out was the mayoral himself and that no one should inform the authorities. This was when the slave Dionisio went to ring the alarm bell, and the witness grabbed the rope from him, asking him what he thought he was doing, ringing the bell when there was no fire. The mayhem continued, and the people advanced upon the mayoral. He drew his machete and retreated, fleeing toward the master's big house, and locking himself in a room there. ... They did not intend to kill him. They only wanted to scare him, which is why he fled and shut himself in. The mayoral's only shortcoming was that he punished the slaves too much...

D. Statement of Juan Nepomuceno (Pomuceno), Congo, twenty years old, single.

He was hiding in the commons, and he came out because he had no other recourse. Then the mayoral grabbed him by the arm, whipping him severely. The mayoral took him [Juan] to the tendals and ordered him face down in order to punish him. That is when the negrito Francisco Ruiz arrived. Ruiz acted as his sponsor, and then the witness got up from there and he went straight to the well, where he threw himself in. He did not answer the mayoral's calls because he feared being punished over something as trivial as hiding from him. He had not drunk any cane liquor. If he smelled of it, it was only because some cane liquor that he used to massage his neck may have dribbled down his neck toward his mouth. He thought of throwing himself into the well to end his life once and for all because he could not put up with the mayoral any longer. All his fellow slaves said the same thing. He and his fellow slaves were very satisfied with the master, but not with the mayoral. The mayoral only wanted to associate with black women . . .[18]

ANC, Miscelánea de Expediente, 223/F.

5.15. JUAN BAUTISTA AND CEFERINO, BOTH MINAS, ABET THEIR COUNTRYMAN RAFAEL

Tapaste, July 28, 1830

A. Statement of Manuel de Montes, over twenty-five years old, single, administrator on the cafetal Nuestra Señora de la Asunción owned by Dolores de Miralles de Ibáñez.

. . . At two thirty or three in the afternoon on the twenty-fifth of this month, he was trying to put the Negro Rafael Mina, a slave on this cafetal, into the stocks as punishment for having disobeyed orders. The slave resisted, brandishing his machete de calabazo and eager to make use of it, causing the witness to take certain precautionary measures. All this took place in the courtyard. Given the situation, the aforementioned slave Rafael, along with Juan Bautista and Ceferino, all members of the same tribe, took flight and made for the paddock there on the farm. . . . The next day, at around seven in the evening, the twenty-sixth, that is . . . two slaves, both carters, from that very paddock came upon their fellows Rafael, Juan Bautista, and Ceferino, all Minas, who had been wounded as a result of having taken up arms against the mayoral and several other white men in the very paddock. . . . He immediately ordered that they be sent to the infirmary. . . . The slave Juan Bautista died between eight and eight-thirty that same night, the twenty-sixth. With respect to the other two, it seemed to him that they were not in any immediate danger.

B. Statement of Rafael Mina, thirty years old, single.

. . . he could not identify the person or persons who wounded him because, besides the many white men confronting him, just as the dispute began he received a blow to the head that bled profusely and impaired his vision. He was sure that he was struck by a *machete de cinta* [long blade with a shell-shaped scabbard]. The incident came about because the previous Sunday, at about three in the afternoon, he went off to a garden plot to eat some mangoes. When he returned to the courtyard, the administrator Don Manuel de Montes directed the contramayoral Mateo Lucumí to put him into the stocks over this trifle. The witness put up a fight, because the punishment seemed unjustified. Reacting straightaway, the administrator drew the saber that he had cinched at his waist and gave him three blows with the flat part of the broadsword and also sicced a dog on him. The witness defended himself with a work machete [*calabozo*] he was holding. Straightaway, he fled, along with his fellow slaves Juan Bautista, Ceferino, and Felipe, making for the fenced paddock on La Leyva. They all intended to ask Don Francisco de Paula Sánchez for the paperwork to look for new masters, which he had in his possession. They did just this, making their request as they prostrated themselves before him. He consoled them, telling them that he would write to their mistress asking that she grant their request. With this, they all left, except for Felipe, who promptly returned to the cafetal. The others waited by the pigeon coop for the promised arrangements to be made. They remained there until the next day when, at around four in the afternoon, some eleven men appeared. They had spent the night there and some others arrived just then. They sicced a number of dogs they had with them on the men. This was why they had to use their work machetes, so as not to be overrun by the dogs. In view of this, the men fell upon them with their machetes, leaving them in the state in which they were found . . .

He had no quarrel with anyone, nor had there been any instigation by a third party. He did what he did because he had worked here, on this plantation, for ten years now, just like his fellow slaves, and they were not so much as given small plots or access to any resource whatsoever that would permit them to come by anything, as slaves everywhere else were allowed to do. Nor were they free to enjoy privileges customarily given to slaves on other establishments, such as not being forced to sleep under lock and key. So, what he wanted was to look for the means to be free of so much oppression . . .

C. Statement of Ceferino Mina, twenty-five years old, single.

. . . He was provoked at the sight of the administrator Don Manuel de Montes trying to put his fellow slave Rafael Mina in shackles just because on Sunday, at three in the afternoon, he went to a garden plot to eat some mangoes. He took off, with the intention of going to the paddock on La Leyva in order to ask Don Francisco Sánchez for papers. . . . The witness, along with his fellow tribesmen Juan Bautista and Felipe, followed him, although some slaves from the same farm followed them as well, prompted by the administrator's bad temperament. The witness managed to escape, along with the three above-mentioned men, and came before the aforementioned Sánchez. . . . He was obliged to do so because of the oppressive circumstances in which he found himself. He had worked there for the past ten years and was deprived of any means whatsoever by which to work toward his freedom. He was not even allowed other privileges typically granted other men, as so commonly seen, and which he knew were extended elsewhere. What he wanted was to improve his lot.

D. Statement of Felipe Mina, twenty years old, single.

. . . the only reason he wants to leave this farm is the harsh way he is treated, even after having worked here for ten years. He does not have a garden plot to work, as is customary elsewhere, and they are absolutely deprived of any means to raise livestock in order to raise some money and improve their lot . . .[19]

ANC, *Miscelánea de Expediente*, 936/33031.

5.16. THE LUCUMÍS OF ARRATIA RISE UP IN SOLIDARITY WITH THEIR FELLOW SLAVES TO PROTEST THEIR PUNISHMENT

Macurijes, July 22, 1842

A. Statement of Vicente Echavarría, native of Vizcaya, legal adult, single, administrator of the ingenio Arratia property of Salvador de la Paz Mariartu.

. . . days ago, the slave Jorge disobeyed the mayoral, and accordingly the witness ordered that he be dealt twenty-five lashes and be shackled. This slave resisted, and they had to forcibly bind him, administer the flogging, and shackle him. Once the fetters were on, those slaves who were part of the Lucumí slave crew congregated in the factory courtyard and requested that the witness order Jorge's shackles removed. Because they did not create a scene or seem particularly threatening, the witness agreed to remove the leg irons, on the condition that the crew return to the fields to work. He offered to send Jorge to them, which was exactly what he did.

(He informed the owner of the ingenio of what had happened, and the latter responded) by ordering the witness to find out who the ringleaders were and punish them severely as a lesson to the others. (The local commandant was only ever on the ingenio intermittently. The administrator took advantage of his presence on that day in order to seize the ringleaders Gregorio, Jorge, and Facundo and punish them) believing that, at the sight of a troop of soldiers, no one would dare make a move, and they all would be suitably intimidated. But the moment he laid a finger on Jorge and Facundo, the Lucumí crew that had been out in the fields suddenly materialized with its machetes, sticks, and baskets laden with stones, shouting loudly, and creating a tumult, saying "Kill whitey" . . .

B. Statement of Manuel Acosta, native of Güines, legal adult, married, mayoral.

. . . it is true that, on the twelfth of this month, he ordered the slave Jorge to pacify a fellow slave. Jorge disobeyed the order and turned his back on him, despite three separate requests. On one of those occasions, he attempted to escape. He pushed him, turned him face down, dealt him twenty-five lashes, and put him into a pair of fetters. Just as he finished putting the leg irons on him, some forty Lucumí slaves created an uproar, asking that he remove the fetters from their fellow slave Jorge, and that he come with them. The administrator was cognizant of the fact that there were only four white men on the entire ingenio and feared an insurrection. He told the hostile slaves to go on back to work. He agreed to order the irons removed from Jorge shortly, and he would send him back out into the fields with them. They all left, except for two who stayed behind to see to it that the administrator's pledge was carried out. Once Jorge was released, they all went back to work.

(The administrator believed that, once the troops were present,) if he lined up all the slaves out in the factory courtyard, it would be possible to single out the guilty parties and administer the appropriate punishment in the presence of their fellow slaves. But, shortly before ringing the bell to call in the field hands, they tried to apprehend the ringleaders Jorge and Facundo, the agitators behind the prior acts of insubordination, who were in the infirmary, although they were not ill. They were armed with their work machetes, and they fought ferociously to avoid being taken prisoner before the Lucumí crew arrived. (Sabers in hand, the troops attacked) but, by that time, the slaves already had disappeared into the cane fields. The slaves assailed the troops using sticks and machetes, impervious to harm from any bullets fired from the carbines. Finally, six slaves were wounded and apprehended. With this, the rest of the slaves began to disperse into the canebrake. Beating a retreat, they set fire to the ingenio's tile works. Others wanted to go by way of the *guardarraya* [an ingenio's tree-lined boundary road], where the rest of the slaves calmly awaited them in the house being made into an infirmary while others chose to flee their huts.

C. Statement of Limbano Carabalí, legal adult, single, contramayoral.

. . . on the day in question, he was in the fields working with forty-nine slaves weeding the canebrake. The cane was quite high and overgrown with weeds. He had a good number of Lucumís, he does not remember how many . . . and suddenly he heard a noise and saw them making for the guardarraya, running. He tried to tell them "Watch it! Watch it!" but they paid him no heed. All of them scattered, including those who had been working with him. The witness found himself all alone, standing on the guardarraya, until a white man found him, and he took them [sic] to the houses . . .

D. Statement of Anselmo Carabalí, legal adult, single.

. . . (in Limbano's crew there were) Carabalís, Lucumís, Minas,Ararás, and Congolese. . . . They were working in the cane fields when the slave Beltrán arrived. He had been in the casa de purga weeping and saying that the soldiers had tied up Facundo and had wounded him in the head. That was when the Lucumí slaves ran toward the buildings with Beltrán, while those of other nationalities remained where they were . . .

E. Statement of Jorge Lucumí, twenty-two years old, single.

. . . (the mayoral apprehended him) on Friday of last week, around noon. The witness was in the infirmary, with the slave Facundo, whom they also had seized. . . . The mayoral came in along with many whites and soldiers, bludgeoning him on the head with a stick, resulting in his injury. They also wounded Facundo in the head again. They tied them both up, and took them to the stocks. . . . Neither he nor Facundo had machetes, cudgels, or any other type of weapon. They did not put up even the least resistance, nor did they have an opportunity to do so. . . . He did not know why they seized him, for he never gave them cause. He never had any trouble with the administrator or any other laborer. The mayoral had only recently come there to the farm. The mayoral went to the infirmary, intending to punish the black Gumersindo, and he ordered the witness to restrain him. He replied that he could not, because his hand was swollen. That is why he was punished. The witness endured the punishment without saying a word. He forgot to say that in the infirmary, when the soldiers seized them, they cut the finger of his left hand, and now he has that injury. . . . He had the irons on for some hours, but they removed them later that same day, and the administrator did it on his own account, without anyone asking him to do it. . . . He had not been conspiring with any slave there on the ingenio, nor did he know of the rumored mutiny, because, as soon as they apprehended him on the day in question, they took him to the boiler house, where they locked him up. He did not see or know anything.

F. Statement of Gregorio Lucumí, single, age unknown.

... on Friday ... the witness was with many of his fellow slaves, just how many he did not know, working in the fields weeding cane under the supervision of the contramayoral, Limbano. ... He confessed that he was certain that the other slaves who acted as advocates for the slave Jorge, the ones who arranged to have his leg irons removed, were among those who came in from the fields. But the confessor was not part of that group [that came in from the fields to act as a *padrino* (sponsor, advocate), even though he is a Lucumí] because he was in the infirmary at that time. He left the infirmary as soon as the others came into the factory courtyard, and at that point he joined them to appeal to the administrator, as an advocate [for Jorge], to remove Jorge's leg irons ...

At around midday, they heard some shouts and other noise coming from the ingenio factories. They could not make out anything, because they were so far away, so they all stopped work and strained to listen. They saw soldiers on horseback coming toward them. The witness, along with the slave Donato, immediately took off running toward the scrub. They hid there, and he heard the shots ...[20]

ANC, *Comisión Militar*, 28/1.

6. The Labor Relations of Coartado Slaves

⚜ 6.1. JOSÉ ANTONIO AVILÉS CONGO CANNOT PAY HIS MISTRESS THE DAY WAGES THAT HE OWES HER

Havana, October 5, 1837

A. Statement of the slave José Antonio Avilés Congo, property of Ana Avilés, thirty to thirty-five years old, single, resident of the La Salud neighborhood, shoemaker by trade.

. . . On Tuesday, the third of this month, he was unable to come up with his daily wage of four reals that he was obliged to hand over to his mistress. A stranger, a moreno with a full beard, apparently English, purchased half a dozen pairs of shoes from him for a total of nine reals, and then he did not pay for them. The deponent recalled that the aforementioned black man had told him that he was a cook on the English vessel Pontón. So, Antonio set out with two men in a small pilot boat for the ship in question. . . . There were many blacks there on the ship's deck, but the deponent did not understand what any of them were saying. When Antonio told them that he was Congolese, they fetched a black woman who supposedly spoke his native language, but he was unable to understand her either. Then he asked for the captain, and a white man came forward. The deponent begged him to take him back ashore and intervene on his behalf with his mistress, for he feared that she would punish him for the missing wages. . . . The English captain told him that he could not be an effective advocate for him there [in Cuba], and he immediately took him back to Havana . . .

B. Statement of the slave Matías Urrutia Gangá, twenty-five years old, single, resident of the San Lázaro neighborhood, shoemaker, and employer of the previous deponent.

. . . he said that he knew him [Antonio, above] because they had worked together in his own quarters just recently. The last time that he saw him was on Saturday, the week before last, when the deponent paid Antonio his wages . . . [the goods that they sold] belonged to the deponent, and he paid

Antonio weekly wages for his labor. . . . He said that at first Antonio would go out to peddle shoes on his own. Now, the deponent accompanies him, because of an incident in which Antonio came back with only eighteen reals for a dozen pairs of shoes, instead of the three pesos that he should have sold them for. . . . He said that it seemed to him that Antonio did not pay his wages to his mistress in a timely fashion, for that lady had been to the deponent's quarters only a few days before the last time that he saw Antonio, and she told him that Antonio owed her back wages and asked the deponent if he paid him regularly, to which he replied in the affirmative.[1]

ANC, *Gobierno Superior Civil*, 938/33095.

6.2. GUMERSINDA REQUESTS AN ACCURATE APPRAISAL OF HER SKILLS

Havana, August 8, 1853

Gumersinda, morena slave belonging to Mrs. María Martínez . . . states:

. . . on August 5 of this year, before the *alcalde primero* [chief alcalde], a fair appraisal established her coartado price at 650 pesos and was duly recorded, the honorable syndic and her mistress being in agreement on this amount. That valuation was based on erroneous information concerning her abilities. On the paper that her mistress gave her, her mistress lists skills that the deponent did not possess, and this almost certainly accounted for the high price for which she was appraised.

This is exceedingly prejudicial for her and, furthermore, makes it impossible for her to find another master. Therefore, in consideration of what has been stated above, she requests a new appraisal . . .[2]

ANC, *Gobierno Superior Civil*, 948/33472.

6.3. MARÍA MAGDALENA'S MISTRESS USES HER TO PAY OFF A DEBT

Havana, September 18, 1853

María Magdalena Santa Cruz, Cuban-born slave belonging to Doña María de la Trinidad González, . . . states that, before her mistress died, she surrendered her to Doña María de la Concepción Santaella in order that her wages be used to satisfy a certain debt that she owed her. Her mistress died, and for more than twenty years the deponent worked for her former mistress's creditress, never knowing whose property she rightfully was. For this reason, and this reason only, she recurred to the deputy syndic in order that he make the appropriate inquiries.

She is in the process of procuring her freedom but does not know who her real owner may be and, despite her endeavors, still has been unable to discover what she is so eager to learn. The deponent, Excellency, is coartada for 282 pesos. She believes that, to date, she has worked an adequate amount of time to satisfy the debt owed to Mrs. Santaella by her mistress, given that she has worked in her employ since 1833. Before she died, her mistress told her that she would have to remain with the aforementioned Santaella, although she only owed her a small amount of money. Unfortunately, her mistress died intestate. The petitioner has no idea what is to become of her . . .[3]

ANC, *Gobierno Superior Civil*, 948/33471.

6.4. MANUEL CÓRDOVA WANTS TO USE HIS DAY WAGES TO PURCHASE HIS FREEDOM

Havana, February 13, 1854

. . . he states that his current master, Don Francisco Ceballos, had him coartado in 1842, as attested to in the attached document. Since that time, he has continued to work at his trade as a baker. As those working in this occupation typically earn wages of twenty reals a day, he soon will have put aside some two thousand pesos. By working on Sundays and all the religious holidays that are celebrated during the course of the year, he is some nine hundred pesos to the good, besides. For these reasons, he requests that Your Excellency deign to forward this case to the deputy syndic so that he may represent the deponent . . .[4]

ANC, *Gobierno Superior Civil*, 949/33590.

6.5. MARÍA DE JESÚS INTERCEDES ON BEHALF OF HER DAUGHTER, A DAY LABORER

Havana, March 9, 1854

María de Jesús, morena, slave belonging to the parda Petronila Quesada, states that she has a daughter who was born and raised as a slave in the same house as her mistress. The daughter always has been placed out somewhere or earned wages as a day laborer.

Six months ago, because the daughter was three weeks behind in her wages, her mistress turned her out, depriving her of shelter and neglecting to provide documents attesting to the daughter's status as either slave or free.

Because of this, the daughter now finds herself in desperate straits, forced by this situation to live in a house of corrupt women, at the mercy of circumstance. For this reason, she implores that Your Excellency compel her daughter's mistress to appear in court and state whether her daughter Petrona Olabe be slave or free, and, if she be slave, she asks that Your Excellency order her daughter be fetched and admonished, and, if she be free, she asks that Your Excellency make provisions for her by placing her daughter in an establishment where they teach her to work until she is of legal age. Her daughter is eighteen years old and has no other trade than that of being confined to a house of women of ill repute, residing at present at 51 Monserrate Street without the benefit of either pass or permit . . .[5]

ANC, *Gobierno Superior Civil*, 949/33550.

6.6. PEDRO REAL CONGO, CAPATAZ OF THE CONGO ASSOCIATION, INTERVENES ON BEHALF OF HIS COMPATRIOT, MARÍA LUISA GONZÁLEZ

Havana, April 21, 1854

The freedman Pedro Real Congo, moreno, chief capataz for the association of his fellow Congolese, resident of the Chávez neighborhood, Gloria Street, widower, and tobacconist by trade, states before Your Excellency that:

Maria Luisa González, morena, Congolese, owned by Ángel Árrechasabaleta, appeared before him with a two-day pass to look for a new master. She had been coartada at 350 pesos and arrears and was owned by Don Ángel Árrechasabaleta. At said slave's request, Don Ángel Árrechasabaleta issued her documents allowing her the two days to look for a new master.

[In his own words:] I sought out Lic. Don José Fornaris to purchase her. This gentleman waited for said Árrechasabaleta to make out the bill of sale. The aforementioned owner did not go to the notary's office but, instead, seized the slave woman and sent her out into the rural countryside to be punished, [this, the fate of] a coartado slave enjoying the privilege of refusing to be sold for an amount not to her liking, and [a privilege to be] even more strictly observed should she have a buyer . . .

In the capacity of capataz of her nation, I beseech that Your Excellency issue an order immediately requiring her master to locate the slave woman so that the buyer may execute the bill . . .[6]

ANC, *Gobierno Superior Civil*, 948/33540.

6.7. JOSÉ ISABEL GALAINENA OFFERS HIS SERVICES AS LIEN

Havana, April 19, 1861

The slave José Isabel Galainena respectfully appears before Your Excellency and states:

In San Cristóbal de los Pinos, Don Justo Paula, resident of that town, gave him his certificate of manumission for the purpose of having him work for him for four years, as agreed, executing said letter before the notary public of the referred to town.

[In his own words:] Upon the death of Don Justo Paula (the agreement being with him alone), I passed to the service of Don Justo's partner, Blas Bale, to whom I gave 204 pesos with which to cancel this obligation, once and for all. That money was a loan to me from Don Pedro Llaranas, which I intended to repay with my service to him. I have served Llaranas for one year, and it would seem that that period of time was sufficient to cancel the debt that I contracted with the gentleman in question . . .[7]

ANC, *Gobierno Superior Civil*, 954/33668.

6.8. NICOLÁS DE AZCÁRATE INTERCEDES ON BEHALF OF AN INGENIO SLAVE

Havana, February 5, 1862

Yesterday the Negro Paulino, a Cuban-born slave belonging to Don Francisco de la Vega, residing on his ingenio Ecuador situated, according to the slave, in the jurisdiction of either Colón or Cárdenas, appeared before me.

The slave is coartado at 250 pesos, and, as a coartado slave, the law accords him the legal right to leave his master's service for a position elsewhere earning daily wages, and paying his master only at the rate of one strong real per 100 pesos of his set price.

The slave complains that his owner keeps him isolated on his ingenio, treating him as if he is a full slave [rather than a coartado slave], keeping him far away from anywhere he can exercise his rights [to earn money]. He states that he distrusts being attended to by the syndic in his own jurisdiction. For this reason, he has come all the way to Havana, on foot and without means . . .⁸

ANC, *Gobierno Superior Civil*, 954/33742.

6.9. MANUEL CONGO PROTESTS THE CONTROL THAT THE SYNDIC EXERCISES OVER HIS MONEY

Havana, February 13, 1862

Manuel Congo, slave belonging to Don Gabriel García, resident of the city of Bejucal . . . states that, desiring to change owners, he had to ask his master for the appropriate permit to search for one to his liking. The reasons compelling him to take this action were just. Therefore, he sought the syndic's intervention in order to force his master to execute the permit, something the deponent had been unable to do. The syndic, Excellency, not only failed to carry out the request that he was obliged to act upon in his official capacity as syndic, but, at one with the claimant's improvident master, he collected the sum of 436 pesos of the deponent's own cash from Don Nicolás Pineiro. Without his [the petitioner's] consent, they drew up a deed of coartación, stipulating his value at 800 pesos. The syndic [who controls the money] should have borne in mind that the interest income that the 436 pesos produced for the petitioner was, assuredly, the sole asset that he possessed as a slave, and with which he aspired, within a certain number of years, together with any other paltry resources that he might licitly attain, to gain his freedom, the singular desire of every slave.⁹

ANC, *Gobierno Superior Civil*, 954/33745.

6.10. AN ELDERLY SLAVE IS SUBJECT TO A FLAGRANT INJUSTICE

Havana, April 4, 1862

The slave José Mina, belonging to Don Bernardo Bravo, complains that, upon aspiring to be free, after more than half a century of slavery, with five ounces of gold that he has scrimped and saved, real by real, they want to raise his appraised price, disregarding the fact that he is over eighty years old and suffers from three illnesses: asthma, a broken bone, and erysipelas on his legs, which scarcely allow him to do any sort of work whatsoever. He was purchased twelve years ago for two hundred pesos . . .¹⁰

ANC, *Gobierno Superior Civil*, 943/33734.

6.11. PEDRO CRIOLLO BUYS HIS FREEDOM AND WANTS TO CONTINUE WORKING ON THE INGENIO

Havana, July 13, 1864

... the slave Pedro Criollo, owned by Mrs. Gutiérrez and Mr. Casal, with Mr. Julián del Casal present.... (Pedro stated) that by dint of his own hard work and by observing great economy, he was able to raise five hundred pesos in cash from a promissory note issued to him by Julián ... ? [sic] ... and an additional nine ounces [of gold]. He gave the promissory note and the money to the governor of Cárdenas, who forwarded them to that city's syndic. The syndic sent them back to the governor. The governor sent them to the governor of this capital, who sent them to the syndic of same, an apothecary living on the Plaza of Belén, who should be holding that money in trust [at present], and, by virtue of which, he requests that his owners, being in receipt of said amount, grant him his freedom, and allow him to continue to work on the ingenio without prejudice.

He wishes to remain there because he has three children living on that ingenio, and he is satisfied with the treatment that he receives there.

Mr. Casal stated that he would have no objection to granting the slave Pedro his freedom for whatever amount he might be appraised for, if only he did not take seriously his own obligation to look out for the interests of his slaves, to whom part of the money Pedro presented as the price for his freedom belonged. In the paperwork submitted, it turns out that some of his [Casal's] servitors had given him [Pedro] amounts of money to safeguard on their behalf and that today he pretended to apply toward his own freedom.

Pedro demonstrated that the money belongs to him, that he and several other slaves won the lottery, in the amount of four hundred pesos. The mayordomo Juan Gutiérrez divided it up, giving seventy-five pesos each to the petitioner and his three children, and another seventy-five pesos to his fellow slave Antonio, the tinsmith. Pedro raised the rest of the money by working and by selling some twenty pigs to the mayoral for fourteen pesos and to the mayordomo for seventeen pesos, and selling fourteen bushels of corn to Pedro Gutiérrez for three and a half pesos.

He has no objection to an inquiry into any contractual arrangements his owner may have entered into ... .[11]

ANC, *Gobierno Superior Civil*, 1056/37612.

6.12. TAKING UP A COLLECTION FOR MAMERTO SALAS

Puerto Príncipe, May 17, 1865

Mamerto Salas, pardo, slave, resident of the city of Puerto Príncipe, with due respect states before Your Excellency:

He found himself held in captivity under the most grievous of circumstances. Several individuals offered to look after him and raise the money necessary to procure his freedom. He recurred to the brigadier of that city to grant permission to begin taking up a collection to raise enough money.

The brigadier has ordered that the matter be directed to his superiors for approval, and he is confident that his merciful heart will not oppose making use of this recourse to quit such oppression, doing so, of course, in the most humble and deferential manner. He requests that Your Excellency intervene and deign to concede the permission as explained herein, seeing to it that the lieutenant governor understand it accordingly, and impose no impediment to raising the money that he needs for his manumission . . .[12]

ANC, *Gobierno Superior Civil*, 961/34067.

6.13. ANTONIO QUESADA CONGO CANNOT EARN HIS DAILY WAGES DUE TO ILLNESS

Havana, November 21, 1866

Antonio Quesada, Congolese, approximately sixty-seven years old, slave belonging to Don Carlos Madrazo, in his service for more than ten years, states:

The aforementioned gentleman purchased him coartado for three hundred pesos, and ever since that time he [Antonio] has scrupulously handed over his wages. On June 6, 1864, he had the misfortune to fall ill from a serious case of dropsy and a problem with his vision. He notified his master, who attended to him during his illness for over four months in 1864. But, once his owner saw that his slave's illness would be protracted, he told him that he could no longer pay the doctor nor the apothecary for lack of funds. Then Antonio told his master to send him to the hospital. The master refused this as well, telling him that he could not afford the cost of one peso per day and that he would have to get along as best he could. Then Antonio contacted his relatives, other Congolese like himself, asking them to take up a collection of alms for him, which they did. Antonio sent for

Doctor Granados, who treated him until his dropsy was cured, although his vision still was not completely restored and remained blurred.

It is for this reason that he is disabled. Excellency, his master has not contributed even one cent toward his care for two years and five months. Therefore, even though he still does not find himself in good health, he wants to sell himself off as a field hand, although he never has done work of this type and understands nothing about farm work.

Also, he informs Your Excellency that the capataz of his nation is willing to contribute one hundred pesos toward his freedom, and to continue assisting him during his convalescence, to see if, with God's favor, he finally finds himself in good health . . .[13]

ANC, *Gobierno Superior Civil*, 968/34190.

7. The Master's Violent Hand

⚜ 7.1. A LOCAL COMMISSARY INTERVENES IN A CASE OF BRUTALITY

Havana, September 25, 1818

The local commissary of Ursulinas reports to you that last night, at approximately eight o'clock, María Ignacia Ayala, parda, registered a complaint with me that in the local grocery next door to her house a black man was being brutally beaten, [the beating] being administered in an outrageous, absolutely intolerable, merciless manner. . . . I found that the report was absolutely true . . . the punishment was extremely harsh, and I found the slave's feet and hands tied to a ladder, where his master, José Mediavilla, had beaten his buttocks with a manatee leather whip. I ordered that he be examined by physicians . . . and had the black man admitted to a ward in the hospital of San Juan de Dios . . .

(The owner stated) that after having overlooked a number of repeated transgressions that his servant Torbicio had committed while in his service, he had no choice but to attempt to discipline him once and for all . . . having him punished in such a way that would teach him a lesson without exceeding the limits of moderation.

In effect, the slave had developed a false sense of security as a result of the kindness and consideration with which he had been treated in the past, [his master] deliberately feigning ignorance of his aforementioned offenses and choosing to overlook them. This encouraged the slave to be openly defiant, boldly and arrogantly resisting whatever punishment was imposed. . . . The master ordered two underlings from his household to restrain the slave and make certain that he offer no further resistance. The slave shouted and wailed, but it was nothing that would have disturbed the peace or constituted any sort of uproar. On the contrary, they observed the greatest moderation and orderly conduct dictated by the situation. Despite this, someone with a grudge against the deponent's family or servants who heard the servitor's lamentations, the expected result of any punishment, reported it . . .

He stated (before the syndic Manuel Benítez) that whenever the slave Toribio Piñeiro . . . was punished, it was on the buttocks only, the customary place that those of this class inflict punishment on slaves, and even on one's own children, when they need to be disciplined for some offense that they may have committed.

Although the aforementioned master might have been somewhat overzealous with Toribio, as indicated on the physicians' certification . . . perhaps this was a consequence of the owner getting overly worked up, always somewhat understandable, because a man who is aggravated is incapable of containing himself, and, perhaps contrary to his own sentiments, [later] repenting of them and greatly remorseful [of his actions] while consumed by wrath . . .

It seems to me that no legal action should be taken . . . it being sufficient, in my judgment, that the slave remain hospitalized . . . until he is fully recuperated, and that, at that juncture, the owner be compelled to transfer ownership for a fair price, and that the slave never again come into his possession under any circumstances whatsoever.

ANC, *Miscelánea de Expedientes*, 1197/T.

7.2. A MODERN VERSION OF THE CHASTITY BELT

November 1834

Your Excellency:

Florencia Rodríguez, parda, with all due respect, appears before Your Excellency and states: that she has been informed of the outcome of her prior allegations in the suit she filed against her master Don Ramón Sáinz, in which she requests that he grant her freedom and alleges that he has committed several excesses against her. Your Excellency has resolved, in consultation with the assessor general, that by virtue of the testimony of the mayor of the hamlet of San Antonio[1] and [in consideration of the fact that] the case is ongoing there, that all the judicial procedures be remitted to that judge to administer justice to her and that all be in accordance with the honorable syndic procurator from that locality.

[In her own words] I would not hesitate, Excellency, to appear before that judge to claim justice for myself unless the following events had, indeed, taken place. My master so ravaged me that I appeared before the mayor, seeking his protection. This gentleman was well aware of [both] my master's wayward nature and, what is more, of his persistent commission of atrocities. The most serious of those was that of having inserted three rings into the innermost private parts of my fellow slave, Inés the mulatto, after having taken her for his woman for a period of time. This is the reason that the first thing that the mayor did when I appeared before him was to ask me if I, too, had rings in my privates. Then, I recounted to him what was happening with me, and he dismissed me, simply telling me to go home, that he would speak with my master.

Such indifference upset and confused me, especially when, purely by chance, I was able to escape my master's furor. As I stated previously before Your Excellency, he seduced me some ten or twelve years ago in order that I service him with my person, giving his word that after three years he would grant me my freedom. I was fourteen years old at the time. The only things that I received from him in return were routinely being dressed in men's clothing, working in the ironworks, and training as a calash driver, beating me all the while.

I endured all of this, Excellency, right up until the moment when he wanted to insert rings into me as well. He went up into the upper room and called me to bring up a candle to him, which I did. To my surprise, upon entering the room, I saw a cot that had been made up, with a rope on it, and on the bedside stand a silver ring, some needles threaded with scarlet-colored silk thread, some scissors, a needle, a dagger, and a whip. Such preparations horrified me, and I quickly took the precaution of staying near the door. He approached that door, intending to close it, and I, naturally, objected. We began to struggle, and I was able to throw him to the floor because he was extremely drunk. Accordingly, I descended the staircase in such haste that I injured my backside. These were the very events that I recounted to the mayor, and which compelled me, in view of the skepticism with which that gentleman looked upon them, to leave that town and make for this city, to stand at the feet of Your Excellency, father of the wretched and the destitute, in order to avail myself of any consolation that the law, both divine and human, grants or accords.

Now then, the greater part of all the witnesses whom I have mentioned and many more are currently living in this capital. For this reason, I believe that the case should take place here rather than in San Antonio. As badly off as I am, not even they will want to take the trouble to travel from here to there, nor will I be able to pay the necessary costs in order to transfer the evidence.

On the other hand, I must advise Your Excellency that if ultimately you compel me to go to San Antonio, I will go obediently, but I most certainly will fall victim to my master's wrath. And the reason for this is none other than that my master has money, and, consequently, he has a close relationship with all the leading residents of that town. This is why they all look the other way concerning his continual transgressions, which is to say that they will not take my case seriously, and, in the end, they will hand me over to my master, leaving me with no other alternative than to die.

This is the truth, Excellency. Is it possible that I, under the protection of Your Excellency as father of the destitute, in search of the alleviation of my afflictions, will not achieve so much as the consolation of seeing Your Excellency protect me even here? Is it possible that through the offices of the syndic general procurator of this capital that you will not even hear the evidence of the eleven witnesses who find themselves here today, whose testimony I am sure will be even more compelling than that I already have related? No, Excellency. The petitioner serenely waits for Your Excellency, by virtue of the wide-ranging faculties accorded you by law, to grant this entreaty, even if you do nothing more than come to fully understand these events that Nature itself finds repugnant. And then, only then will Your Excellency understand the just grounds for my resistance, or, better said, why I fear to go to the town of San Antonio where all kinds of crimes committed by my master are tolerated.

Likewise, I know that in Your Excellency's rulings on my case that you have strictly observed the letter of the law; but, as Your Excellency cannot fail to acknowledge, there are certain cases in which it is necessary to distance oneself from those findings in order to avoid abuses that unduly burden the destitute. That is why I have resolved, as a final and sole solution, to make this petition to Your Excellency in [your] capacity of highest authority on the island, and because you are capable of administering justice as with the scales of Astrea. In this way, and confident of all I have related herein, as well as what Your Excellency has kindly set out, which is all any claimant for justice puts before you, submit:

To Your Excellency, beseeching that you order the suspension of any remittance of the judicial formalities to the hamlet of San Antonio, and that the case continue right here under the conduct of the syndic procurator general, before whom I will appear the instant Your Excellency may so order, providing that the presentation of evidence requires no longer than eight days, unless Your Excellency himself wishes to examine the witnesses further, for the other mulatto, Inés, with the rings, finds herself in this city and is ready to appear the moment she is so ordered. She who longs to attain mercy from Your Excellency, at whose feet this wretched creature prostrates herself in the interest of justice. Havana, November 5, 1834.

Subsequent petition: I beseech Your Excellency that, in the case of having remitted the judicial proceeding to San Antonio, that you dispatch an official letter [ordering] the mayor to return them to the political secretariat in order that they be forwarded to the syndic procurator general, in the event that Your Excellency grants this forlorn creature's petition. This, in that I look forward to Your Excellency reviewing much more of my testimony, and that he become persuaded of this unfortunate woman's just cause for objecting to the restoration of the proceedings to San Antonio, which she also hopes to be granted . . .

Excellency:

Florencia Rodríguez, parda, with due respect appears before Your Excellency and states: that my latest official request, in which it was clearly established for Your Excellency that dispatching me to the town of San Antonio was tantamount to surrendering me [to my master], was ordered forwarded to the general assessor. Your Excellency must not doubt for even one moment that the instant that I arrive in town I will be handed over to my master and will fall victim to his furor, because no less than the syndic procurator himself is an intimate friend of my master. This I know for a fact, which is the reason why you protected me and that I continue to enjoy the benefit of Your Excellency's righteousness.

More than fifteen days ago, in the secretariat, I was informed that the legal proceedings have been transferred to the assessor general. Without giving me any notice whatsoever, an individual has come with an order from San Antonio to take me to my master's house in bonds, completely defenseless. Consequently, I submit myself before Your Excellency, seeking your protection. This is a grave matter, nothing less than accusations of horrific deeds and my freedom are at stake, after having enjoyed more than ten years of freedom. I ask that you deign to suspend the order dispatching me to San Antonio, as long as I offer not only to prove to Your Excellency, before eight days have elapsed, the truth of what I have maintained ever since my initial testimony, but also [to disprove] the [charges] against me, filed for the sole purpose of pleasing my master, who has money.

The blow that awaits me, Excellency, is such that today, as I see the very individual who is to transport me back to San Antonio, who even has traveled here on one of my master's beasts, I would be fully capable of renouncing all of my legal rights in order obtain my freedom. I only request that, here and now, he [the master] give me the document to look for a new master. Otherwise, I would rather die than endure the bitterness, pain, and toil that will be mine.

I prostrate myself before Your Excellency, and I long to be safeguarded and liberated from the ambush awaiting me in San Antonio, swearing all the same that if, in any manner or in the least detail, my evidence be disproved, I am ready to suffer the harshest of punishments. I will give evidence right here, and if you are resolute in your decision that it must take place there, at the proper time, I ask that I not be torn away from this city until such time as the above evidence has been heard.

I find myself wandering from place to place, Excellency, vulnerable, fearful of returning home, where I have remained until now with Your Excellency's full knowledge, lest he who is charged with the task of taking me to my master's house, he who constantly intrudes to see if I am there in order to forcibly remove me, accomplish his purpose.

It is not in my nature to jeopardize others or myself, but it is in my nature to trust in Your Excellency's righteousness, in which I have invested all of my hopes for you to both console my misfortunes and check the devastation that threatens me. Yes, Your Excellency, it is you who can free me in your capacity as the defender of the innocent. For this reason:

I beg that Your Excellency order that until such time as what I have recounted here and the recent judicial proceedings have been resolved, that the order removing me to San Antonio be suspended, and that you take a moment to direct serious attention to the testimony on the record in order to familiarize yourself completely with the evidence in this case that compels me to take this step and that I am sure that has horrified Your Excellency. [I beseech Your Excellency] as well to order that the remittal of the judicial proceedings be suspended and to hear the evidence in the case here. I await the thanks and justice bestowed by Your Excellency. Havana, November 20, 1834.

ANC, *Gobierno Superior Civil*, 936/33047.

7.3. THE DUNGEON ON THE HACIENDA LA CUABA

Santiago de Cuba, November 11, 1834

A. Statement of Eduardo, appearing to be about twenty-five years old, "very ladino."

... (he came to appear before the governor) in order to inform him of the punishment that his master Don José María de Águila administered with the utmost cruelty to five black slaves on his hacienda La Cuaba on Monday of last week, the third of this month, which resulted in the death yesterday, the tenth, of the slave called Marino, who was buried in the paddock.... Those punished were Patricio, Juan Bautista, José Jobino, and the slave woman Lucrecia, from that very same hacienda La Cuaba.... Marino, Patricio, and José Jobino were punished because they lost a kid goat. The master believed that they had stolen it, even though the huts of all slaves involved were searched straightaway and neither the kid nor any trace of him was found.... The mayoral himself, upon orders from his master Don José María de Águila, who lives on the hacienda full time ... (they punished them and) they were dealt a great many (lashes) and, on several occasions, [in a grievous fashion] involving flaying of the skin. He added that he punished the slave Juan Bautista because he failed to make certain that no one crossed the fences while he was on sentry duty. [However,] he allowed someone to go through the fence because the royal highway was impassable due to the rains. He also punished the slave woman Lucrecia because the mayoral alleged that she had stolen a bit of codfish.

Even when the master did not so order, the mayoral Eugenio Abreu cruelly punished [the slaves] because the master would tell him to kill them, that he had more than enough money to pay the consequences.... Marino and Patricio, shackled with chokers and chains, were down in an underground pit or crypt in the mayoral's quarters. At about ten o'clock yesterday morning, Patricio cried out that Marino had died. The slave Graciano heard him and went up to inform the mayoral ... Patricio remained down in the crypt, along with Juan Bautista ...

B. Statement of Silvestre, probably about twenty years old, "quite ladino."

... the other four are on the same hacienda, harshly beaten, especially two of them who have maggot-infested wounds on their backsides ...

C. Statement of José de Jesús Anaya, native of Santiago, forty-five years old.

... (the mayoral has been on the hacienda for two years) and has always been harsh in his punishment of the slaves....

D. Statement of Patricio, thirty years old.

... he says that his master blames the slaves over any trifling matter and orders them punished frequently.

E. Examination by two doctors, Hilario de Cisneros Saco and the syndic Juan Bautista Sagarra:

... the site in question was a little over three yards long and just over two yards wide, its walls fashioned out of rubble masonry, with almost no ventilation, and two old panniers on the floor. The place was absolutely detrimental to one's health due to the lack of fresh air to breathe.... (referring to Patricio) finding that he had a great many enormous sores on his upper and lower back, his buttocks, as well as all over his legs, these greatly inflamed. The lesions of the second [victim], Juan Bautista, were identical, lesions, but were in a more advanced state of decomposition on the lesser gluteal muscle of the left buttocks, partially maggot infested. The third, José Jobino, also had some smaller more superficial abrasions, with fewer on the lower back and both buttocks, and Lucrecia, the last [victim], had the same type of lesions, but on the buttocks only . . .

F. Statement of the mayoral Eugenio Abreu, native of the hamlet of San Carlos on the Island of Santo Domingo, thirty-two years old, single.

. . . (the escape of the two slaves making the charges) presumes that they were motivated to do so because a slave named Marino died yesterday on the hacienda in question; he had been punished, he became unresponsive, and lost consciousness . . . they had flogged him, meting out some fifty or sixty lashes with a woven rawhide crop. They dealt him more lashes again the next day and thereafter in order to revive him, as is necessary with slaves. He [the mayoral] cannot say with any certainty when he [Marino] went cold, for one cannot always trust slaves, as they feign illness. The seizure was discovered yesterday morning, and he died at about ten, with no doctor in attendance. The deponent, on his master's order, applied oil and Castile honey several times to the wounds on the slave's buttocks that were a result of the beating, washed them with cane whiskey, [but] administered no other remedy. . . . The slave was being held in an underground cell in the mayoral's quarters where slaves were restrained so as not to escape and dressed in nothing more than breeches and an iron collar . . .[2]

ANC, *Miscelánea de Expedientes*, 224/G.

7.4. DOMINGO VERDUGO, LIEUTENANT GOVERNOR OF CÁRDENAS, TAKES ACTION

February 1861

Most Excellent Captain General:

On January 29 last, an anonymous source informed me that Pablo Hernández was meting out dreadful punishments to his slaves on his ingenios Osado, Dolores, San Juan, and San Fernando. This drove several slaves on those establishments to the brink of despair, electing to [commit suicide by] hanging themselves or hurling themselves into wells rather than submit to any further punishment. It also was reported to me that some had succumbed to the ruthless blows dealt at the behest of the owner.

Although the *alcalde mayor*'s [administrator of a provincial division usually smaller than that of a *corregidor* (magistrate)] office was in the process of drawing up an indictment for the death of some slaves on the aforementioned farms, who had been discovered hung days before, I ordered that the *ayudante de plaza* [lieutenant], Joaquín Beltrán, move to initiate the necessary legal proceedings in order to investigate the grounds for the anonymous charges, above. The findings, Excellency, are attached in the dreadful summary, below.

By virtue of this, I immediately ordered Don Pablo Hernández, resident of Matanzas, owner of the ingenios in question, detained, and I forwarded the aforementioned judicial proceedings to the office of the alcalde mayor. Although, as I have stated, the court was to rule on this matter expeditiously, I did not believe that Hernández should remain for even one minute [at large and] in a position to commit new crimes . . . adding that I took the necessary precautions in order that such scandalous scenarios as those that already had taken place not be repeated on the farms in question.

Cardenas, February 3, 1861.

This proceeding was initiated by an anonymous report, [subsequently] corroborated by two official letters directed to the [proper] authority of Your Honor by the members of the lower courts of justice of Cimarrones and Lagunillas, in which they reported finding two black men from the ingenio San Fernando, owned by Pablo Hernández, hung by the neck. . . . The farm doctor, Lic. Blas Rocafort, stated that, while in the company of the lower-court official from Lagunillas and the Lic. Dr. Basilio García Negrete, he examined four brutally beaten black men from the ingenio San Fernando who had been hung by the neck. They also ascertained that some sixty others had been beaten in an equally brutal manner. The remainder of the farm's slaves were dealt somewhat fewer blows, thanks to their good conduct. These slaves were good, respectful, and adept at their work.

On folio eight, the mayoral Eusebio González stated that he had been on the farm for five days. Even though the slaves were well maintained, they did not have enough strength to do their work due to excessive punishment. Many of the young slaves appeared to be much older than they really were, for they were unable to walk upright due to wounds on their buttocks, which obliged them to walk in a stooped fashion. When he [the mayoral] first came to the farm, he found that four slaves had recently hung themselves for this very reason, weary of the continual beatings they were dealt.

The sugar master Manuel Morgado, folio nine, stated that he had been on the farm since December 8 of last year. He had worked in the sugar industry for many years, and had experience on countless ingenios there on the island. Never had he seen such brutality toward the slaves as there was on this farm. He was revolted by the incessant beatings, which were so unremitting that the crack of the whip flaying the buttocks of the wretched slaves ever resonated in his ears.

Antonio Ramón Cuevas, a carpenter, folio eleven, stated that he had worked on the farm for three years and could attest to the fact that the four slaves who recently hung themselves did so due to the severity of the beatings. Weary of their torment, they embraced this way out. The owner ordered these punishments when he was on the farm. Since the beginning of sugar-grinding season, he unleashed the wrath of God (his words) even against the employees, who were relieved after some hours, and the poor slaves. The employees became accustomed to the constant echo of the crack of the whip and the wretched victims' pitiable entreaties. He attributed it all to the master's depraved nature and believed that the master suffered from some sort of mental derangement alleviated only by watching the slaves being punished or by disciplining the unfortunates himself. . . .

The black woman Francisca, a nurse, folio thirteen, said that, when she took charge of the infirmary, she found it full of patients who were there as a result of a punishment they had received. Their master ordered them to go out to work in that condition. She herself endured such a harsh beating that she could not don clothing again for many days. Florencia Lucumí, the black nurse who relieved the latest nurse, stated on folio fifteen that, when she handed over the infirmary to Francisca Criolla, there were five patients suffering from fever and some twenty patients recovering from vicious face-down beatings. The slaves José Rosario Lucumí, Luciano Gangá, . . . Trinidad Congo, Perico Bibí, Lorenzo Lucumí were prompted to hang themselves because of those punishments . . . and, along with the slave woman Rosalía Criolla, who hurled herself into the well to drown, remaining there for six days [until] they removed her and buried her in the yard next to the big house.

The slave Ceferino Lucumí, folio seventeen, related the same incidents and completely agreed with the prior declaration. He added that his master could not have slept, because at four o'clock in the morning he already was in the barracks, lining the slaves up. He made them go out single file, ordered them to turn face down, and lower their drawers. Four black men grabbed them by their arms and legs. Everyone was given fifty lashes, providing he did not lose count. If some contramayoral let up because he became fatigued, he was subjected to the very same treatment himself, with his own whip. When the master could go on no longer, he ordered another to continue in his place. This is how the contramayorals were punished more than any other slave. All this lasted two hours, or, rather, until six, when they left to go work out in the fields. At nine, the master went out and repeated the same punishment there [in the field], and began the same process all over again in the barracks when the slaves came in to eat at noon. This is why the people became so fed up with such unjustified cruelty and opted to hang themselves, just as the five previously mentioned black men and the black woman Rosalía chose to do . . .

In her statement, the black woman Luisa, folio nineteen, said that she was sweeping nearby and saw the slave woman Rosalía hurl herself into the well. She stated that she [Rosalía] did it because she had become weary of all the cruel punishment that she had received. She herself [Luisa] had not been punished because she was in the final months of pregnancy, but her two sons were half-dead from beatings. She was sick at heart at seeing her children so cruelly punished without cause.

The slave Eduardo's statement, folio twenty, stated the same thing, and he was in complete agreement with the prior [witness] statements. He added that the punishments meted out on the ingenio San Juan were worse because there they died from them. This was the case with the slave Marcelo Criollo, whose master obliged him to go out to work in the fields after being ruthlessly beaten. He was unable to do so, so they brought him before his master, striking him all along the way, felling him with their blows. When he reached the machine where his master was, he was thrashed again, this time with maguey strips. They put him in the stocks, and he died a short time later.

The slave Ceferino Lucumí, folio twenty-three, agreed with the prior [witness] statements. He stated that when his master was not on the farm, the slaves had a reprieve from the floggings. They prayed to God that he never return . . .[3]

[On the ingenio San Juan, with a total of 268 black slaves and 44 Asians, owned by the same master, the slave Baldomero stated:] . . . that the slave Marcelo Criollo died from the beating, and gave the same account as the mayoral. He added that he [the mayoral] punished him [Baldomero] when he was brought before his master, using three prickly maguey leaves to thrash his buttocks. He stated by name and nationality fifty-five black slaves who had been severely beaten, and denounced the deaths of two other blacks due to excessive punishment, one named Marcelo Mandinga, and the other Francisco, an old darkie from Vuelta Abajo, known as Juan de la Cruz. The rest of the statements from the slaves Joaquín Lucumí, Ricardo Macuá, Francisco Pérez, Sixto Criollo, Celestino Congo, and the mulatto Esteban Criollo . . . affirmed that three slaves named Marcelo Criollo, Marcelo Lucumí, and the old man from Vuelta Abajo, Juan de la Cruz, died from beatings . . .[4]

ANC, *Gobierno Superior Civil*, 954/33754-A.

7.5. A HUMANITARIAN WRITES TO CAPTAIN GENERAL FRANCISCO SERRANO CONCERNING ATROCITIES HE HAS WITNESSED

July 1862

Excellency:

The undersigned, moved by compassion for others, declares before Your Excellency that, ever since Esteban Santa Cruz Oviedo arrived on his coffee farm La Suerte (?), a most atrocious inquisition, perhaps in the history of the world, has been in effect. His wretched servants are whipped to death, as if their demise serves to amuse the aforementioned Esteban Santa Cruz de Oviedo as he watches these unfortunate creatures plead with him [for mercy]. The signatory, as a compassionate gesture, with due respect presents the following for [the exercise of] Your Excellency's benevolence and heartfelt compassion, [seeking] whatever sanctuary and mitigation [of their pain and suffering] that can be found for those wretched creatures. This Esteban Santa Cruz de Oviedo, as Your Excellency will appreciate, undoubtedly has forgotten that the sacred texts instruct him, "Do unto others as you would have them do unto you."

The situation for the aforementioned female slaves is so appalling that they can easily be called martyrs. On that farm known as the coffee plantation La Suerte, his slaves María de la Cruz and Paula are plagued with blows from cudgels and lashes. And why? Because they refuse to submit themselves to him. As for Paula, because some fireflies died while in her care. As Your Excellency appreciates, both acts are contrary to [the norms of] civilization. The undersigned's purpose is to gather [information] and call your benevolent heartfelt attention to the alleviation of the cruelties rained down upon so many unfortunates and [to request] that Your Excellency's sound judgment put a stop to the brutality of the aforementioned Don Esteban Santa Cruz de Oviedo.

Not four months ago, a similarly atrocious punishment killed the slave Enrique on the coffee plantation El Carmen, in spite of the fact that the authorities had been informed of the incident. Several ounces of gold served to cover up his crime.

[On February 14, in a new accusation] I have just received an anonymous tip in which the following barbarous deed has been denounced. I am told that in the paddock on the cafetal El Carmen, district of San Nicolás, jurisdiction of Güines, that the farm's owner Don Esteben Oviedo directed that 560 lashes be administered over the course of three days to the slave Enrique: 250 the first day, a like number on the second, and 60 on the third day. Red-hot irons were applied once he [Enrique] was on death's door. Naturally, he died as a result of such cruel treatment. I am told that the captain of said district was aware of the incident but failed to act, and that the deed took place at the end of January. And, finally, I am told that such inhumane treatment was in punishment for relations between the slave and a mulatto there on the farm . . . [he orders an investigation].

Statement of Paula from the coffee plantation La Suerte, Alacranes.

. . . She was on the farm working as a wet nurse for newborn infants. The little parda Paulita had been assigned to care for fireflies on the ingenio Trinidad. When they brought her to the coffee plantation La Suerte, she was assigned to the nursery. She heard that they had Paulita out in back of the big house, where they turned her face down to beat her for her carelessness with the aforementioned little creatures, and everyone on the farm knew about it. Her master ordered Don Pablo Molina to deal her five blows with a riding crop, and he remained to witness the punishment.

Before he was married, her master wooed the young slave girl María de la Cruz. For refusing him, he flogged her countless times. Soon afterward, she had with her master a daughter named Julia, who now would be seven years old. They took the child to Havana some five or six months ago. The slave girl María de la Cruz now works in the big house as a house slave. Whether she completes her chores or not, her master constantly beats her, sometimes lashing her face down and, others, cuffing her about the head.

Her master treats his slaves badly. He gives the men but one plantain apiece, just half a plantain to the women, and a little jerked beef. He provides no clothing. When slaves sell one of the hogs they have raised, he takes half the money. He beats them all a great deal, and they have a room full of whips, horse crops, and thick whips of manatee hide that they call *mandinga*, or "the devil," because of its heft and the pain it inflicts. He continually threatens her [María], and, although he watches her being beaten, he has never himself administered any floggings . . .

Statement of María de la Cruz:

. . . She explained in detail how her master forced himself on her while she was still but a child and constantly threatened and punished her. She had relations with him until he married. When she asked whether the child she bore would be slave or free, he said that it would belong to him. When she had her first mulatto daughter, her master gave her the bassinette, but her mother provided her with all the rest [of the things for the baby]. Despite this, he always has made her work and has punished her a great deal by his own hand, and the mayoral Molina has administered a bocabajo. During the time he was with her, he had relations with the mulatto Paulina, the black women Asunción and Rufina, and the mulattoes Paula and Florentina. He has two children with Paulina and one with Asunción. He also had children with the slaves Micaela and María del Rosario, and with other women whose names she does not recall. He had children with Natalia, Adelaida, Jacoba, and others from the cafetal El Carmen. He punished them all the same. The black man José Luis said that he witnessed the beating that killed Enrique, according to what the mulatto José Luis said. The reason for the mortal punishment was because he made the mulatto Jacoba pregnant.

Statement of the mulatto Paulina:

. . . Ever since she was little, she had been Oviedo's slave. She had three children and finds herself pregnant again. Her master fathered the first two, named Josefina and Helénida. The slave Joaquín Gangá was the father of the third. Sotero Criollo was the father of the unborn child. Her master took advantage of her against her will when she was but a child, by dint of force, using the whip, as her body attests. She could not love someone who treated her so badly. He punished her in every conceivable way and at his whim, with the exception of the bocabajo. He ordered the slave Jacobo to thrash her when her master arrived from the north and found her four months pregnant, then put her feet into leg irons fastened together with a wooden shaft, which she wore for nine months, as everyone knew. . . . As an act of kindness, the mayoral removed them when she went into labor . . .[5]

ANC, *Gobierno Superior Civil*, 954/33752.

7.6. EXCERPTS FROM THE PROCEEDINGS OF A LAWSUIT EXECUTED IN SAGUA LA GRANDE ON APRIL 28, 1864, AGAINST ANDRÉS MENA AND HIS SON JUSTO FOR ATROCITIES

The black slaves Eduardo, Diego, Bernardo, Pedro Congo, Mariana, Leonor, Hilaria, Isabel, Francisco, Antonio, and the Asians Achon, Miguel, and Julio [stated] that on Saturday morning, August 22, the ox herd beat Luis over his entire body with a leather whip and a stick until he collapsed. Some of the slaves involved asserted that that punishment took place on Sunday the twenty-third . . . later they amended [their statements]. Nevertheless, Luis's wife maintained that he had told her that the drover had pummeled him on Saturday and that, on the morning of the Sunday in question, the mayoral also had struck him. At about twelve o'clock that day, when she left Luis, he was complaining a great deal that his head was hurting from the blows that he had been dealt. Some of the above witnesses added that they saw Luis plowing the land or working after he had been punished . . .

Once the mayoral and the drover were jailed, the twelve slaves who had escaped returned, nine of whom had been away about a month. Mena and his son managed the farm. Upon being questioned, [the runaways] stated unanimously that they ran away because they could not stand their [the Mena's] extremely harsh treatment of them, relentlessly flogging them with a doubled lash and beating them with sticks. The mayoral would release those who were in the stocks, only to send them out to work under a rain of blows. The slave Eduardo was shackled in the stocks with a large sore on his right foot rife with vermin . . . the drover had put him into leg irons when he found him fleeing this cruel regimen. After punching him and beating him with a doubled lash, he sicced the dogs on him. They bit him in his private parts, and this is the reason that there was still blood in his urine. He had been in the stocks for the last three weeks. They tied the slave Diego to a forked stake, [forced him to] bark like a dog, and flogged him if he stopped. They took him into the rural countryside, his neck bound and his legs in irons, and obliged him to intone vulgarities. The slave Hipólito, who had fallen ill in the countryside, was put into a wasp's nest. They excited the wasps into a frenzy with the whip, and when he [Hipólito] emerged he was almost totally swollen and . . . (?) . . . [sic] The drover and the mayoral also had administered the bocabajo to the pickaninnies Florencio and Tomás, the latter only about six years old. The first boy [was punished] because had failed make fast a calf, and the second boy because he had refused to tell the mayoral who had stolen a turkey. And the dogs horribly disfigured the black slave Vidal. According to the statement, the drover deliberately sicced the dogs on him. All of this was confirmed not only by the statements of the black slaves, but also by four neighbors and five Chinese coolies who were working there on the farm . . .

In addition, the slave woman Mariana stated that the drover had forced the slave woman Matilde to live with him. The mayoral had fastened the slave woman Irene to a chair in the large salon in the courtyard. In full view of everyone, he tucked her clothes up, put on his glasses, and set about inspecting to see if she had any vermin in her private parts, hurling obscenities as he did so. On another occasion, in a vault, the mayoral in question ordered the slave woman Isabel restrained and had a slave woman named Hilaria tuck up her clothes and urinate into her mouth. Hilaria was revolted, prompting the mayoral to whip her soundly, and leaving him no other alternative than to urinate in Isabel's mouth and face himself . . .

The slave Antonio Barriga stated . . . that the mayoral in question had made him and the slave Eduardo clean out their own and their fellow slaves' bodily refuse with their bare hands, because he did not take them out to attend to their necessities. Once he saw that their hands were completely soiled, he forced them to hit each other in the face, eat the filth, and then he flogged them with a doubled lash and sticks . . .[6]

ANC, *Miscelánea de Expedientes*, 1391/A.

8. Freedom Road

8-1. The Rights of Slaves Who Travel to Countries without Slavery

8.1. THE SYNDIC RULES THAT CATALINA IS FREE

Havana, January 13, 1852

The syndic reports that in his opinion the slave woman Catalina is free and so finds in his ruling.

When she was taken to Spain, where slavery was forbidden, she effectively was free from the moment that she set foot in that land. An individual reduced to serving as a slave to another [in Spain] would have constituted an anomaly. Indeed, if she were free, and if freedom were a perpetual state, she hardly could become a slave once again by returning to this island. Whether or not she was given leave to go to Spain with the permission of one of Your Excellency's predecessors has no bearing on this matter either. Moreover, the owner was unable to present any proof concerning that permit, or the terms and conditions under which it was granted. Counsel for the slave owner involved sustained that the original owner's rights remained suspended while the slave was in Spain and were resumed once she [Catalina] returned to the island. This was perhaps the most flawed legal argument, completely contrary to all principles of law and reason that I had ever heard. When Catalina was in Spain, she was either a slave or she was free. She could not have been a slave, because in Spain slavery was neither recognized nor tolerated. Then she was free. Such a status could never be equivocal, lacking character and substance. The right of postliminy was established to promote freedom. An analogous right promoting slavery never existed because, according to the wise and enduring legal code formulated by Alfonso X, "All worldly rights always advance the interests of freedom." Lastly, Rodríguez's status as a slave owner and the enjoyment of any attendant rights thereto were not infringed upon in any way to date. When Catalina appeared before him for the first time, the aforementioned Rodríguez agreed to grant her permission to hire herself out as a journeywoman while the matter was being decided. . . . [Rodríguez] stated, besides, that Catalina gave birth to a son upon returning from Spain and that, given what had been reported here, it was pointless to sustain that her son was free, by virtue of the legal principle that a newborn's status was identical to that of its mother . . .[1]

ANC, *Gobierno Superior Civil*, 948/33463.

8.2. MANUELA DE LA GUARDIA REPRESENTS THE SLAVE JOSÉ AND GIVES TESTIMONY ON HIS BEHALF

Havana, November 26, 1861

Manuela de la Guardia, free morena, native of Africa, member of the Gangá nation, residing in the first district, 88 Amargura Street . . . says that José Ruiz, the moreno slave owned by Don Cándido Ruiz, who currently resides at 96 Amargura Street, traveled from Cuba to the United States of America in May 1859 in his master's company. The deponent in this petition is a witness in this matter, for on that date she, too, found herself in the company of Don Cándido and his slave in North America.

José's master told him that he already was free simply by virtue of having traveled from this country to that. Upon returning here from that country, José found himself greatly abused and subject to slavery just as before. Well, this wretched Negro, deceived by his master, had the good fortune to speak with Your Excellency in the patio of your palace, Your Excellency's residence, three days ago now. You recommended that your secretary investigate the legal status of his claim . . . and yesterday at three o'clock, while in the coach house of Your Excellency's residence, just as Your Excellency directed until such time as your secretary resolved the matter, José Ruiz was brazenly removed, flagrantly violating the sanctity of Your Excellency's abode, in violation of proper decorum and in complete disregard for your superior rank as most illustrious representative of Your Majesty the Queen, God save her. . . . He was bound, and taken to the home of Don Cándido Ruiz . . . where he is at the present time, his feet thrust in the stocks and threatened with being banished to a farm far out in the rural countryside, as punishment for nothing more than making a just claim for justice in the name of the laws of heaven and earth . . .[2]

ANC, *Gobierono Superior Civil*, 954/33678.

8.3. THE MULATTO DÁMASO SAILS FOR MEXICO AND FREEDOM

Santiago de Cuba, September 6, 1864

My beloved and esteemed mother:

I will be so happy to find you enjoying full and complete good health, just as is my wish. I find myself in Veracruz. The trip took five days and was quite enjoyable. The captain had high regard for me, and so far everything has gone very well for me. I found a compatriot in the port of Veracruz, who has been like a father to me, and more. He asked me several questions. My answers assured him that I truly was a compatriot, and so he proceeded to take me to his house. I was so grateful to him that I did not know how to repay him. He got me a job on the railroad and I earn twelve reals a day. I am very happy with everyone here in this country, because they think well of me. Whenever I am out of work, they take it upon themselves to look for work for me. And so, I am never without a job. I think about my country every hour of the day. But, there is no other alternative but to trust in God's will. Here, in this country, they do not distinguish between white and black. Everyone is equal, because we are living in a republic. I have spent the religious holidays honoring Santiago and Santa Ana[3] working, because these days are not celebrated here. I have been to some dances that have been given here, in this country, and I have enjoyed myself quite a bit.

I ran into López Serena here, the clerk at the secretariat, and he said I was right about Silvia and Amalia. Antonio Gullón [assistant to the port captain Francisco Ros],[4] asked me to inquire whether Celia has given birth yet, and asked that you tell his mother to write him, for he is anxious to receive a letter from her. Whenever she wants to write him, she should give the letter to you [to forward to me]. Ask Matilde to write as well, and tell her that she is to give the letter to you to forward it. Give my sincere regards to my buddy Juan Mulatto and a kiss to my daughter Prudencia. I am very eager (a piece of the letter is torn off here, apparently in the interests of privacy.) . . . Antonio Gullón and warm regards to Florencia and Rosa and Ramón, to everyone. Ask Sixta what is happening with the wedding, and tell Florencia that I was right about the masked balls. Marcelina's most esteemed son sends his blessing. Tell my brother, Juan de Mata, that I remember him always, and that it is difficult to endure the hardship of never seeing him again. And make sure that you address the letter to me in Veracruz. Best wishes to all of my friends.

Dámaso Portuondo Bravo.[5]

ANC, *Gobierno Superior Civil*, 961/34031.

8.4. THE SLAVE GIRL ÁNGELA DÍEZ AND HER VISIT TO VENEZUELA AS GROUNDS FOR PETITIONING FOR HER FREEDOM

Havana, January 20, 1865

Ángela Díez, eleven years old, parda, and Puerto Rico born, claims her freedom because she has resided for more than six months in the capital of Venezuela in the company of her mistress, Juana Díez. She explains that her mistress works as a member of Robreños's Compañía Cómica, as a stewardess. In this capacity and as companion, her mistress took Ángela along on all of the company's tours. Despite this, Juana Díez has just sold Ángela to Merced Valdés, after just having received three ounces of gold toward Ángela's coartación purchase price of 450 pesos, or some 900 escudos [colonial gold coin] . . . thus, committing an act of criminal kidnapping.

Another slave belonging to Juana Díez named Caridad Armenta, a Lucumí, made a similar claim and was very graciously granted a certificate of manumission on exactly the same grounds as Ángela Díez, i.e., for having accompanied and served her mistress while in Carácas, on the very same trip as the petitioner. This proves that Juana Díez was familiar with the law and that the law could not have failed to apply to the slave girl Ángela. . . . presumably, because the girl was no more than four years old at the time, she would have remained ignorant of the right that she was now hers.[6]

ANC, *Gobierno Superior Civil*, 967/34165.

8-II. Maroons and Palenque Dwellers

8.5. ACCOUNT BY FRANCISCO (PANCHO) MINA, CAPTAIN OF THE MAROONS

Cayajabos, August 31, 1835

The deponent states that he is a Mina, single, of legal age, owned by Don José Rubio Campos, and that he ran away more than twenty years ago. . . . (He fled because his former master had sold him to a coffee plantation. He was unaccustomed to that type of work — he is a cart driver — and the mayoral punished him a great deal. . . . He had been in Vuelta de Abajo and a place they call Guanes. . . . He never was the leader of the palenque. He lived with only four Negro men and two Negro women, with no one acting as leader, each individual governing their own fate . . .)

The runaways survived by eating *jutías* [Cuban rats] and *majaes rabones* [Cuban snakes also known as Santa Marías]. . . . Don Miguel Herrera, the mayoral from Borbón, two white youths, and two mulattoes apprehended him on the coffee plantation Santa Teresa, also known as Landot. . . . There were ten maroons in all, four of them there together in the scrub on the coffee plantation Plumas. They were on that particular coffee plantation because formerly they had been very friendly with those on this estate . . .

Those maroons accompanying him were: José de Jesús Gangá, from the ingenio owned by the Countess de Lombillo; Nicolás Carabalí, property of Don Antonio Duarte Zenea; Toribio Mina, owned by Don Jacinto González Larrinaga; Bartolo, property of Don León Blen; Remigio, from the ingenio San Isidro; Aniceto Macuá, owned by Don Manuel Díaz of the [ingenio] Bejucal; and the black women Gertrudis Conga, property of Don Antonio Duarte Zenea; María Filomena Carabalí, owned by Mrs. Condesa de Lombillo; and Tomasa Criolla, about sixteen years old, born and raised in the scrub, and her mother, property of the ingenio San Francisco owned by Alfaro. They came to the coffee plantation Landot because the slave Pablo Criollo had run away from there. He proposed that they go back there with some of their beeswax and barter with it for truck. There was very little chance that they would get caught on that coffee plantation. . . . Pablo was with them for a week, because he went to take the black woman Rosalía Lucumí, a slave owned by Don Miguel Herrera, to the black man Hilario Mandinga, who had been a contramayoral from the coffee plantation Borbón but ran away into the scrub and was waiting for said black woman for his wife. Once he saw that she had reached her destination, Pablo returned to his house in order to wait for the others to bring the wax. They finally came about two weeks later. They stayed for eight days, hiding right there in the slave quarters on the coffee plantation Landot. They learned that the mayoral there on Borbón tried to send for the captain to search those huts, so they set out for the scrubland to wait until the others came with the wax. They dealt with the slaves Antonio Gangá, León Gangá, and another whose name he did not know about the wax. They gave a crude cake of wax to each of the two contramayorals . . . in return they gave them only lunch and a little cane liquor, agreeing to pay for the wax later. That is when the mayoral on Borbón showed up along with some others, and seized them and captured them . . .[7]

ANC, *Gobierno Superior Civil*, 616/19688.

8.6. FUGITIVES FROM THE INGENIO SANTÍSIMA TRINIDAD

Guanajay, August 1837

A. Statement of Agustín Carabalí, sixty years old, slave on the ingenio owned by María Asunción Goicoechea.

. . . it is true that he escaped from the ingenio El Mariel this past May, just after all the sugarcane had been ground. He ran away because the mayordomo threatened him and pummeled him over at the big house, where he was mixing mortar. He escaped alone. He hid himself in the mango orchard on that very estate, where he remained for a day. The following night, he went on to the coffee plantation Santo Tomás, owned by Don Nicolás Zacanini, who had been his owner at one time. He hid among the coffee shrubs there for about a month, more or less. At the end of that time, he came upon a woman from the ingenio El Mariel, who was in the company of Vicente and Antonio, other runaways, whom he [Agustín] had found on that cafetal, and she took them to the mayoral under her protection.

B. Statement of Gabriel, native Cuban, fifteen or sixteen years old, single, ox herd on the same ingenio.

. . . he ran away from the ingenio El Mariel in March of this year because the contramayoral there at the sugar mill beleaguered him. His job was to haul the sugarcane as quickly as possible, which he was unable to do satisfactorily because there was something wrong with his foot. . . . He subsisted on plantains from that very coffee plantation (Zacanini), roasting them over a fire at night. He would lay in wait, on the lookout for the sentries on their rounds, and then pilfer candles . . .

C. Statement of Antonio Mina, sixty years old, single, and slave on the same plantation.

(He ran away because) he had been assigned to guard some prisoners, who escaped by breaking down the door to the jail, and he was afraid of being punished by the mayoral . . .

D. Statement of Vicente Bibí, thirty-two years old, single, and slave on the same plantation.

. . . he ran away from the ingenio in question in the midst of the latest milling season, he did not know exactly what month that was. He ran away not because the work was disagreeable but because he had no clothing. He escaped on his own. . . . He managed to survive for about four months (on the Zacanini coffee plantation, where he came from). . . . he turned himself in to his mistress on the ingenio, along with Agustín and Antonio. . . . this lady reproved them and arranged for the mayoral, who was there when they were brought in, to look the other way concerning any infractions they had committed . . .

E. Statement of Hilario Congo, fifty years old, single, and a slave from the plantation.

. . . he ran away from the ingenio in question a month before the end of sugar-milling season, making for the coffee plantation Santo Tomás that very same day. He hid among the brush twenty some days, at the end of which he came out and went home.

As he approached the canebrake, the carter . . . captured him and turned him over to the mayoral. The owner of the ingenio, who happened to be there at the time, sent him to the infirmary, assuming that the carter's dogs had injured him. He remained in the infirmary until he had recuperated. Once he was able bodied, the mayoral ordered him back to work in the fields along with the others. And so he went. After about a month back at work and a little more than two months after his capture, he ran away again. This time he was gone for twelve days, more or less, when he was taken prisoner by a Negro who farmed on leased land adjacent to the coffee plantation Santo Tomás. That farmer turned him in to the watch commander, who in turn handed him over to the captain of the town of Mariel.

On both occasions, he escaped alone. He ran away the first time because his previous owner, Don Nicolás Zacanini, did not honor a promise he had made. Don Nicolás had said that he would not remove them from the coffee plantation to put them up for sale. At most, they would be taken to work on the ingenio El Mariel for six months, after which they would return to the coffee plantation. This did not happen, even after working for more than a year on El Mariel, [so] this was the reason for his first attempt . . .

The second time, he attempted to escape because the contramayoral José Criollo harassed him tremendously, constantly punishing him. . . . the only person he met out there was Vicente Bibí from the coffee plantation Santo Tomás, of whom he asked, "Vicente, what are you doing around here," and he [Vicente] replied: "Yes, I too am a fugitive because the ingenio work is difficult. . . ." (They captured him the second time because) of the black man Lorenzo Criollo. The deponent went to Lorenzo's house to collect four reals that he was owed for two chickens that he had given him to sell when he was a slave there on the coffee plantation . . .[8]

ANC, *Miscelánea de Expedientes*, 604/M8.

🌿 8.7. THE INHABITANTS OF EL CEDRO TALK ABOUT PALENQUE LIFE

Santiago de Cuba, August 1838

A. Statement of Josefa Rita Bibí, slave owned by Doña Francisca Estrada, resident of the hamlet Bayamo, twenty-six or twenty-seven years old, single, laundress and presser.

. . . there were more than thirty shanties, each containing a runaway and his wife. The captain in charge was named Manuel Matoso and his deputy was Lorenzo. . . . there was a council building where the runaways often met. She did not know what they used to talk about in there, for the women did not go in there. . . . They staved off hunger by working on their estancias, sowing all kinds of victuals to feed themselves, catching jutías and wild boars . . .

B. Statement of Genoveva, native of Curazao, thirty years old, slave owned by Don Joaquín Ceferino Rodríguez, resident of the hamlet Bayamo, single, laundress.

. . . she ran away because her master, Rodríguez, mistreated her by dint of harsh punishments, such as the blow he dealt her with the heel of his shoe which caused a morbid swelling over her right eye. Unable to put up with it any longer, she decided to go away, out into the rural countryside. . . . Only the men ever left the palenque. They did not tell the women anything about what happened to them away from there . . . (they sold the wax) half of them made for this city and the rest for the hamlet of Bayamo . . .

C. Statement of Dionisia Calás Gangá, twenty-nine or thirty years old, single, day laborer, slave belonging to Doña Antonia Zayas, resident of Bayamo.

. . . when someone lied or gossiped there in the palenque, the captain ordered them flogged. Lorenzo carried out the lashings with a horsewhip that he had for that purpose . . .

D. Statement of Manuela Calás Gangá, thirty years old, single, grazier earning two reals a day, slave owned by Don Andrés Calás.

. . . she was an associate of the Negro slave José del Carmen, who himself belonged to the priest Don José Antonio Leiva in Bayamo. She ran away one night after evening prayers . . . because her master mistreated her, inflicting harsh punishments. She was obliged to pay her master two reals a day, plus feed and clothe herself. One day, she found nowhere to earn the daily wages he demanded of her. She became fed up with such rigor and took off, intending to rest from her toils right there in the scrub. . . . (there was) a large council building where they used to meet in the morning at

Matoso's request. He would advise them that when they made forays in small parties they must not do harm to any whites, to only pilfer what they needed. At night they played drums . . .

E. Statement of Federico Bibí, forty years old, slave owned by Don Narciso Tamayo, resident of the hamlet of Bayamo, tiller.

. . . the deponent believed that the main purpose [of the large house] was as a place to hang up the tobacco that they cut out in the field, because it was full of that leaf. . . . they had no clothing other than what they made from the bark of the *jagüey* [woody liana] tree . . .

F. Statement of Bartolomé Portuondo Congo, fifty years old, slave belonging to Don Vicente Portuondo on his ingenio Jicotea.

. . . he fled the hacienda Jicotea alone, heading out into the scrubland there, where he came upon several other slaves belonging to his master who had run away earlier, named Luis, Federico, Desiderio, José Caridad, Carlos, Sebastián, Eduardo, and Celestino. All together, they embarked upon their march deep into the scrubland. . . . they made for Demajagual, because there were wild yams there that they could live on, and built their shantytown settlement there. As soon as they ran out of yams, they pushed farther on, settling down wherever they found more of them. They remained in the backlands of Demajagual for about a year, until the day that the black men Ignacio, Estéban, and Vicente showed up. They invited them to go with them to the fugitive shantytown of El Cedro, where they told him that there was plenty to eat. . . . He ran away because his master did not give him anything to eat but ground corn, the mayoral made them work a lot, and he cruelly punished him . . .[9]

ANC, *Miscelánea de Expedientes*, 1107/F.

8.8. ALEJANDRO CONGO RECOUNTS HIS EXPERIENCES AS A MAROON

Candelaria, August 21, 1844

. . . he was brought to this island many years ago, when he was very young. Upon his arrival, Mr. Magín Borí, now deceased, purchased him. Upon his master's death, Alejandro passed to his current master, Don Manuel Villalón, as the former's heir. All the while, he worked as a slave on the cafetal Desierto.

. . . the captain of the district of Candelaria captured him three days ago. . . . the deponent ran away from the coffee plantation Desierto eight months ago because the mayoral, Monsieur Beroc, mistreated him. The day he ran away, the mayoral had put him in leg irons for spending one day of the Easter holiday at Villanueva, the cafetal that had belonged to his dead master, Don Magín Borí.... He removed his shackles out in the scrubland by striking them with a rock. He ran away on another occasion as well. Appearing before his master . . . he ordered him bound and dispatched him to that very same coffee plantation Desierto so as to be at the mayoral's disposal. They beat him over a three-day period, dealing him fifty lashes the first day, thirty on the second, and another thirty on the third. While free of his master's authority, he spent a month in the scrub on the cafetal Villanueva and later he spent time in the backlands on Songuito, owned by Monsieur Fablé. Somarise Borí, from the coffee plantation Monserrate, lived there with him, and was captured along with the deponent. Camilo was also with them. The deponent did not know who Camilo's owner was, because he never told him his name, only that he was from Havana. Other slaves, known as Rafael and Tomás, did not know who their owners were either, but he did hear them say that they were from the city of Havana. The slave Luciano was also a slave belonging to Magín Borí, owner of the cafetal Villanueva. He did not know the whereabouts of his fellow runaways, as they ran off when the deponent was captured and it was difficult to know which way they went.... they were pursued and the deponent was apprehended upon going down to the hacienda Candelaria to gather mangoes . . .

. . . The deponent and his fellow slaves used to gather at night in the scrubland of Songuito. To this end, they reinforced their sleeping quarters with palm bark and their shanties with palm leaves. They survived solely on jutías and wild yucca, together with the honey they removed from beehives deep in the scrub. They never went down to the farms to pilfer foodstuffs, meat, or any other type of sustenance. Conversation revolved around how to survive while avoiding detection and capture. Camilo was their leader, and he insisted that they "be careful not to damage the farms or any animals roaming about in the scrub." Camilo customarily sold the wax that they gathered in the scrub to the darkie José, a muleteer belonging to Juan the Catalán . . . next to the coffee plantation Songuito. There, on Catalán's establishment, they customarily planted coffee trees on one side and tobacco on the other. Of all the slaves there on the property, José was the only one they knew. The only weapons they had were their work machetes, taking them with them when they ran away . . .

Camilo kept the money from the sales, never dividing it up among them, telling them that he was saving it to take to the main palenque. The deponent did not know its name, for he never went there and did not know where it was. Camilo used to go to that cimarrón settlement quite frequently, accompanied by Rafael. He refused to take any of the other fugitive slaves with him. He heard him say all the time that they kept it a secret from any newly arrived runaways, because he feared that they might be disloyal, trusting only those who had been there for quite some time. Camilo and Rafael were usually away for many days when they went off to deliver the money. When they came back, Camilo and Rafael showed the others that they returned empty handed. In Camilo's absence, Longorio acted as captain.

ANC, *Miscelánea de Expedientes*, 943/33261.

8-III. Waging War, Winning War

8.9. INSURRECTION ON THE COFFEE PLANTATIONS OF MATANZAS

June 1825

A. Confession of Tom or Tomás Mandinga, over twenty-five years old, slave on the cafetal La Yaba owned by Juan Fouquier.

... long before [the insurrection] took place, Lorenzo de Sateliens would come by every Sunday, urging them to join in his scheme to rise up and kill all the whites, arguing that they were fed up and did not want to work anymore. All the slaves on the farm where he lived pledged themselves to the undertaking and agreed that he would contact them about the date. Lorenzo added that they could count on all the slaves belonging to Sabanazo and, according to Cristóbal, the contramayoral, those from other farms as well. He was going to be one of the captains, along with Federico, who was owned by the Armitages. They both were brujos and were busy concocting some special charms that would harm only whites and not affect the slaves. Lorenzo came about a month before the uprising, returning frequently, continually fine-tuning the plan and monitoring its progress. Federico came along, toting a sack of yams and a jug of cane liquor. They said that they had come from Taylor's house, where they had worked on the scheme. They used the yams as a pretext, telling their masters that they had gone to buy them so as to account for their absences and prevent their masters from becoming suspicious. On that day they met for a while, and everyone drank the cane liquor that they had brought with them. Lorenzo added that Pablo de Tosca was a captain, and, because he frequently would go to Matanzas, he was charged with acquiring the bullets and gunpowder, as he effectively was doing. On another of his trips, Lorenzo revealed that the uprising would be soon, all was ready, and showed them some of the new lead bullets that he said were just like the ones that Pablo was bringing. Pablo did not speak to them about the plan, even though he often went to the deponent's house to court Josefa, a native-born black woman.

That same day he told Lorenzo and Federico not to work in their garden plots... that they should go ahead and eat their hens and whatever else they had on hand, for once war came, all would be lost. The slaves on Satrán del Sabanazo, Gómez, Peletier, and others already had done so. The uprising took place Tuesday night, just days after that Sunday when Lorenzo warned that the outbreak of hostilities was imminent. Lorenzo and Federico led the slaves from Satrán del Sabanazo, Gómez, Sateliens, Pancho Lima, and other farms he never had heard of. The rebels called at his house. He did not know what was going on until his wife called him and he immediately went out, not even taking the time to put on his breeches. That was when he realized that the slaves had surrounded his house and were creating an uproar. Some slaves were attempting to quiet the mutineers, so that the whites did not hear them and get up. Just then, he heard some rebels breaking down the door to his master's big house. The house slaves inside kept insisting to those outside that it would be better to start somewhere else, and that they would follow later. They said this so that their master could escape in the interval. They [the rebels] refused. There were a great many slaves everywhere, milling about in complete chaos, working at cross-purposes. That was when he heard the wails of his mistress. As shotgun blasts were fired, the deponent ran over to his mistress. He saw slaves swarming over the entire big house. They already had killed the master. The deponent attempted to signal his mistress to quit the house, but she could not see him for the horde. At this, his mistress was able to escape with the slave woman Petrona. The slaves began to rummage the house, looking for weapons and munitions. The deponent entered and told them not to touch the crystal and the porcelain, and they obeyed. And in the course of the sacking, he noticed that Guillermo and Miguel, his fellow slaves, and Leisi, along with others he cannot recall, did the bulk of the looting.

When the deponent was asked whether Lorenzo and Federico had told them who had devised the scheme to go to war, he said that it was no less than Lorenzo, Federico, and Pablo de Tosca. It was they who had laid the plans for war, and they alone. They originated the idea, or talked it up, and carried it out. He did not know of any other persons who were involved...

They inquired who was responsible for the deaths and other destruction in the course of the war. He replied that afterward they continued on to Paire's house, that they already had attacked him, and that José María de Fouquier grabbed him by the hand and gave it to him. He does not know who might have killed Paire's son or Monsuit either, although he heard that Lorenzo did it. Afterward, they went to Tosca's house. When they got there, they found Pablo, who had two horses with him and was looking for corn. They admonished him for his actions. How could he, a captain, run off and leave them? The war had begun, and he should come with them because everything was his idea in the first place. Then Pablo left the horses and set off toward the big house with all the rebels in tow. When Pablo arrived at the big house, he entered, feigned surprise, and approached his mistress, "Miss, the slaves are coming to kill the whites." With that, the woman hid herself and ordered Pablo to see that they did her no harm. Just then, one of Tosca's former shipmates who was owned by Sabanzo covered him with a gun, enabling him to escape. Immediately, Pablo began to ransack the big house, distributing any weapons and munitions that he found to the others, breaking open a small keg of gunpowder belonging to his master and allotting portions. After plundering the big house, Pablo took the powder horn, a blunderbuss, and a saber, mounted his master's honey-colored horse, and left along with everyone else, going off toward the Morejón house.

There they set fire to the factory buildings [as a diversion], because they were afraid of the whites there in the big house and expected them to take flight once they saw the fire. The deponent saw Pablo set fire to a coffee bean shelter, and Pablo ordered the deponent off to set fire to the coffee mill. The deponent did it, because he was afraid of Pablo. Just then, they heard someone moaning, and they all hurried toward the tavern, only to realize that a white youth had been killed. They went on to the Webster cafetal, where they found the slaves assembling and their master. As the rebels came in, the slaves joined them. At this point, Lorenzo shot the master. Later, Felipe de Fouquier told him that he had killed Monsieur Batle. The deponent went at once to where Batle already lay dead and struck him several blows, all the slaves and the rebels following suit. From there, they set out for the Arce tavern, passing other coffee plantations along the way and ransacking a house. At this point, the whites fell upon them, and they divided up into groups. One band went off toward the Chapeaux and Taylor cafetals, where they killed two people. Roberto killed a mason named Mirson who worked at the Chapeaux house. Cristóbal, the contramayoral on the Taylor coffee plantation and one of the leaders who had counseled for war, killed a white man, an American.

Although the deponent did not witness these deaths, Isidoro and others told him all about it at the time. The prisoners spoke of it right there, in the very jail where they were being held, all of them swearing never to reveal the truth. After the scene at the Arce tavern, where they were routed, the deponent hid himself out in the scrub, later turning up at his house, where they apprehended him.

B. Statement of Clemente Gangá, twenty-two years old, slave belonging to Tomás Peiton on his coffee plantation Arcadia.

... four or five days ago [Antonio Congo] was sleeping in his hut because that was what his contramayoral, Sandi Gangá, had ordered.... when said slave Antonio got out to where people were working cutting brush around sunset, this same slave Antonio was speaking with said contramayoral. Later, the latter [contramayoral] ordered the pickaninny Sesé to call the slave Bosen. Everyone was talking. So, when this Bosen got there, the contramayoral asked everyone if they were ready to rise up against the whites when called upon to do so, and they all said yes. ... Last Sunday, he saw him [the contramayoral] speaking with three slaves owned by Don Luis Larrentrín, one named Tomás, another called Carlos Gangá, and someone else whose name he did not know. Those three told Sandi, Bosen, and the deponent that today, Saturday, they were going to revolt against the whites, along with Mr. Junco's slaves and the slaves on Monsieur Monet's ingenio. Four [other] blacks would come to notify them ...

C. Statement of Francisco Mandiga, twenty-five years old, slave owned by Luis Larrentrín.

... the deponent was working on the camino real when a darkie passing by told him that he was the ox herd from Mr. Monet's ingenio. He told the deponent that the king of the whites and the governor of Havana had given orders to kill all the seasoned slaves here in this land. Bozals would be brought in to work instead. His mayoral had told him so. Thus, in order to live, they all must rise up, when they were least expecting it, and they would take them all prisoner and decapitate them ...

D. Statement of Carlos Gangá, twenty-one years old, slave on the same plantation.

... he told Sandi that he did not want to get involved in any wickedness ... and Sandi said that he was very green and they must not wait any longer. He said that he would go to speak to Francisco, a courageous man, and that if the other slaves did not want to mutiny, well, there on Don Felipe's ingenio there were many others, also very determined ...

E. Statement of Sandi Quisi, twenty-five years old, contramayoral for Tomás Peiton's widow.

He was asked who first persuaded him to participate. He replied that his mistress's son, Don Enrique, was the first to tell him that a vessel was coming from his homeland, loaded with people coming to fight on behalf of the slaves against the criollos and the whites and that everyone should make ready their weapons. A free black, Joaquín, who lives in Caobas, also told him the same thing. . . . this freedman told the deponent that he too would go to war with them and that there was fighting in Vuelta Arriba as well. The mason on his farm, Don Guillermo, had told him the same thing as his master Enrique . . .

F. Statement of José Luis, slave owned by Antonio Gómez on his cafetal El Solitario.

. . . on the Sunday before the war broke out, the deponent was doing chores along with everyone else, when it was his turn to go with Vicente to inspect the condition of the fence next to Laguna. Federico, from Sabanazo, the Englishman's slave, showed up there, and he told him, "Compadre, weeze goin' ta war ta kill all da whites, daze more than 'nuff blacks for dat." At this, the deponent and Vicente replied that they did not get involved in things of that nature, that they did not want to harm the whites because the whites always held the upper hand and would kill them, and that he absolutely should not count on them. Federico replied that a darkie from Vuelta Arriba had come to tell him that they could not abide the whites any longer, that they were subjecting them to many bocabajos, killing blacks, burying them way out in the jungle, forcing them [the blacks] to make war . . .

G. Statement of José Felipe Navarro, native of Maracaibo, thirty-five years old, single, slave on the cafetal belonging to Monsieur Sateliens.

. . . the slaves themselves told him that they were in agreement with a lot of people from this town [Matanzas] and even from Havana. Buoyed by such feelings of assurance, their first decision was to set out for this city in order to take it, but they were forced to change course because they encountered troops on the road . . .

H. Statement of Carlos Gangá, twenty years old, coachman for Tomás Peiton's widow.

. . . [the slave Bosen told him] that he was going to take off with the slave Antonio, because he was sick and tired of this master, and he did not want to serve him any longer. He was going to Vuelta Arriba with Antonio, who knew the way, and join up with those slaves who were killing whites because he did not want to serve the whites any more . . .

I. Statement of Ramon Mandinga, legal adult, slave owned by Webster on his coffee plantation Santa Ana.

. . . the morning after all the tumult, when he went to Justo's [Lucumí, from the cafetal Carolina] garden plot with Félix, the deponent told Justo that his fellow slave Juan had been killed in the war with the whites. As Juan was the padrino of the deponent, and the deponent looked upon him as a father, he had tried to go to look for him in order to give him a proper burial. He had been unable to do so for fear of being killed himself. That was what Ramón *El Manco* [One-Handed] told him. Then Justo told him that God would provide him with an unforeseen opportunity to kill his master. He had a shotgun and a large horn of gunpowder in his hut for this purpose. The deponent told him not to do it and asked him what he would accomplish by killing his master, telling him that it was a very wicked thing to do. He did not want to talk about it, because he greatly respected his master. Justo replied that he, indeed, would kill him . . .

J. Statement of Lucía, native of Virginia, United States, forty years old, widow and slave owned by Monsieur Armitage on his coffee plantation Sabanazo.

. . . everyone there unanimously stated that they were going to kill all the whites and create a free state, taking control of Matanzas and Havana to that end . . .[10]

ANC, *Comisión Militar*, 1/3, 4, 5.

8.10. WAR IN THE LANDS OF MARIEL

Banes, August 13, 1833

A. Statement of Diego Varreiro, thirty-two years old, mayordomo on the cafetal El Salvador owned by Francisco Santiago Aguirre.

. . . on the thirteenth, sometime between eight and nine in the evening, around the time they went to bed in the big house, he heard a voice in the factory courtyard that repeated the words *Hó=bé*, which is Lucumí for "meeting." Very soon thereafter, a number of blacks rushed onto the house's covered way, amid a great deal of uproar. He feared an unfortunate incident and, as he made for the infirmary, he asked the slave Alejo what it meant. Alejo replied, "Damn it, we want freedom," suddenly hitting his left arm with his machete. . . . [He was forced to flee] and, arriving at the tile works, he came upon the slaves Francisco Gangá, Roque, and Domingo, Gangás as well, who accompanied him to the ingenio El Fénix.... [Later the mutineers were attacked by the troops] and the deponent himself shot and killed the black contramayoral Luis Lucumí, who had commanded them and led them, carrying an open red silk parasol as his emblem, with no other weapon...

B. Statement of José Baquero, twenty-five years old, illiterate and the nurse on the coffee plantation.

... he fled into the field and hid amid the cornstalks. He heard them shouting "*Hotnú* Baquero!" which is to say that they wanted to kill him.

C. Statement of Guillermo, known as Ayuso in his country (through an interpreter).

... three days before his master left for Havana, he noticed that the contramayorals Joaquín and Fierabrás and the slaves Agó and Bale were speaking confidentially. When the deponent drew near, they told him to back off, because he would go and report what they were saying to Mr. Baquero later. They went over by the well to continue their conversation. Fierabrás, known as Edu in his homeland, and Joaquín incited the slaves and bullied them into following their lead. They told them that in the morning the whites would kill anyone who remained behind. Many left with Fierabrás and Joaquín, who went to Banes on horseback. He did not know who set the houses on fire there or killed the whites. They returned to the farm at daybreak, and continued to inflict property damage and loot until the troops fired on them later that morning, dispersing them. Some of their comrades returned fire, ensconced in some houses containing firearms and white women.... As captains, [Joaquín] and Fierabrás carried opened dark red parasols...

D. Statement of Eguiyove, as he is called in his country, or Matías, as he is called here, appearing to be between thirteen and fifteen years old, slave on the cafetal El Salvador.

... the day before the black contramayorals Joaquín and Fierabrás mutinied, they went along with the other folks to load stones for work purposes. They separated out the young and the women from the adult men. He believed that was when the most seasoned men began plotting some sort of conspiracy. The deponent knew nothing of it, because he had been made a contramayoral in charge of a number of pickaninnies. On the following night, Joaquín and Fierabrás created an uproar and forced all the slaves to leave, arming them with sticks, stones, and machetes for their assault on the big house. The slaves Margarita, Guadalupe, and Nicolás wanted to lock the doors to the big house. Fierabrás was going around the factory courtyard and the slave quarters, threatening to kill anyone who took flight or was hiding. Meanwhile, Joaquín and those known in their homeland as Ayai, Churipe, Bale, and Agó, along with Alejo, gathered the people together and forced them to arm themselves, steal from their master, and destroy his things. Immediately, all the bucks, including the deponent, made for Banes, leaving the women, the pickaninnies, and the sick behind. . . . they all returned to the farm, and at first light they made everyone come out, even the women, pickaninnies, and the ill. They set out for the neighboring ingenio Catalina to the beat of two drums and the tune of a flute. Several of the slaves traveled by horseback, including, among others, Fierabrás and Luis, the contramayoral, who had donned a woman's dress and bonnet. They rifled houses and seized some old machetes at that ingenio, before continuing on toward the neighboring coffee plantation, where they did the same thing. Agó set fire to a house with a shotgun blast. They drank fresh milk right there, and continued on to the next ingenio. There, in broad daylight, the whites fired on the slaves . . .

E. Statement of Margarita Lucumí, over twenty-five, servant in the big house.

. . . (When she heard them enter the house) she spoke to them in their native language, asking them what they were doing. Some of them, she did not know who, replied that they wanted to make war. She asked them against whom they were waging this war. A black man she knew and whom everyone knew as Labrao seemed to be the leader. He responded that the war was against the whites, because they were the ones who made slaves of them, forced them to work, and punished them, and that with the war they were going to be free. And although the deponent wanted to dissuade them, they did not listen to her and stoned her twice. Unable to contain them, she shouted at the whites to leave. . . . (Then she grabbed) her two small criollo children, Domingo and Julián, by the hand. By that time, her husband Joaquín Lucumí had arrived. He was the contramayoral responsible for the bozalons. He told her to come with them because they were going to kill the whites and be free in Vuelta de Abajo. But the deponent resisted and tried to convince him and the others of their wickedness. Her husband dealt her a violent blow and snatched her oldest son away from her. They became even more agitated and a large contingent left the farm, while another remained behind, inflicting further damage and arming themselves with stones. . . . (Later, the first contingent returned, and, observing smoke over toward the town of Banes,) the deponent asked Joaquín if they had set fire to the houses. He replied, "What was he to do, for he was no white man's son." He told her once more to come with them, chiding her for defending the whites. Seeing that she continued to defy him, he told her, "Well, once the master comes, he will give you your certificate of manumission" . . .

F. Statement of Francisco Gutiérrez, native of Álvarez, married, fifty-five years old, mayoral on the cafetal Santa Catalina.

. . . [There was] a black man who was Aguirre's calash driver . . . with peacock feathers symbolizing the king; and a black woman with a red sash with a black man at the animal's haunches carrying a doll in a black smock, and, if he remembers correctly, it had a white face. This same man acting as king carried a machete de cinta, and he used it to pull a cord to ring a bell . . . which sounded three times, tolling the signal calling the mayoral. When he did not appear, all those on horseback began riding around the slave quarters. Finding no one, they began to ransack the huts. At this point, another larger throng of slaves arrived on foot. They began to sing and to dance in the courtyard to the beat of three drums and several horns made from shells. Straightaway, they went into the chicken coop and began to kill birds and eat them raw, fashioning a fence and parading around inside it, the king and the queen . . .

G. Statement of Pascual, known as Ayai in his homeland, from the coffee plantation El Salvador (through an interpreter).

He was asked if he knew that to rob, kill, commit arson, and resist arrest were sins punishable everywhere by the most severe penalties. He replied, through the interpreter, that in Guinea they also kill those who kill others and commit such crimes, and that here, if it had not been for the ladinos, the bozals would not have done any harm . . .

H. Statement of Prudencio, known as Fangua in his homeland, twenty years old, from the same cafetal.

. . . Fierabrás incited all the slaves, arming them, and telling them that he was going to take them to the land of the blacks. He was not aware of any other motive for his actions, other than not allowing them to eat all they wanted, especially sweet corn, which was plentiful on the farm . . .

I. Statement of Gonzalo Mandinga, over thirty, from the same coffee plantation.

When he was asked where they were going and what the insurgent slaves proposed to do, he replied that they wanted to go to the scrubland to be free . . .

J. Statement of Romualdo, known as Churipe in his homeland, seemingly around forty years old, from the same cafetal (through an interpreter).

... two days before the uprising took place, the contramayoral Joaquín proposed to Fierabrás, capataz of the bozalons, to take everyone to the land of the blacks to be free, an idea that he had had for a long time and had not been able to carry out because of the few blacks on the farm. Now that there were many more, they would be able to take the project forward, although some whites opposed it. He assured them that nothing would happen to them even if they were killed, because he would put them in a place where they would not be able to do them any harm. Fierabrás made this proposal to the deponent and to other of his fellow slaves. They agreed to it because they wanted to be free. With this objective in mind, they mutinied on the evening of the thirteenth, at bedtime ...

K. Statement of Agustín, known as Chobó in his homeland, eighteen years old, from the same coffee plantation (through an interpreter).

... the contramayoral Joaquín spoke to him about the scheme that he had for all the slaves on the farm, together with those from other nearby farms, to mutiny and kill the whites, become free, and establish themselves in Banes ...[11]

ANC, *Miscelánea de Expedientes*, 540/B.

8.11. THE TERRIFYING REBELLION ON THE INGENIO EL TRIUNVIRATO

Santa Ana, Matanzas, November 5, 1843

A. Statement of Domingo Eusebio Madan, native of Matanzas, thirty-two years old, administrator on the ingenio El Triunvirato owned by Julián Luis Alfonso.

... [on the fifth], at about eight thirty [in the evening] the deponent was seated in the doorway of the big house along with Don Benito Manresa, the farm doctor, and Don Felipe Manresa. One group of slaves was engaged in the task of moving brick fragments needed to patch the guardarraya and another was fitting out carts for hauling firewood. One of the slaves who had been patching the road began shouting, "Seize that slave!" The deponent got up and took off running to find out what that slave was shouting about, and then that same man cried out to him, "Kid, get your master into the big house and barricade yourself there, because they have killed the mayoral." Then, the deponent returned to the house, grabbed his cutlass, and headed for the throng of slaves, accompanied by the two aforementioned individuals. But a short distance from the house he came upon the farm's mayoral, who had been wounded and was being carried by two slaves. The mayoral said to him, "Don Domingo, they have slain me." The mayoral made his way toward his quarters, which were nearby, under his own power, for the slaves who had been helping him had left.... [Once more, the same slave counseled him to go home for his own safety,] then the deponent ordered another slave to put him [the first slave] into the stocks. That slave's excessively officious manner caused the deponent to suspect him of being guilty of some sort of involvement. Straightaway, four slaves advanced, leading the biggest group of slaves, and one of them clutched the mayoral's unsheathed machete. At this, the deponent and the farm doctor hollered at them to return to the barracks. Except for the man bearing the machete, everyone else stopped short, and made a show of compliance, decidedly taking the barracks road.

The slave brandishing the machete, seeing that those who accompanied him hesitated as to whether to follow or retreat, urged them on, calling particularly to one. This was when the doctor, a cocked pistol in hand, told the slave carrying the machete that if he did not let him go, that he would shoot him. The slave replied, "Shoot." When the doctor saw the slave's impudence, he asked the deponent if he should shoot him, to which the deponent responded, keeping in mind the bad example that this seditious Negro was for the others, "Go ahead and shoot." Then the doctor [Benito] fired... but, regrettably, he missed his mark. Straightaway, the slave dealt the doctor a blow with his machete, although it was thwarted, blocked by Don Felipe, the doctor's brother, as he dealt the slave a counter blow with his machete, wounding the slave in the arm. With this, the slaves retreated...

B. Statement of Francisco Delgado, forty years old, the mayoral on the ingenio.

... on Sunday, the fifth of this month, at about eight fifteen in the evening, he was with people at the kiln in the tile works, loading some brick shards to pave the guardarraya. He felt it as they dealt him a machete blow from behind that landed on his neck, just below his right ear. He immediately fell to the ground, was rendered unconscious, and did not come to his senses until he woke to find himself near his quarters, being carried there by some slaves...

He only became mayoral on this farm three months ago. Previously, he had been an ox herd here. Between the two jobs, he had worked there altogether for a year. He swears that the slaves on this ingenio did not do chores for any more than one and a half or two hours on Sunday mornings and religious holidays, and that they only worked occasionally in the afternoons, and even then never for more than an hour. He says that the work done on that Sunday of the uprising was an exception, to prepare the guardarraya in order to allow the passage of carts hauling firewood late at night, which was being stockpiled for the sugar harvest season.

C. Statement of Zacarías, over twenty-five years old, carter, plowman, occasionally working as a contramayoral on the ingenio.

... [On Sunday] at about four in the afternoon, he was out behind the boiler house pulling weeds, along with a slave crew. They did not finish until nightfall, when they sent them to load some brick shards to use as filler for the guardarraya. As soon as that chore was finished, which would have been at about eight thirty that night, the mayoral told all the slaves, "Let's go grab some food." They all made for the refinery courtyard, and the deponent was one of those in the forefront. Shortly after getting underway, he heard a voice behind him saying, "Get back!" The deponent turned his head and saw the slave Bonifacio, proceeding with great strides at the head of the throng of slaves, carrying the mayoral's machete. Upon seeing this, the deponent began to run toward the house to warn the administrator ... [then] he took off in search of the patrol commander to inform him of what was going on ... and it was he who ordered the deponent to remain there until morning ...

D. Statement of Ramon Lucumí, twenty years old, and ox herd on the ingenio Triunvirato.

... the deponent had been a sentry at the trapiche for some seven weeks. ... it was at some point after midnight when Bonifacio Gangá showed up there. The deponent asked him what it was that he was looking for at that hour. Eduardo and Nicolás, both Gangás, and Zoilo and Ulpiano, both Lucumís, also suddenly appeared. This aroused his suspicions, and he interrogated them once again, telling him that "if you come to steal, watch out, because [I] am on guard duty." Then, Zoilo tried to ring the bell, but the deponent stood his ground. He went at once to report this incident to Narciso, the contramayoral. The latter arranged for him to fetch the slaves Filomeno, Nazario, Bartolo, and Diego in order to seize those people. The four slaves came along with the deponent, and, when they saw the persons involved, one of the four cried "Don't touch them!" ...

E. Statement of Nicolas Gangá, over twenty-five, carter, field hand at the ingenio.

... planning for the rebellion began some two months ago ... [the meetings] were in different places, sometimes in the huts, other times in the cane fields, sometimes in the sugar mill, and sometimes in the very fields where they were working.... The purpose and objective of the uprising were to go to the farms, gather together the greatest possible number of slaves, make war on the whites, become free, and not do any work...

F. Statement of Manuel Gangá, over twenty-five, cartwright and field hand.

... the slaves Eduardo, Bonifacio, and Santiago, the leader, encouraged the others to abandon the farm and go off to the ingenio El Acana.... [They came upon] the farm manager on the road, and he said to the slave Bonifacio, who was in the lead, "What is this, Bonifacio, what are you going to do?" and the slave responded, "I come to fight you."... the slaves reaching the ingenio's outer limits... making sure that the slave Bonifacio and others out in front shouted upon leaving the ingenio, "Fellow slaves, let's go to El Acana to kill whites and to look for more people."... When the people arrived at that ingenio and were gathered around the bell post, the slave Cristóbal Lucumí made an appeal to all the slaves there on that farm to come and join forces with them. Those from the infirmary were the first to do so, and then some of those who lived in the huts agreed to join them as well. Altogether, about half of all the slaves on the ingenio joined forces with the insurgents. Then and there... they made for the big house, which they found locked. They tried to force the door, finding it easier said than done. A slave from the ingenio El Acana, who stood out because he had lost his left hand, appeared. He was toting large baskets for them to load with bagasse [as tinder] to set fire to the house. He also brought a firebrand for this purpose. Just then, the slave Cristóbal from El Triunvirato broke into [the house] through the window, repeatedly knocking it in using a watering trough [as a battering ram]. By this time, they had piled the bagasse up against at the door.... [Upon entering, Bonifacio killed a white man who had assaulted him, and then they killed another who put up no resistance.] Straightaway, they saw two women behind the bed, one seated and the other squatting next to her, with a small child, not yet weaned, at her feet. The slave Nicolás approached the women, and killed them then and there with his machete. The slave Santiago killed the child.... [They set fire to the factories on El Acana] and the slave Cristóbal from El Triunvirato set fire to the slaves' hovels, saying "Because those inside the huts did not want to join [us], we are burning their pigsties"...

The ringleaders ordered the entire group of rebel slaves to set off toward the ingenio La Concepción to kill whites and assemble the slave force.

... When they arrived at La Concepción, they came in by way of the street through the slave quarters. They did not find any slaves until they passed by their kitchen, where they found a slave named Julio, a Gangá, who joined them. Later, upon passing by the door of the purging house, they found a group of some eight to ten slave women standing around, who also joined them. The rebels asked the slave women where the mayoral and the rest of the whites on the farm stayed. They responded that all of them had gone off on horseback.... Because this ingenio was deserted, the ringleaders gave orders to continue on to the ingenio San Miguel [where they found only one white man in the courtyard, and he fled].... immediately thereafter, they spoke to the slaves there on the farm, who had been locked in the purging house, encouraging them to join forces with them and abandon the farm.... everyone who had been locked in the [purging] house came out and formed ranks, according to their custom, but separate from the rebels. At this, the slave Cristóbal harangued those from San Miguel to join them. They replied that they were going to their huts to gather up their clothes, and that they would return. Very few actually did so, those who remained sent a message that they would follow them at daylight.

Then the rebels ordered them to begin the march for the ingenio San Rafael, and, in order to avoid any further delay, the deponent and the others decided not to take the time to set fire to the factories on San Miguel, leaving those bringing up the rear to do it instead. Passions unloosed, they went on to the ingenio San Lorenzo with the same purpose in mind. Once they arrived there, they heard that all the slaves on that ingenio had run off into the canebrake. The rebels called out to them to stop and not to hide. Out behind the building containing the fornalla, they saw a group of white men on horseback. The rebels advanced to attack them, but everyone in the group turned tail and took off running. Then, seeing that no one was joining forces with them, they decided to turn toward San Rafael. Cristóbal broke away, on the one hand urging the slaves onward, and then remained behind to set fire to the bagasse house, which was what he did.

... They continued traveling until [they reached] the ingenio San Rafael, finding the slaves from that farm gathered together in the house. Bonifacio, the deponent, and the others asked where the whites were, and they replied that everyone had gone to the little town of Santa Ana. The rebel slaves urged the slaves from San Rafael to follow them, but they responded that they were going back to take their clothing to the huts, and never came back, and no one knew where they were hidden. That was when the rebels paused in the factory courtyard for the purpose of awaiting those who were coming up from behind and to rest a little. In their repose, they were attacked from several different directions at once by a troop of cavalry and some countrymen. They completely dispersed all of the mutinous slaves. The deponent only remembered seeing Bonifacio die at the hands of a soldier. . . . [The rebels] had their work machetes, some long ones, and almost all of the Lucumí slaves carried leather hides as shields. Narciso had one of the pistols that they took away from the farm carpenter. Nicolás carried a long iron pole as a lance. They had no banners and no more than two war drums . . .

. . . The ringleaders spoke to the deponent sometime last September about their plan to wreak havoc. The deponent asked them what they intended to accomplish by creating such a tumult. They responded that they did not want to tell him until it was imminent, because he was a slave of long standing there on the farm [and might betray them]. He does not know whether the ringleaders were talking to outsiders when they would go out along the roads adjoining the farm on Sundays . . .

G. Statement of Gonzalo Lucumí, older than twenty-five, mason on the ingenio.

. . . [He went to alert the mayoral on El Acana of the uprising, and that is when he was surprised by the sudden arrival of the mutineers. Then he went into the house with the whites.] . . . he peaked out and told them what the doctor asked him to. The slave Cirilo Lucumí from El Triunvirato responded, "[W]hat they wanted were the whites' machetes and so they would not kill them." At the same time, the slaves Bonifacio, Santiago, and Narciso, also from El Triunvirato, shouted at him, "Hi, you are the whites' snitch, eh. Well, we will kill you as well." . . . he is sure that the slave who was beating the drum was Adán Gangá, from the ingenio El Triunvirato . . .

H. Statement of Adriano Gangá, over twenty-five, coppersmith and field hand, from the ingenio El Acana, with a work force of 270 slaves, owned by José Eusebio Alfonso.

. . . the slaves from El Triunvirato arrived at the slave quarters making a great deal of racket, flinging open the doors to all their rooms, ordering them to get up and join them. Then they [the slaves from El Acana] came out, and asked what was going on. Their [the slaves from El Triunvirato] response was, "Let's go make war and kill the whites. We already have killed the mayoral on our ingenio." The deponent and most of the rest of the slaves there on the farm, tremendously affected by the rebels' evil intent, replied that they in no way shared their intentions, and they began to scatter out into the canebrakes. . . . At that time, seventeen slaves had been locked up for having attempted to escape. One of these was named Adán, a Lucumí, and he began to shout, imploring the mutineers for help. [When the rebels became] aware of their clamors, they immediately forced their way into the room, released the prisoners, and took them over to the mayoral's house. They already had the house surrounded, and they proceeded to remove the prisoners' bonds. . . . [The deponent and a fellow slave, Eleuterio,] found the mayoral's two daughters, one wounded and the other unharmed, who were fleeing from a group of slaves that was pursuing them. The deponent and his companion saw that, and they each grabbed one of them [the girls]. The deponent carried his (the wounded one) to the pigsty belonging to the sentry for the banana grove and covered her with fronds from that tree. The deponent led his [girl, uninjured] to a place where there was a horse, helped her mount it, and took her to where the mayoral was. . . . The mayordomo, his wife, and a child, the mayoral's nephew, the carpenter's sister, and another woman who was a stranger to him [were assassinated on El Acana] . . .

I. Statement of Juliana Criolla, twenty years old, from the ingenio El Acana.

. . . [She was in the infirmary because she was tending to a child], and the deponent and the rest of the women were waiting for their husbands to tell them what to do. In effect, the deponent's husband arrived (Juan de la Cruz Gangá) along with other husbands from the farm. They told them to go to a place, La Sidra, right next door to this ingenio . . .

J. Statement of Camila Criolla, twenty years old, assistant in the infirmary on El Acana.

. . . She saw and heard the black woman Fermina, one of this ingenio's slaves, telling them that the whites were escaping over there. Right away, she observed that Fermina was approaching the banana grove, ordering some slaves around, and telling them, "Grab this fat white man and hit him with your machete. He is the one who puts us in irons." The deponent believed that [Fermina] was referring to the farm's mayoral . . .

K. Statement of Marina Criolla, eighteen years old, field hand on El Acana, and wife of Fabián Carabalí.

. . . When she went to the front of the house under attack, she saw the slave woman Fermina calling a Lucumí slave, known in his homeland as Uyó, and she was loudly shouting for a sledgehammer to remove the shackles from the slaves who were imprisoned on this farm . . .

L. Statement of Anastasio Mina, over twenty-five, field hand on the ingenio San Lorenzo owned by José Alfonso and Martina García.

... The rebels appealed to those on that ingenio to join forces with them in their undertaking to kill whites and be free in order to work no more as slaves. The slaves on this farm, well informed of their true situation and their duties toward their masters, told them that they were not going with them under any circumstances, because they were well dressed and well fed and they did not want a ruckus of any kind ...

The slaves on the farm work willingly, without complaint, because they are good and he never heard them engage in discussions about disturbing the peace on the farm ...

M. Statement of Mariano Gangá, over twenty-five, field hand on the ingenio San Rafael with forty-nine slaves, owned by Blas Cuesta.

... He was sleeping in his hut like everyone else when the master called him. He got up, and the master told [the slaves] that wicked people were coming to set fire to the houses, the huts, and the pigpens. If they were able, they should resist them and not allow them to do any such thing on this farm. They immediately went to the factory courtyard, and from there they could already make out the fire at San Lorenzo. On seeing this, they resolved to defend the interests of their master and themselves to the death. They advanced to meet the aggressors, but as they were only a few men and they saw a large mob of mutineers approaching the ingenio, they had to cede ground and retreat to the ingenio factories. The rebels entered the factory courtyard from two different directions. Some tried to put a torch to the bagasse houses, and others wanted to enter the master's big house, but the ingenio's slaves were able to dissuade them, offering to follow them in their undertaking, just as the mutineers had hoped. At this, the rebels continued their spree, abandoning the ingenio, coming to rest quite a distance from there. At almost the same time, the troop of cavalry and many other compatriots on horseback arrived and went through the ingenio, engaging the rebels in battle, inflicting many casualties ...[12]

ANC, *Comisión Militar*, 30/3.

8.12. AN ABORTED GENERAL INSURRECTION

Cimarrones, February 16, 1844

A. Statement of Ramón Criollo, field hand on the ingenio La Luisa, owned by Baró y Barraqué:

... they seized him today at dawn, and he imagined that it was due to the attempted slave uprising on the farm, of which he was to be a leader.

... They intended to do it on Wednesday of this week, at midnight. The main conspirators were Desiderio Criollo, Anselmo Carabalí, and Ignacio Lucumí. They were going to fight and kill all the whites on the ingenio, even the master. The following individuals came to Manuel Carabalí's hut on several different evenings: Agustín Jiménez, freedman, sawyer, middle-aged, regular build, thick beard, resident of Palo Seco; Agustín, oriental-looking mulatto, sawyer, who lived and worked with the latter, and lives with him, promised to supply firearms and gunpowder; Julián, another Negro, also a sawyer, who lived with the black woman Mercedes in the same place in Palo Seco; Guadalupe, another Negro, had worked on La Conchita; another a black farmer, an associate of Güelche, regular build, toothy, whose name he did not know.

Those were the men who met in Manuel's hut. They advised them to go in the direction of Sierra Morena, where there was a road that would take them to a place where they could embark directly for Guarico (Haiti), killing all the whites they possibly could. They told them that the slaves on the ingenios El Atrevido, La Conchita, Genes, El Toro, Cuabalejo, and many others he did not recall were going to do the same. Nine months ago, while he was with his fellow slave Desiderio in Matanzas, where their master had sent them, the freedman Cirilo Reyes, a mason, spoke with them and counseled them about their escape and flight. No one else was involved ...

B. Statement of Desiderio Criollo, field hand, from the same ingenio.

... the objective was to kill his master and all the other whites on the farm, to escape by way of Macagua, the La Palma river, and embark for Santo Domingo, killing all the whites they met along the way. ... The red banner that Ramón was to have carried was in Anselmo's hut ...

C. Confession of Antonio Criollo, contramayoral on the ingenio Santa Ana, owned by Pablo Antonio de Salas.

... León Lucumí, Rafael Mina, and Remigio Lucumí intended to do it, they were the leaders. José Lucumí, from the big house, and the deponent also were involved in this affair. They were going to mutiny for the purpose of killing their master and his entire family, along with the rest of the hired help there on the farm. ... The free Chinese sawyer Agustín Jiménez, who worked on this ingenio about four months ago, talked to them about the uprising, advised them to be insubordinate, and promised to bring them store-bought trinkets, so that, when the situation presented itself, they could count on their fellow slaves. Perico Criollo, slave from the ingenio El Asiento, also used to come to that farm for the same purpose, and when he could not get there, he stayed in the tile works and sent for León and Rafael to talk. The freedman José Criollo, who was employed as a plowman on the ingenio, used to tell them that they were nobody's fools, that they should fight, kill, and get away . . .

D. Statement of Tiburcio Criollo, married, works with roof maker on the ingenio El Asiento owned by José María Morales Sotolongo.

He was asked which blacks in the area regularly would come to the tile works, and he responded that usually it was Ambrosio Carabalí, from the ingenio El Atrevido, and Gerónimo Lucumí and Baldomero, also a Lucumí, from the ingenio Pichardo. The first one would come to look for earthen cooking vessels and the others to visit black women. . . . One night, when the deponent was there, five or six slaves from El Atrevido came on down, and he heard them talking about the uprising . . . that must have been three or four months ago. The Negro Perico Carabalí, freedman, formerly a slave on this farm, spoke to him several times in the tile works about the uprising. He advised him that his master's slaves should join forces with those from the rest of the farms to rebel, kill the whites, and become the owners of the land themselves. Sometimes Melchor Naranjo, free moreno sawyer, would come looking for him at his hut with the same purpose in mind. He thinks that it was Ramón Gangá, the tile maker from La Luisa, who also would come around about the same time of day, and the mulatto Antonio, who had a position working on Don José Pérez's carts . . .

E. Confession of Román Lucumí, appearing to be about thirty-five years old, single, and worker on the ingenio San José owned by Isabel Caballero:

. . . Patricio Lucumí and Eusebio Lucumí from El Atrevido found him in the scrub looking for bejuco. They told him that he should look for [things to make some] magic charms for them and that they were thinking about rising up to fight against the whites. . . . He scraped the root of the *pendejera* bush [*Solanum gersifolium*], yerba root, bitter broom, a root from the *yaya* [annonaceous plant native to the Antillas] tree. He ground all these leaves and put them into a leather pouch that he had sewn and took it to the ingenio El Atrevido, where he sold it to those slaves . . .

F. Statement of Telésforo Lucumí, about fifty-five years old, from the same ingenio:

. . . [No freedman] brought any witchcraft, for the deponent was the very person who made them up to sell . . . making them from the roots from the *yagruma* [tree native to Cuba belonging to the araliaceas family] and yaya trees. He would put them into a little cow's horn and he would wrap it up in a piece of leather that he would sew. He had sold them to the slaves from the ingenio El Toro . . . so that they would be able to do battle and fight better. He does not remember how many charms he sold, since the slaves did not want to pay him for them until the actual uprising . . .

G. Statement of Félix Mina, who denies that he is a Mina and states for the record that he is Cuban born, thirty years old, single, and a field hand from the ingenio San Ramón, owned by Petrona Milián:

. . . [They were going to rise up for the purpose] of killing the whites and becoming free . . . those from this plantation were going to join forces with those from El Olimpo, La [sic] Ceres, El Asesor, currently the property of Cándido Ruiz and Don Ignacio Hernández, and San José owned by Barbería. Cristóbal Gangá, chief captain, told them that it was best to leave the moment the town of Cimarrones was taken, because it was easier to kill whites there in town than to lie in wait for them in the rural countryside . . .

H. Confession of Cristóbal Gangá, about forty years old, single, from the same ingenio.

. . . Ángel Gangá, Lorenzo Mandinga, Isidro Lucumí, Félix Criollo, and myself were captains in charge of persuading the rest of the slaves there [on the farm] to join forces with them when the uprising broke out. . . . their former ship mates were in the warehouses near the Camino de Hierro . . . (and among them Mateo Lucumí who) told them that he and those from the Camino de Hierro had their people ready . . .

I. Confession of Ángel Gangá, fifty years old, single, from the same ingenio.

. . . The black referred to as Santiago Carabalí came around at the very end of milling season, looking for an earthen pot of honey in the boiler house. He told them that he was already free, thank God! The whites would not mess with him anymore. He had a witchdoctor, you bet, to hassle the whites, and they, in turn, could neither catch him nor do him any harm . . .

J. Statement of Benito Carabalí, fifty-five years old, single, field hand on the ingenio Ceres, owned by the Delmonte family.

. . . his fellow slaves Francisco Lucumí and Antonio Abad told them that they were going to mutiny. Some slaves from neighboring ingenios would come to that farm some nights . . . they all were in touch with one another to get together over Lent and to do battle with the whites. Some months ago, another fellow slave, Francisco Lucumí, stole a black cow from his master and gave it to the slaves from Brufao, and a hog as well, in order to buy implements of war . . .

K. Confession of Cornelio Congo, thirty years old, from the same ingenio.

(Francisco Lucumí) told him repeatedly that his master was always overburdening him with a great deal of work. This was the reason he wanted to kill his master and rebel. When the whites came with shotguns to shoot them, that was when they would advance upon them and use their machetes to take away their shotguns. They were to sit tight and not run away at the first shot, [so as] to fearlessly fall upon them as one . . .

L. Statement of Francisco Mina, thirty-two years old, field hand on the ingenio Asunción, owned by Cándido Ruiz.

. . . Pancho Gangá was the king, and the deponent was the chief captain. . . . they were going to confirm [the uprising] the very same night that the judge . . . came and seized them [March 4]. After they killed all the whites on the farm, they were going to set fire to the sugarcane and the factories. Everyone was going to leave by way of the Camino de Hierro that cuts through the farm in order to join up with other slaves, and continue fighting against the whites . . .

M. Statement of Longino Lucumí, thirty years old, field hand on the ingenio La Rosa, owned by Cristóbal Madan.

. . . Jorge, Napoleón Lucumí, and Hilario were those who had advised his master's slave to rebel. Hilario and Napoleón wanted to go fight last year,[13] when the slaves were waging war in Bemba. . . . Napoleón was the captain of the Lucumís, and everyone did what he said. Jorge was the leader of the Gangás . . .

N. Confession of Jorge Gangá, twenty-eight years old, field hand on the same ingenio.

. . . every Sunday that year, he was in La Cumbre, near Matanzas, where his master had taken him for medical treatment. The mulatto Perico Criollo, his master's calash driver, used to talk to him on those occasions. He would tell him that the slaves on the ingenio El Triunvirato had risen up, along with those from other farms, and had killed the whites. What were those slaves on the ingenio La Rosa doing? Why, they must be numbskulls, good-for-nothings. The mulattoes and the freedmen were going to get involved in fighting the whites, and they would become the landowners. . . . Shortly after arriving, while working one night in the boiler room, Miguel Prado, moreno freedman, came to see him, and told him that the slaves there on the farm were prepared to fight. What were they waiting for? Didn't they know about the slaves fighting over on the ingenio Alcancía . . .[14]

ANC, *Comisión Militar*, 33/1.

Notes

INTRODUCTION

1. For a description of this process, see Instituto de Historia de Cuba, *Historia de Cuba: La Colonia, Evolución socioeconómica y formación nacional de los orígins hasta 1867* (Havana: Editora Política, 1994), chap. 6.

2. Francisco de Arango y Parreño, *Obras* (Havana: Publicaciones de la Dirección de Cultura del Ministerio de Educación, 1952), vol. 1, 13.

3. For an analysis of the continued importance of the island's slave trade, see José Antonio Saco, *Historia de la esclavitud desde los tiempos más remotos hasta nuestros días*, 2nd ed. (Havana: Editorial Alfa, 1944), vol. 5. Also see Hubert H. S. Aimes, *A History of Slavery in Cuba, 1511 to 1868* (New York: G. P. Putnam's Sons, 1907), chaps. 3 and 4.

4. Philip D. Curtin, *The Atlantic Slave Trade: A Census* (Madison: University of Wisconsin Press, 1970). María del Carmen Barcia reproduces several estimates of that trade. See her *Burguesía esclavista y abolición* (Havana: Editorial de Ciencias Sociales, 1987), 161–62.

5. José Luciano Franco, *Comercio clandestino de esclavos* (Havana: Editorial de Ciencias Sociales, 1980), 389.

6. Juan Pérez de la Riva's *El barracón y otros ensayos* (Havana: Editorial de Ciencias Sociales, 1975) is a collection of several of his works on the traffic in Chinese laborers.

7. The Güines population rosters are available for consultation in the Archivo Nacional de Cuba (hereafter ANC), *Gobierno Superior Civil*, 862/29188.

8. Table 4 includes the parishes of Batabanó, El Cano, Güines, Managua, Río Blanco, and Guanabacoa, all located in the vicinity of Havana.

9. The theoretical literature on the plantation system, as is well known, is extremely far flung, and we cannot do justice to all the notable contributions over the past forty years in a mere footnote.

10. The physical deterioration of this document made it extremely difficult to read some of the numbers. For this reason the totals in table 6 do not coincide with the original. The original table shows totals of 235 established ingenios, 309 newly established operations, and 1,142 cafetals, worked by a total of 111,232 slaves. Be advised that the figures are not precise because the parishes of Matanzas, Río Blanco, and Remedios did not remit their respective documentation on tithing.

11. Manuel Moreno Fraginals, *El ingenio; el complejo económico social cubano del azúcar* (Havana: Editorial de Ciencias Sociales, 1978).

12. ANC, *Miscelánea de Expedientes*, 629/Af. See also chapter 3, document 3.2, "The hacendado Jacinto González Larrinaga explains his methods. San Antonio de los Baños, April 14, 1842."

13. Ibid.

14. ANC, *Miscelánea de Expedientes*, 609/R.

15. In 1837 Francisquillo was sentenced to eight years in prison. He was to be auctioned off upon his release in order to pay court costs.

16. In Eugene D. Genovese's landmark work on slavery, *Roll, Jordan, Roll: The World the Slave Made* (New York: Vintage Books, 1976), he documents the proactive role the slaves themselves played in the formation of such a system.

17. See Pérez de la Riva's essay "Barracón" in his collected works, *El barracón y otros ensayos*. Also see Moreno Fraginals, *El ingenio*, vol. 2.

18. Statement of Clemente Díaz, assistant sugar master, ANC, *Gobierno Superior Civil*, 941/33163.

19. Ibid.

20. ANC, *Comsión Militar*, 27/3.

21. Esteban Pichardo, *Diccionario provincial casi razonado de voces y frases cubanas* (Havana: Editorial de Ciencias Sociales, 1976). The book originally was published in 1836.

22. This was deduced from Rosa Lucumí's statement in the suit initiated in 1842, ANC, *Comsión Militar*, 28/2.

23. Herbert G. Gutman, *The Black Family in Slavery and Freedom, 1750–1925* (Oxford: Basil Blackwell, 1976).

24. ANC, *Miscelánea de Expedientes*, 267/M. The confession is reproduced in chapter 5, document 5.12, "Pedro Criollo confesses to the murder of his sweetheart, María del Rosario Gangá. Pipián, April 2, 1837."

25. ANC, *Comisión Militar*, 1/3, 4, 5. See chapter 8, document 8.9, "Insurrection on the coffee plantations of Matanzas. June 1825."

26. ANC, *Gobierno Superior Civil*, 1056/37612. See chapter 6, document 6.11, "Pedro Criollo buys his freedom and wants to continue working on the ingenio. Havana, July 13, 1864."

27. ANC, *Asuntos Políticos*, 12/9, suit of 1812.

28. ANC, *Miscelánea de Expedientes*, 113/Ad.

29. ANC, *Asuntos Políticos*, 135/15.

30. ANC, *Comisión Militar*, 29/5.

31. Ibid.

32. It is curious that in the rural countryside there is no reference to "godmothers." In cities, on the other hand, those relations were explicit, especially in cases presented to the *capitanía general* (captaincy general).

33. See chapter 3, document 3.3, "Excerpts from the slave code, November 14, 1842," Article 25, and, also, the circular dated July 20, 1843, reiterating the obligatory nature of its observance in ANC, *Gobierno Superior Civil*, 942/33246.

34. Ibid. and Pérez de las Riva, *El barracón y otros ensayos*.

35. See chapter 3, document 3.1, "Survey by Captain General Gerónimo Valdés, Havana. February 23, 1842."

36. Letter to the Captain General, August 15, 1843, in ANC, *Miscelánea de Expedientes*, 3585/Cu.

37. Ibid., letter, August 19, 1843.

38. ANC, *Gobierno Superior Civil*, 1056/37607.

39. See Julia Ward Howe, *A Trip to Cuba* (Boston: Ticknor and Fields, 1860), 75.

40. Among other authors it is worthwhile to consult are Genovese, *Roll, Jordan, Roll*; Richard Hart, *Esclavos que abolieron la esclavitud* (Havana: Casa de las Américas, 1984); and Gabriel Debien, "La nourriture des esclaves sur les plantations des Antilles françaises aux XVIIe et XVIIIe siècles," *Caribbean Studies* 4, no. 2 (July 1964): 3–27.

41. See Abiel Abbot, *Cartas; escritas en el interior de Cuba, entre las montañas de Arcana en el este, y las de Cusco, al oeste, en los meses de febrero, marzo, abril, y mayo de 1828* (Havana: Consejo Nacional de Cultura, 1965), 5.

42. See files concerning the development of security policies for slaves in *Real Consulado de Agricultura, Industria, y Comercia o Junta de Fomento*, 184/8330.

43. ANC, *Gobierno Superior Civil*, 941/33186, letter to the captain general, May 19, 1842. See chapter 3, document 3.2, "The hacendado Jacinto González Larrinaga explains his methods. San Antonio de los Baños, April 14, 1842."

44. ANC, *Comisión Militar*, 46/3, Testimonio de 1844.

45. See Abbot, *Cartas*, 211–12.

46. José Luciano Franco, *Los palenques de los negros cimarrones* (Havana: Departamento de Orientación Revolucionaria, 1973). The work comments on the relations between bands of runaways with slaves from both ingenios and cafetals.

47. ANC, *Gobierno Superior Civil*, 616/19688. See chapter 8, document 8.5, "Account by Francisco (Pancho) Mina, captain of the maroons. Cayajabos, August 31, 1835."

48. Arango y Parreño, *Obras*, vol. 2, 218–19.

49. ANC, *Intendencia de Hacienda*, 960/3.

50. Ibid.

51. See Herbert S. Klein, *Slavery in the Americas: A Comparative Study of Virginia and Cuba* (London: Oxford University Press, 1967), 199.

52. See in this respect the suggestive study of Leslie F. Manigat, "The Relationship between Marronage and Slave Revolts and Revolution in St. Domingue-Haiti," in *Comparative Perspectives on Slavery in New World Plantation Societies*, ed. V. Rubin and A. Tuden (New York: New York Academy of Sciences, 1977), 420–38.

53. Gabino La Rosa Corzo, *Los cimarrones de Cuba* (Havana: Editorial de Ciencias Sociales, 1988). Another source for the reconstruction of escape attempts on a month-by-month basis is the administrative farm records or the records kept by individual mayorals, but these lack the systematization of the fugitive slave register.

54. Pedro Deschamps Chapeaux, *Los cimarrones urbanos* (Havana: Editorial de Ciencias Sociales, 1983).

55. See chapter 8, document 8.7, "The inhabitants of El Cedro talk about Palenque life."

56. See chapter 8, document 8.3, "The mulatto Dámaso sails for Mexico and freedom. Santiago de Cuba, September 6, 1864."

57. ANC, *Gobierno Superior Civil*, 96/34036. José Bibián was apprehended on April 15, 1864, aboard a British vessel about to go out to sea. He was detained on the pontoon Ebro until his owner claimed him. According to the functionary reporting on the case, José fled once again and "was found the next morning on another British ship that was about to set sail, which proves his intention to leave the island for abroad was premeditated."

58. See Pedro Deschamps Chapeaux, *El negro in la economía habanera del siglo XIX* (Havana: UNEAC, 1971).

CHAPTER 1

1. This is a reference to the Siete Partidas, a seven-part medieval legal code compiled by Alfonso X the Learned of Castile. Translator.

2. A residence trial was a legal process by which all public officials had to justify their acts at the end of their tenure. Translator.

CHAPTER 2

1. Torn in the original.
2. Torn in the original.
3. Torn in the original.
4. Torn in the original.
5. Torn in the original.
6. Torn in the original.
7. Torn in the original.
8. Torn in the original.
9. Torn in the original.
10. Torn in the original.
11. Torn in the original.
12. Torn in the original.
13. Torn in the original.
14. Torn in the original.
15. Torn in the original.
16. Torn in the original. Probably "tobacco." Translator.
17. Torn in the original.
18. Torn in the original.
19. Torn in the original.
20. Torn in the original.
21. Torn in the original.
22. Torn in the original.
23. Torn in the original.
24. Torn in the original.

25. Torn in the original.
26. Torn in the original.
27. Torn in the original.
28. Torn in the original.
29. Torn in the original.

30. Neither I nor any of the various persons I regularly consult could find a satisfactory translation of this term. While the compiler favors an interpretation dealing with the transmigration of souls, I tend to believe that the term is related to the literal physical transmigration from Africa to the New World, that is, the ocean passage. Alejandro de la Fuente has suggested that a proper translation requires further research. Translator.

31. Torn in the original.
32. Torn in the original.
33. Torn in the original.

CHAPTER 3

1. The circular was sent to the following hacendados: Domingo Aldama, José Manuel Carillo, Count de la Fernandina, Joaquín Gómez, Jacinto González Larrinaga, Ignacio Herrera, Patricio de Laguardia, Sebastián de Lasa, Marqués de Arcos, Juan Montalvo, Joaquín Muñoz Izaguirre, Rafael O'Farril, and Wenceslao Villaurrutia.

CHAPTER 4

1. The case concluded with the return of the slave to his master for punishment, and the owner paid court costs.

2. On September 7, in 1835, a doctor at Havana's Real Hospital de San Juan de Díos reported that Juan Gualberto died of ague. Rita was sent to the infirmary, where she gave birth to a baby girl.

3. See translator's preface on the translation of racial terms. Translator.

4. There is no resolution noted in the file.

5. There is no resolution noted in the file.

6. She presented her petition again on December 18, 1837, and February 13, 1838, until she finally prevailed the following month, when her daughter was sold to a new owner.

7. Romualdo paid 350 pesos to the syndic, but her owners asked for 450. On December 1, Damiana Macuá obtained her papers.

8. Sobrado continued to appeal, and on June 27 the captain general reported that "the syndic has thrown the case out without further comment." There is no resolution noted in the file.

9. There is no resolution of the case in the file.

10. The secretariat of the captain general forwarded the suit to the syndic for resolution.

11. On December 24, the syndic Francisco de Goyri informed the captain general that the matter had been concluded to the satisfaction of the interested parties.

12. The secretariat of the captain general forwarded the case to the syndic Miguel de Estorch, who had processed the first petition, "recommending that the matter be attended to with the utmost dispatch."

13. There is no resolution of the case in the file.

14. There is no resolution of the case in the file.

15. On June 14, the secretariat of the captain general refused to grant Palomino's petition. According to baptismal documents, the child was born on October 23, 1843, in Guatao, to Petrona Medina, slave belonging to Josefa de León, and her father was unknown.

16. On September 14, she resubmitted her petition but was told that this petition was a legal matter between the buyer and seller and not a matter for the Gobierno Superior Civil.

17. The government secretariat ordered that the syndic report and proceed according to regulations.

18. This was an obligatory review of certain sentences by a higher court. Translator.

19. See translator's preface on racial terms. Translator.

20. See translator's preface on racial terms. Translator.

21. According to what can be deduced from the notes in the file, on April 11, the petitioner stated her demand once more, until, at long last, in August, she was granted her son's certificate of manumission for less than nine hundred pesos, due to a persistent ulcer on one leg.

22. The petition, as was standard practice at the time, was forwarded to one of the syndics in the capital for review. Nevertheless, given that Valenzuela did not leave her address nor the name and address of her owner, the suit remained unsettled.

23. The file abruptly ends with a letter from the syndic from Santa María del Rosario in which he throws doubt on Valerio's statement and added that the latter had a permit to look for another master and that, as of September 2, still had not returned to his master.

24. There is no resolution noted in the file.

25. The syndic Antonio María de Zayas said that the slave did not wish to be appraised.

26. Carlota Polo returned to court on October 18, November 15, and, lastly, December 4. Meanwhile, the syndic reported on November 7 that the master had the right to send his female slave to give birth wherever he chose and that, "according to information that I have been able to acquire confidentially, one of the owners of the hardware store located on the corner of San Rafael Street and Aguila got Asunción pregnant while she worked there when she had been hired out by her master. Not satisfied with the harm that this punishable offense would cause Mr. Meireles, it was he who gave the twenty-five pesos to the negress Carlota to redeem the freedom of the unborn child and make it appear that it was she who was behind the claim filed with the government." Carlota Polo's petition is rejected by the secretariat.

27. There is no resolution noted in the file.

28. The syndic, in another report, said that on September 14, Dimas paid eighteen ounces of gold in order to free his mother. Acosta said that she was appraised on the

ingenio, and the court ruled in favor of the syndic in the sense that she was brought into the city in order to do it. Dimas demonstrated that the money constituted his entire life savings and that he had used it to free his aged and ailing mother. Upon proceeding to look for her at the ingenio, Acosta replied that she was in the infirmary and did not hand her over. It was necessary to send guards to the ingenio to inquire about Lorenza's whereabouts. The inquiry included Mercedes, mother of Lorenza, who said that, three or four months before the interrogatory, her owner ordered a white man to take her to Havana. Confidentially, it was learned from neighbors that the negress was at the ingenio La Rosa in Cimarrones. She was found there on March 18, 1867. On March 27, she obtained her certificate of manumission for three hundred pesos.

CHAPTER 5

1. In Cuba in particular, slaves had a great fear of dogs, who were used to viciously hunt them down like prey. See Demoticus Philalethes, "Hunting the Maroons with Dogs in Cuba," in *Maroon Societies: Rebel Slave Communities in the Americas*, ed. Richard Price (Garden City, N.Y.: Anchor Press, 1973), 49–59. Translator.

2. Feliciano was sentenced to twenty-five lashes and ordered shackled for six months. The thirteen others were given the same number of lashes and ordered shackled for three months.

3. In general, planting should be done in cool, cloudy weather. The best seedlings are those with a straight taproot. Larger seedlings also grow more slowly. For a review of the labor issues peculiar to tobacco operations, see chapter 2, paragraph beginning "Regarding Chapter II," to review growers' concerns. Translator.

4. As a rule, it is always better to transplant smaller rather than larger seedlings. Larger plants must have a much larger root ball and require a greater amount of rain than smaller seedlings. Thus, unless there is sufficient rain, the larger plants tend to wither. This is the reason for the planting instructions. Translator.

5. The hands need to be careful not to remove the soil from the root ball. Hard soil may stubbornly adhere to the delicate roots and damage them. Translator.

6. Álvarez was a free pardo. The judge criticized him for violating the regulations that disallow persons of color from occupying such posts.

7. Benigno was condemned to six years in shackles. Víctor, Gregorio Viví, and Canuto were sentenced to four years in shackles. The rest of those implicated received a year in shackles and were assigned the most grueling jobs on the plantation.

8. Nicolás, Francisco, and Esperanza were condemned to two hundred lashes each, sentenced to serve ten years in prison in Africa, and permanently exiled. Ambrosio, José María, Fernando, and Federico were sentenced to be bound and shackled for six years, and received fifty lashes apiece. The same fate, except the floggings, awaited Dionisio and Adolfo. Geraldo was to be bound and shackled for two years. The slaves Fermín, Carlos, and Pablo died in jail during the legal proceedings.

9. There is no resolution in the file.

10. The death was ruled a suicide. The file contains no statements from the slaves.

11. Ceferino was sentenced to hard labor and four years in prison.

12. It says in the case file that Francisco's real name was Antonio de la Cruz (alias Chico) and that he was Cuban born and some forty years old.

13. José del Rosario was sentenced "to suffer the usual penalty of gallows, being dragged to them, and once dead, of course, to have the executioner cut off his hand and proceed to display it publicly at the scene of the crime."

14. Boticario was sentenced to be hung by the neck until dead.

15. Claudio contracted tetanus from his machete wounds and died. He was buried on August 26.

16. Pedro was sentenced to death by means of a garrote, or strangulation with an iron collar.

17. The file abruptly ends.

18. An adviser to the governor, Ildelfonso Suárez, was of the opinion that Buenaventura and Simón should be condemned to two years in prison on that very farm, while the fiscal believes it is preferable to leave the penalty up to the hacendado.

19. There is no resolution in the file.

20. When the trial ended, Gregorio was condemned to one hundred lashes, ten years in prison in Ceuta, and then sent into exile. Genaro and Beltrán were sentenced to one hundred lashes and ten years in prison in Cuba, while Facundo and Jorge received eight years in jail. Others participating in the uprising were sentenced to fifty lashes.

CHAPTER 6

1. The court deemed a sentence of twenty-five lashes an appropriate sentence for José Antonio because, in addition to denying everything, "he has done nothing but lie, according to the statement of the slave Matías, and as other coloreds tend to mimic such behavior, it can be very detrimental for the country," resolving to impose the aforementioned punishment.

2. The syndic as well as the alcalde both agreed that Gumersinda's petition not proceed any further, given that it was fully within the owner's rights to set her price.

3. On December 24, the syndic at that time, Francisco de Goyri, reported to the secretariat of the captain general that, "by agreement of the parties, a permit to seek out a new master was issued to the servitor Magdalena for her coartado value of 282 pesos, obliging her to pay separately 17 pesos in back wages and an excise fee, because it was she who asked to change owners without just cause."

4. The office of the Gobierno Superior transferred the case to the syndic Miguel Estorch. There is no resolution noted in the file.

5. There is no resolution in the file.

6. The syndic, Miguel Estorch, reported that, on May 16, she was given a three-day pass. Although it was renewed for two additional days, she did not find a master. Instead of returning home, she ran away for four days until she was apprehended and sent to the

countryside as a punishment. He was of the opinion that "for now" the petition should not be granted, "mostly because Lic. José Fornaris did not seem to be prepared to purchase her."

7. The file was forwarded to the capital and decided in Galainena's favor.

8. Azcárate's petition to the government asking for authorization for him to represent Paulino was granted.

9. There is no resolution in the file.

10. The office of the captain general, upon sending the case to the syndic, stated, "Such a stance on the part of the owner, if the facts the old slave relates are true, fly in the face of humanity. For this reason, the case is forwarded to the chief syndic so that, if what the slave contends is indeed true, it is assured that the appropriate authority acknowledges the facts of the case, and, according to the slave's physical state and what regulations currently in force recommend, current moral and cultural mores favoring freedom, that he be conscientiously appraised, as has been the custom in this country; whose humanity and fundamental decency in the treatment of slaves and in the means adopted by the government with that end in mind have come to the attention of all civilized nations."

11. There is no resolution in the file.

12. The lieutenant governor of Puerto Príncipe ruled in favor of Salas, who, it was said, was a slave doing domestic service for the heirs of Agustín José de Varona, an old and sick man. Nevertheless, on October 27, the office of the Gobierno Superior Civil determined that permission must not be given "both because these subscriptions are involuntary and because they set a bad precedent."

13. The secretariat said that it was unable to rule on the case, because the black man could not be located at his stated address.

CHAPTER 7

1. The town of San Antonio de los Baños is in the jurisdiction of the province of Havana. According to the 1827 census, it had 9,346 inhabitants, 3,116 of whom were slaves.

2. The file concludes with the imprisonment of Abreu. The file does not contain the final ruling in the case.

3. The doctors said that, of the 320 slaves on the ingenio San Fernando, only 8 or 10 showed no signs of punishment, concluding that "the slaves on this plantation have been quite mistreated."

4. The doctors said the same thing concerning the second group of slaves. The cases of the owner as well as that of the employees guilty of these atrocities went to court. Hernández remained in prison until the end of the proceeding. There is no information on his sentence.

5. The indictment was passed on to the Audiencia Pretorial (Magistrate) for his consideration. No final resolution to the case was noted in the file.

6. The mayoral and the drover were found guilty of abusing the slaves on the ingenio San Rafael in Bejucal. The court sentenced them to twelve months in prison and prohib-

ited them in perpetuity from engaging in any employment which gave them the authority to discipline slaves. The culprit Andrés was sentenced to an additional six months in prison for obscene words and deeds, and another six months more for calumnies against the district's public officials, plus a fine of two hundred pesos, or, alternatively, four more months in jail. The offenders also paid court costs.

CHAPTER 8

1. Catalina was on the Iberian Peninsula with a previous owner from 1846 until late 1847. The file does not contain a final resolution to the case.

2. It appears that, at last, the master agreed to coartación. The document does not mention where he traveled in the United States. Since the journey was in 1861 and preceded the Civil War there, one must assume that they traveled somewhere in the North, where slavery had already been abolished.

3. These saints' days are celebrated on July 25 and July 25 and 26, respectively. Translator.

4. Antonio Gullón was an assistant to the port's captain, Francisco Ros.

5. His master had accused him of "contemplating an escape attempt from this city and had come up with the daring idea of embarking on one of the ships that set sail frequently from our port for abroad." Dámaso's letter was intercepted. The case caused the captain general to send a note to the French counsel, relating what had happened and begging him to take measures to prevent other similar incidents, because Dámaso boarded a French steamship belonging to the Saint Nazaire–Veracruz line.

6. There is no resolution in the file.

7. José Ildefonso Suárez, adviser to the governor, argued that it had not been proved that Pancho Mina committed any crime and, therefore, that he must be returned to his owner "to keep him in jail for four to six years so that he may serve as an example to the rest of the servitors. As soon as possible after his release, his ownership must be transferred to a neighbor or a hacendado as far away as possible from the hills of Cuzco, in order to make it both difficult and impractical to return to them." The captain general Miguel Tacón agreed with this ruling.

8. The file does not contain the sentence that was imposed.

9. The file does not include the ruling, but it is assumed that the slaves were returned to their masters.

10. The uprising's key ringleaders, Lorenzo, owned by Monsieur Sateliens, and Federico, owned by Monsieur Armitage, were both dead. Eight others were found guilty and sentenced to be shot in the back: Vicente, owned by Antonio Gómez; Guillermo, owned by Juan Fourquier; Cristóbal Gangá, owned by Samuel Taylor; Ramón Criollo, also the property of Taylor; Pedro Carabalí, owned by Monsieur Armitage; Justo Lucumí, belonging to Jorge Batle; Leisi Mina, owned by J. Fouquier; and José María Gangá, owned by A. Gómez. Many others were sentenced to shackles and tether for several years and floggings.

11. Troops killed the rebellion's three ringleaders in battle: Luis Lucumí, Joaquín Lucumí, and the man called Fierabrás. The total number of slaves who perished reached fifty-seven, while eight were sentenced to be shot in the back: Pedro the carter, Gonzalo Mandinga, Eusebio Gangá, Luis Gangá, Pascual, Romualdo, Atilano, and Hermenegildo, all Lucumís.

12. The combat on the ingenio San Rafael effectively snuffed out the rebellion. All the slaves on the ingenio Triunvirato — 240 — and some from the ingenio Arcana — 270 — participated, while the slaves on the rest of the ingenios involved did not back them up. Manuel Gangá, Narciso, Zoilo, Cirilo, Adán, and Fermina — Lucumís all — and Agustín Carabalí, Niclas Gangá, and the fugitives Cristóbal, Santiago, and Eduardo were condemned to be shot in the back. Also, two slaves each from the ingenios Triunvirato, Acana, La Concepción, and San Miguel were condemned to death, "their cadavers to be incinerated, the respective ingenio slaves and ten Negroes from each of the adjacent farms to witness their executions." A number of other slaves were condemned to lashings, shackles, and incarceration on their respective farms.

13. This alludes to the uprising that occurred in the ingenio Alcancía in the early morning hours of March 27, 1843.

14. During the course of the proceedings, the slaves Ramón and Félix, both Cuban born, Anselmo Carabalí, Antonio Abad, and the Lucumís Francisco, Hilario, and Napoleón all died. The fugitive Agustín Jiménez, José María López, Tomás Álvarez, and Pedro Morales, all freedmen, were imprisoned in Africa for ten years. The freedman Miguel Prado also was sent to Africa for four years, and Domingo Gangá and the sawyer Rafael were sent there for two years. Others, almost all slaves, were sentenced to two, four, six, eight, or ten years in prison in Cuba. The uprisings at Triunvirato and La Alcancía and the conspiracy discovered at La Luisa and other ingenios presaged the tragic episode of the conspiracy of La Escalera and the extensive repression unleashed against the black population, both slave and free.

Bibliography

Abbot, Abiel. *Cartas; escritas en el interior de Cuba, entre las montañas de Arcana, en el este, y las de Cusco, al oeste, en los meses de febrero, marzo, abril, y mayo de 1828*. Havana: Consejo Nacional de Cultura, 1965.

Acosta Saignes, Miguel. *Vida de los esclavos negros en Venezuela*. Havana: Casa de las Américas, 1978.

Aguirre Beltrán, Gonzalo. *La población negra de México*. Mexico City: Fondo de Cultura Económica, 1946.

Aimes, Hubert H. S. *A History of Slavery in Cuba, 1511 to 1868*. New York: G. P. Putnam's Sons, 1907.

Aptheker, Herbert. *Las revueltas de los esclavos negros norteamericanos*. Madrid: Siglo XX de España Editores, 1978.

Arango y Parreño, Francisco de. *Obras*. 2 vols. Havana: Publicaciones de la Dirección de Cultura del Ministerio de Educación, 1952.

Barcia, María del Carmén. *Burguesía esclavista y abolición*. Havana: Editorial de Ciencias Sociales, 1987.

Corwin, Arthur F. *Spain and the Abolition of Slavery in Cuba, 1817–1886*. Austin: University of Texas Press, 1967.

Curtin, Philip D. *The Atlantic Slave Trade: A Census*. Madison: University of Wisconsin Press, 1970.

Debien, Gabriel. "La nourriture des esclaves sur les plantations des Antilles françaises aux XVIIe et XVIIIe siècles." *Caribbean Studies* 4, no. 2 (July 1964): 3–27.

Deschamps Chapeaux, Pedro. *El negro en la economía habanera del siglo XIX*. Havana: UNEAC, 1971.

——— . *Los batallones de pardos y morenos libres*. Havana: Editorial de Arte y Literatura, 1976.

——— . *Los cimarrones urbanos*. Havana: Editorial de Ciencias Sociales, 1983.

——— . "Los negros curros." *Historia* (Publicación de la Comisión de Activistas de Historia Regional), October 10, 1972, 33–42.

Deschamps Chapeaux, Pedro, and Juan Pérez de la Riva. *Contribución a la historia de la gente sin historia*. Havana: Editorial de Ciencias Sociales, 1974.

Duharte Jiménes, Rafael. *El negro en la sociedad colonial*. Santiago de Cuba: Editorial Oriente, 1988.

Franco, José Luciano. *Comercio clandestino de esclavos*. Havana: Editorial de Ciencias Sociales, 1980.

——— . *Los palenques de los negros cimarrones*. Havana: Departamento de Orientación Revolucionaria, 1973.
Genovese, Eugene D. *Esclavitud y capitalismo*. Barcelona: Ediciones Ariel, 1971.
——— . *Roll, Jordan, Roll: The World the Slaves Made*. New York: Vintage Books, 1976.
Guerra Sánchez, Ramiro. *Manual de historia de Cuba (económica, social, y política)*. Havana: Editora del Consejo Nacional de Universidades, 1964.
Gutman, Herbert G. *The Black Family in Slavery and Freedom, 1750–1925*. Oxford: Basil Blackwell, 1976.
Hart, Richard. *Esclavos que abolieron la esclavitud*. Havana: Casa de las Américas, 1984.
Howe, Julia Ward. *A Trip to Cuba*. Boston: Ticknor and Fields, 1860.
Iduate, Juan. "Noticias sobre sublevaciones y conspiraciones de esclavos: Cafetal Salvador, 1833." *Revista de la Biblioteca Nacional José Martí*, January–August 1982, 117–52.
Instituto de Historia de Cuba. *Historia de Cuba: La Colonia; Evolución socioeconómica y formación nacional de los orígenes hasta 1867*. Havana: Editora Política, 1994.
Klein, Herbert S. *African Slavery in Latin America and the Caribbean*. New York: Oxford University Press, 1986.
——— . *Slavery in the Americas: A Comparative Study of Virginia and Cuba*. London: Oxford University Press, 1967.
Knight, Franklin W. *Slave Society in Cuba during the Nineteenth Century*. Madison: University of Wisconsin Press, 1974.
La Rosa Corzo, Gabino. *Los cimarrones de Cuba*. Havana: Editorial de Ciencias Sociales, 1988.
——— . *Los palenques del oriente de Cuba; resistencia y acoso*. Havana: Editorial Academia, 1991.
Manigat, Leslie F. "The Relationship between Marronage and Slave Revolts and Revolutions in St. Domingue-Haita." In *Comparative Perspectives on Slavery in New World Plantation Societies*, edited by V. Rubin and A. Tuden, 420–38. New York: New York Academy of Sciences, 1977.
Moreno Fraginals, Manuel. "Aportes culturales y deculturación." *Africa en América Latina*. Mexico City: Siglo XX Editores, 1977.
——— . *El ingenio; el complejo económico social cubano del azúcar*. 3 vols. Havana: Editorial de Ciencias Sociales, 1978.
Ortiz, Fernando. *Los negros curros*. Prologue and explanatory notes by Diana Iznaga. Havana: Editorial de Ciencias Sociales, 1986.
——— . *Los negros esclavos*. Havana: Editorial de Ciencias Sociales, 1975.
Pérez de la Riva, Juan. *El barracón y otros ensayos*. Havana: Editorial de Ciencias Sociales, 1975.
Pichardo, Esteban. *Diccionario provincial casi razonado de vozes y frases cubanas*. Havana: Editorial de Ciencias Sociales, 1976.
Rubin, Vera, and Arthur Tuden, eds. *Comparative Perspectives on Slavery in New World Plantation Societies*. New York: New York Academy of Sciences, 1977.

Saco, José Antonio. *Historia de la esclavitud desde los tiempos más remotos hasta nuestros días*. 2nd ed. 6 vols. Havana: Editorial Alfa, 1944. (The last two volumes are dedicated to African slavery.)

Sarracino, Rodolfo. *Los que volvieron a África*. Havana: Editorial de Ciencias Sociales, 1988.

Scott, Rebecca J. *Slave Emancipation in Cuba: The Transition to Free Labor, 1860–1899*. Princeton: Princeton University Press, 1985.

Sosa, Enrique. *La economía en la novela cubana del siglo XIX*. Havana: Editorial Letras Cubanas, 1978.

Torres-Cuevas, Eduardo, and Eusebio Reyes. *Esclavitud y sociedad; notas y documentos para la historia de la esclavitud negra en Cuba*. Havana: Editorial de Ciencias Sociales, 1986.

Villaverde, Cirilo. *Diario del rancheador*. Introduction by Roberto Friol. Havana: Editorial Letras Cubanas, 1982.

Viotti da Costa, Emilia. "Slave Images and Realities." In *Comparative Perspectives on Slavery in New World Plantation Societies*, edited by Vera Rubin and Arthur Tuden, 293–310. New York: New York Academy of Sciences, 1977.

Index

Abad, Antonio, 190, 203 (n. 14)
Abadía, Teresa, 102
Abbot, Abiel, 39
Abolitionist ideals, 42, 46
Abreu, Eugenio, 151, 152, 201 (n. 2)
Abreu, María Francisca, 96
Abuse allegations: slaveholders' defense against, 47, 62–64, 67–73, 121, 145–46; and petitions for change in master, 90
Acosta, Manuel, 133
Acosta, Pedro, 104, 199 (n. 28)
Administrators: and hierarchical principles of plantation system, 23; slaves' grievances against, 120, 132–33
African traditions: and slave family composition, 3; and plantation slave community, 24; and native languages, 26; and kin networks, 32; religious practices, 33–34, 66
Age of slaves: and plantation slave community, 28; distinguishing characteristics of, 29; and slave code, 49, 50, 81; and coartación, 141, 201 (n. 10)
Aguado, Matías, 101
Aguiar Mella, José, 120–21
Águila, José María de, 151
Aguirre, Francisco Santiago, 176
Alcancía (ingenio), 33, 191, 203 (nn. 13, 14)
Aldama, Domingo, 197 (n. 1)
Alemán, Juan Antonio, 91
Alfonso, Juan, 186
Alfonso, Julián Luis, 180, 185
Alfonso X (king of Spain), 161, 196 (n. 1)
Álvarez, Tomás, 203 (n. 14)
Álvarez, Vicente María, 114
American South, 9, 22
Anaya, José de Jesús, 151
Angerona (cafetal), 39

Aponte, José Antonio, 46
Apprenticeship system, role of, 2
Arango y Parreño, Francisco de, 6–7
Arcadia (cafetal), 174
Archivo Nacional de Cuba (Cuban National Archive; ANC), 2
Arcos, Marqués de, 38, 197 (n. 1)
Armenta, Caridad, 164
Armenteros, Andrés, 122
Arratia (ingenio), 132–35
Árrechasabaleta, Ángel, 139
Arriendo (rental/lease) system, 40–41
Asunción (ingenio), 191
Avilés, Ana, 136
Avilés Congo, José Antonio, 136–37, 200 (n. 1)
Ayala, María Ignacia, 145
Azcarate, Nicolás, as syndic, 3, 98, 140–41, 201 (n. 8)

Baldés Álvarez, Prudencio, 88–89
Bale, Blas, 140
Balear (ingenio), 117–18
Baquero, José, 177
Barracks system: and plantation slave community, 34–36, 39; and traveling peddlers, 37; slaveholders on, 78; and slave code, 82
Barriga, Antonio, 160
Batey (courtyard), 25
Batle, Jorge, 202 (n. 10)
Bejucal (ingenio), 165
Belén, María, 116
Belén Medina, María, 92
Belén Medina, Simón, 92
Beltrán, Joaquín, 153
Benítez, Manuel, 146
Betancourt, Ramón, 104
Bibí, Adrián, 110–11

209

Bibí, Federico, 169
Bibí, Josefa Rita, 168
Bibí, Perico, 154
Bibí, Vicente, 166–67
Bibí, Víctor, 114
Bibián, José, 45, 196 (n. 57)
Blen, León, 165
Bohíos (huts): and slave marriages, 30, 75, 78, 82; barracks system versus, 35, 78
Borbón (cafetal), 165
Borí, Magín, 169, 170
Borí, Somarise, 170
Boyeros (ox herds/drovers): and hierarchical principles of plantation system, 23; slaves' assaults on, 109–11; and contramayorals, 113–15; and violence against slaves, 159–60, 201–2 (n. 6); as runaway slaves, 166
Bozals (newly arrived African-born slaves): assimilation into plantation slave community, 29; and transactions between slaves, 39; slaveholders' characterization of, 64, 66–67
Bravo, Bernardo, 141
Bravo, Dámaso Portuondo, 163, 202 (n. 5)
Britain: and slaves' holdings in colonies, 38; treatment of slaves, 64; and runaway slaves, 68; wars against, 72
Brujos (witch doctors), 27, 28, 171
Bruzón, José, 97

Caballero, Isabel, 189
Cabildos de nación (ethnic associations), 32, 43, 65
Cafetales (coffee plantation and processing complexes): dominance of, 5–6; income generated by, 6; population density of, 11, 12; slave population on, 14; slave occupations on, 79; and transplanting seedlings, 112, 199 (nn. 3, 4, 5); and slave rebellions, 171–76. *See also* Slaveholders; *specific cafetales*
Calás, Andrés, 168
Calás Gangá, Dionisia, 168
Calás Gangá, Manuela, 168–69
Campo Florida, Marquis de, 35
Campos, José Rubio, 164

Capatazes (foremen), 25, 65, 82
Capitalism, plantation system compared to, 39–40
Carabalí, Agustín, 166, 203 (n. 12)
Carabalí, Anselmo, 134, 188, 203 (n. 14)
Carabalí, Benito, 190
Carabalí, Carlos, 117, 199 (n. 8)
Carabalí, Casimiro, 117
Carabalí, Claudio, 124–25
Carabalí, Cristóbal, 25, 109
Carabalí, Fabián, 186
Carabalí, Feliciano, 105–8, 199 (n. 2)
Carabalí, Francisco, 116, 199 (n. 8)
Carabalí, Ildefonso, 85–86, 197 (n. 1)
Carabalí, Limbano, 133–34, 135
Carabalí, Lucía, 97
Carabalí, Manuel, 188
Carabalí, María Filomena, 165
Carabalí, Nicolás, 165
Carabalí, Pantaleón, 121–22
Carabalí, Pedro, 202 (n. 10)
Carabalí, Perico, 189
Carabalí, Santiago, 190
Carabalí Bibí, Savad, 109–11
Carabelas (shipmates on the transatlantic voyage), 32
Cárdenas y Chávez, Miguel de, 92–93
Carillo, José Manuel, 197 (n. 1)
Carmen, José del, 168
Carolina (cafetal), 176
Carriage drivers, contacts of, 36
Cart drivers, slaves as, 36
Casa Bayona, Count of, 67
Casal, Julián del, 142
Casimoro (Mina), 107–8
Catalina (cafetal), 105–9
Catalina (ingenio), 178
Catholic Church: and plantation system expansion, 14; and slave marriages, 30; and padrinazgo, 33–34; and slave code's provision for religious instruction, 48, 49, 56, 57, 80; and slave code's provision for oversight of mayordomos, 53
Cayetana, María, 96–97
Ceballos, Francisco, 138
Cepero, Joaquín de, 89

210 : INDEX

Cepero, José Agustín, 89
Cepero, Juana, 89
Ceres (ingenio), 190
Chapeaux (cafetal), 173
Chávez, Dimas, 104, 198–99 (n. 28)
Chávez, Lorenza, 104, 199 (n. 28)
Chil, Francisco, 110
Chinese colonos, 9, 126–27
Chronic illness, and slave code, 50, 81
Cimarronería (fugitive slave phenomenon), 2, 44. *See also* Maroons; Runaway slaves
Cisneros Saco, Hilario, 151–52
Claro, José, 88
Clothing provision: and slave code, 48, 57–58, 63, 74, 77, 80; of runaway slaves, 169
Coartación (legal right to be appraised at fixed value and pay down balance): conditional freedom of, 2; and social confrontation, 3; and urban slaves, 41; and masters' power to transfer ownership, 42; and slave resistance, 42, 43; and slave code, 83; and petitions for family members, 98, 100–102, 198 (nn. 21, 25); and labor relations, 136–44, 200 (n. 3), 201 (n. 10), 202 (n. 2); and slaves' grievances, 164
Colonial government: and slaves' kin networks, 33; fears of slave revolts, 34; and barracks system, 36; hostility toward taverns, 37
Colonial legal structure: and scope of medieval legal system, 3; and slave rights, 40, 42–43. *See also* Slave code
Colonos (sugar planters), 7, 8
Commerce: liberalization of, 4–5; and plantation system, 36–40; and rural slaves, 37–40; slaveholders on slave code's effect on, 55, 60, 71
Conga, Gertrudis, 165
Congo, Alejandro, 169–71
Congo, Antonio, 174
Congo, Buenaventure (Ventura), 128, 129, 200 (n. 18)
Congo, Celestino, 156
Congo, Cornelio, 190–91
Congo, Hilario, 167

Congo, Manuel, 141
Congo, Trinidad, 154
Congos (ingenio), 32
Contramayorals (slave gang bosses): in plantation slave community, 24–27; punishments administered by, 25; complicity in late-night family meetings, 31; and boyeros, 113–15; slaves' killing, 122–23; punishment of, 155
Córdova, Manuel, 138
Council of the Indies, 47–48
Cowardice allegations, 28
Criolla, Camila, 186
Criolla, Francisca, 154
Criolla, Juliana, 186
Criolla, Marina, 186
Criolla, Rosalía, 154–55
Criollo, Alejo, 119–21
Criollo, Antonio, 188–89
Criollo, Dámaso, 45
Criollo, Desiderio, 188
Criollo, Esteban, 156
Criollo, Félix, 190
Criollo, José, 25, 167, 189
Criollo, José Eleno, 107
Criollo, Lorenzo, 167
Criollo, Marcelo, 155–56
Criollo, Pablo, 165
Criollo, Pedro, 30, 31–32, 125–26, 142, 200 (n. 16)
Criollo, Perico, 188, 191
Criollo, Ramón, 187–88, 202 (n. 10)
Criollo, Sixto, 156
Criollo, Sotero, 158
Criollo, Tiburcio, 189
Criollo, Tomasa, 165
Criollo, Vicente, 33
Cruz, Antonio de la, 122–23, 200 (n. 12)
Cruz, Juan de la, 156
Cruz, María de la, 156, 157–58
Cuabalejo (ingenio), 188
Cuesta, Antonio, 93
Cuesta, Blas, 187
Cuesta, Bonifacio, 93
Cuesta, Isidro, 93
Cuevas, Antonio Ramón, 154

Delgado, Francisco, 181–82
Demographic trends, 8–10, 29
Deschamps Chapeaux, Pedro, 45
Desierto (cafetal), 169, 170
Díaz, Dolores, 88
Díaz, Domingo, 96
Díaz, Manuel, 165
Díez, Ángela, 164
Díez, Juana, 164
Disciplinary measures, and slave code, 50–52, 66. *See also* Punishments
Domestic laborers: slave labor as source of, 4, 49; urban slaves as, 41
Duarte Zenea, Antonio, 165

Echavarría, Vicente, 132–33
El Acana (ingenio), 183, 185, 186, 203 (n. 12)
El Asesor (ingenio), 190
El Asiento (ingenio), 188, 189
El Atrevido (ingenio), 188, 189
El Carmen (cafetal), 127–30, 157, 158
El Cedro (shantytown), 45, 168–69
El Fénix (ingenio), 177
El Largo, Francisco, 100–101
El Mariel (ingenio), 166–67
El Olimpo (ingenio), 190
El Salvador (cafetal), 176, 177, 179–80
El Solitario (cafetal), 175
El Toro (ingenio), 188, 189–90
El Triunvirato (ingenio), 180–87, 191, 203 (nn. 12, 14)
Errand boys, contacts of, 36
Esteban, Pedro, 91
Estorch, Miguel de, 198 (n. 12), 200 (n. 4), 200–201 (n. 6)
Estrada, Francisca, 168
Ethnicity: in plantation slave community, 24–26; and kin networks, 32; and cabildos de nación, 32, 43, 65; and causes of slave rebellions, 43–44
Export trade, 4, 5–7, 8

Federia, Tomasa, 103–4
Fernández, Domingo, 115
Fernandina, Count de la, 20–21, 197 (n. 1)
Fincas (rural agricultural estates), 14, 23

Florida, 8
Food provisions: and slave code, 48, 57–58, 63, 74, 76–77, 80; and slaves' grievances, 106–7, 108; of maroons, 165, 168, 170
Fornaris, José, 139, 201 (n. 6)
Fouquier, Felipe de, 173
Fouquier, José María de, 173
Fouquier, Juan, 171, 202 (n. 10)
Franco, José Luciano, 39
Free blacks: illiteracy of, 1–2; complaints about treatment of, 14; brujos' contact with, 28; and kin networks, 32, 33; sociopolitical movements of, 34; slaves' contacts with, 36, 40; as traveling peddlers, 37; slaveholders' employing, 61
Freedom: within plantation slave community, 35, 36, 39; and arriendo (rental/lease) system, 40–41; in Mexico, 45–46, 163; and petitions for family members, 89, 90–96, 97, 98, 102–4, 197 (nn. 7, 11), 198 (nn. 12, 15, 26), 198–99 (n. 28); and travel to countries without slavery, 161–64. *See also* Coartación; Manumission
Free labor, 12–13, 23
Frías, María de los Dolores, 90, 197 (n. 6)
Fuente, Alejandro de la, 197 (n. 30)

Galainena, José Isabel, 140
Galarrage, Francisco, 95
Galarrage, Norberto, 94
Galbín, Lorenzo, 123–24
Gangá, Adriano, 185
Gangá, Alejo, 39
Gangá, Ángel, 190
Gangá, Antonio, 165
Gangá, Bárbara, 122–23
Gangá, Bonifacio, 182, 183, 185
Gangá, Carlos, 174–76
Gangá, Clemente, 174
Gangá, Cristóbal, 190, 202 (n. 10)
Gangá, Dionisio, 26–27
Gangá, Dominga, 91–92
Gangá, Domingo, 203 (n. 14)
Gangá, Eusebio, 203 (n. 11)
Gangá, Francisco, 177
Gangá, Gabino, 112–13

Gangá, Joaquín, 158
Gangá, Jorge, 191
Gangá, José de Jesús, 114, 115, 165
Gangá, José María, 202 (n. 10)
Gangá, Juan de la Cruz, 186
Gangá, León, 165
Gangá, Luciano, 154
Gangá, Luis, 203 (n. 11)
Gangá, Manuel, 183–85, 203 (n. 12)
Gangá, María del Rosario, 30
Gangá, Mariano, 187
Gangá, Nicolás, 116–17, 199 (n. 8)
Gangá, Nicolas, 182–83, 203 (n. 12)
Gangá, Pablo, 25
Gangá, Pacho, 114
Gangá, Pancho, 191
Gangá, Ramón, 189
Gangá, Rita, 87, 197 (n. 2)
Gangá, Sabino, 121–22
Gangá, Sandi, 174
Gangá, Tomás, 88
Gangá, Victor, 118
García, Antonio, 89
García, Gabriel, 141
García, Martina, 186
García, Romualdo, 90–91, 197 (n. 7)
García Negrete, Basilio, 153
Genes (ingenio), 188
Genovese, Eugene, 22
Geraldo (native of Curazao), 117, 199 (n. 8)
Goicoechea, María Asunción, 166
Gómez, Antonio, 175, 202–3 (n. 10)
Gómez, Joaquín, 197 (n. 1)
Gongo, Valentín, 126
González, Eusebio, 153–54
González, María de la Trinidad, 137
González, María Luisa, 139–40
González, Pedro, 20–21
González, Regina, 102
González Arando, Joaquín, 90
González Arando, Manuel, 90
González González, Benito, 95–96
González Larrinaga, Jacinto, 76–79, 165, 197 (n. 1)
Gossip, 36
Goyri, Francisco, 91, 197 (n. 11), 200 (n. 3)

Guantánamo, Cuba, 10
Guardia, Manuela de la, 162
Güines, Cuba, 10
Gullón, Antonio, 163, 202 (n. 4)
Gumersina (morena slave), 137, 220 (n. 2)
Gutiérrez, Francisco, 179
Gutiérrez, Juan, 142
Gutiérrez, Luciano, 94
Gutiérrez y Casal (ingenio owner), 31–32
Gutman, Herbert, 30

Hacendados (hacienda owners), 6, 34, 35
Haciendas (large rural estates), 5–6
Havana, Cuba, 10, 14, 41
Hernández, Ignacio, 190
Hernández, Josefa, 86
Hernández, Pablo, 152–56, 201 (n. 4)
Hernández, Rafael, 125
Herrera, Antonia, 110
Herrera, Ignacio, 197 (n. 1)
Herrera, Miguel, 165
Hierarchical principles: of plantation system, 13, 23, 24, 26; of plantation slave community, 24, 29
Holidays, and slave code, 48, 49, 56, 57, 63, 65, 67, 80
Housing: spatial distribution of, 23; and slave code, 49; of maroons, 170
Houssin, Canuto, 94–95
Howe, Julia Ward, 37

Ingenios (sugarcane plantation and processing complexes): dominance of, 5–6; income generated by, 6; population density of, 11–12; slave population of, 14; steam-powered machinery used in, 22; and barracks systems, 36; slave occupations in, 59–62, 77–78. *See also* Slaveholders; *specific ingenios*
Intrépido (ingenio), 113–15
Iznaga, José, 32

Jamaica: and slaves' holdings, 38; palenques in, 68
Jesús, María de (morena slave), 138–39
Jesús María (ingenio), 124–25

Jicotea (ingenio), 169
Jiménez, Agustín, 188, 203 (n. 14)
Jiménez, José, 104
Jobino, José, 151, 152
Journeymen, urban slaves as, 40, 41

Kin networks: and plantation slave community, 29, 32–33; and rural slaves/urban slaves relationship, 33, 40; and padrinazgo, 33–34. *See also* Slave families

Labor supply: sources of, 6–8; and plantation system, 41
La Concepción (ingenio), 183–84, 203 (n. 12)
La Conchita (ingenio), 188
La Cuaba (hacienda), 150–52
Ladinos (culturally adapted African slave), 29
La Escalera conspiracy, 28, 46, 204 (n. 14)
Laguardia, Patricio de, 197 (n. 1)
La Luisa (ingenio), 187, 188, 189, 203 (n. 14)
La Merced (ingenio), 39
Landot (cafetal), 39, 165
La Rosa (ingenio), 191
Larrentrín, Luis, 174
Lasa, Sebastián de, 197 (n. 1)
La Suerte (cafetal), 156–58
Latin American wars for independence, 8
La Trinidad (ingenio), 33
Law, rule of, and colonial policy, 3
La Yaba (cafetal), 171
Leiva, José Antonio, 168
León, Josefa de, 95, 198 (n. 15)
Lima de Elosua, María Teresa, 97
Linares, Félix Cantalicio, 98
Livestock industry: and slave labor, 4; and hacienda system, 5–6; displacement of, 7; and population density, 11; effect of slave code on, 60–61
Llaranas, Pedro, 140
Lombillo, Countess de, 165
López, José María, 203 (n. 14)
López, Manuel, 113
López de Villavicencio, Diego, 87
Loreto (ingenio), 25
Louisiana, and slave trade, 8
Lucumí, Andrés, 26
Lucumí, Benigno, 113–15, 199 (n. 7)
Lucumí, Cerefino, 154–55
Lucumí, Cirilo, 185, 203 (n. 12)
Lucumí, Cristóbal, 112, 183
Lucumí, Domingo, 112
Lucumí, Eusebio, 189
Lucumí, Fermín, 117–18
Lucumí, Fernando, 30, 126
Lucumí, Florencia, 154
Lucumí, Francisco, 39, 190–91, 203 (n. 14)
Lucumí, Gaspar, 111–13
Lucumí, Gerónomo, 189
Lucumí, Gonzalo, 185
Lucumí, Gregorio, 135, 200 (n. 20)
Lucumí, Ignacio, 188
Lucumí, Isidro, 190
Lucumí, Joaquín, 156, 178–79, 180, 203 (n. 11)
Lucumí, Jorge, 134
Lucumí, José, 112, 188
Lucumí, José Rosario, 154
Lucumí, Justo, 176, 202 (n. 10)
Lucumí, León, 188
Lucumí, Longino, 191
Lucumí, Lorenzo, 154
Lucumí, Luis, 177, 203 (n. 11)
Lucumí, Marcelo, 156
Lucumí, Margarita, 178–79
Lucumí, Mateo, 131, 190
Lucumí, Napoleón, 191, 203 (n. 14)
Lucumí, Nicolás, 117–18
Lucumí, Pascual, 112–13, 127
Lucumí, Patricio, 189
Lucumí, Pedro, 108–9, 119
Lucumí, Pedro José, 112
Lucumí, Ramon, 182
Lucumí, Remigio, 188
Lucumí, Román, 189
Lucumí, Rosalía, 165
Lucumí, Simón, 111–12
Lucumí, Telésforo, 189–90
Luz, José de la, 103–4

Macías, Pedro, 91–92
Macuá, Aniceto, 165
Macuá, Damiana, 91, 197 (n. 7)
Macuá, Ricardo, 156

Madan, Cristóbal, 191
Madan, Eusebio, 180–81
Madrazo, Carlos, 143
Mainicú (ingenio), 32
Mandiga, Francisco, 174
Mandiga, Ramón, 31
Mandinga, Ceferino, 121–22, 200 (n. 11)
Mandinga, Celedonia, 128–29
Mandinga, Domingo, 114, 115
Mandinga, Francisco, 114
Mandinga, Gonzalo, 179, 203 (n. 11)
Mandinga, Hilario, 165
Mandinga, Lorenzo, 190
Mandinga, Marcelo, 156
Mandinga, María Guadalupe, 122, 123
Mandinga, Ramon, 176
Mandinga, Tomás, 171–74
Manresa, Benito, 180, 181
Manresa, Felipe, 180, 181
Manumission: slaves saving for, 31–32; slaves' holdings providing cash for, 38–39, 59, 63; and rural slaves/urban slaves relationship, 40; and coartación agreements, 41; figures on, 43; as safety valve, 43; and slave code, 50, 59, 63; for discovering slave rebellion plots, 84
Maritime personnel, punishments for, 70
Maroons: slaveholders' characterization of, 67; accounts of, 164–67, 168, 169–71. *See also* Palenques; Runaway slaves
Marqueti (cafetal), 39
Marriage: and slave families, 30–31, 50, 65, 75, 82, 83; and slave code, 50, 65, 75, 82, 83
Marsá, Gregorio, 98
Martínez, Francisco, 105
Martínez, María, 137
Master/slave relations: and production needs, 15; violence in, 20–21, 145–60; handling of slave complaints, 20–22; and authority of master, 21; and slaves' holdings, 38–39; and masters' power to transfer ownership, 42; and slave code, 51–54
Matanzas, Cuba, 14, 41
Matoso, Manuel, 168, 169
Mayolí, Diego, 123
Mayorals (overseers): and slave rebellions, 22; and hierarchical principles of plantation system, 23, 24, 26; and attraction of taverns, 37; and holidays, 65; and slaves' health, 65; and punishments, 67, 68, 84, 169–70; and slaves' walkouts, 105–9; slaves' grievances against, 106, 107, 109, 116–17, 119, 120, 199 (nn. 2, 8); slaves' injuring of, 111–13; slaves' flogging of, 115–17; slaves' killing, 117–18; and violence against slaves, 159–60, 201–2 (n. 6)
Mayordomos (chief stewards): and slave code, 47, 49, 50, 51–54, 78, 82; inspection of plantation infirmaries, 78; and slaves visiting other farms, 82; and punishments, 84
Mayorga, Pablo, 32
Mediavilla, José, 145–46
Medina, Agustín, 92
Medina, Petrona, 96, 198 (n. 15)
Meireles, Asunción, 102–3, 198 (n. 26)
Meireles, Ramón, 102–3, 198 (n. 26)
Mena, Andrés, 159–60, 201–2 (n. 6)
Mena, Justo, 159–60, 201–2 (n. 6)
Mercantile relations, diffusion of, 4–5
Mexico: as destination for runaway slaves, 45–46, 163; mine work in, 63
Mieres, José, 85
Milián, Petrona, 190
Mina, Anastasio, 186–87
Mina, Antonio, 166
Mina, Ceferino, 130–32
Mina, Felipe, 131, 132
Mina, Félix, 190
Mina, Francisco, 164–65, 191, 202 (n. 7)
Mina, José, 141
Mina, Juan Bautista, 130–32
Mina, Leisa, 202 (n. 10)
Mina, Pancho, 39
Mina, Rafael, 130–32, 188
Mina, Toribio, 165
Miralles de Ibáñez, Dolores, 130
Molina, Josefa, 86
Molina, Pablo, 157
Monserrate (cafetal), 170
Montalvo, Juan, 197 (n. 1)
Montalvo, Rafael, 114

Montalvo y Castillo, José, 35
Montenegro, Bernardo, 101
Montes, Manuel de, 130–31
Morales, Antonio, 111–12
Morales, Pedro, 203 (n. 14)
Morales Lemus, José, 3, 42
Morales Sotolongo, José María, 189
Moreno, Carlota, 88–89
Moreno, Miguel, 92–93
Moreno, Tomasa, 92–93
Moreno Fraginals, Manuel, 15
Morgado, Manuel, 154
Moya, Miguel de, 73
Muñoz Izaguirre, Joaquín, 197 (n. 1)

Naranjo, Melcho, 189
Naranjo, Micaela, 104
Native languages, and plantation slave community, 26
Navarro, José Felipe, 175
Nepomuceno, Juan (Pomuceno), 127–30
New Orleans, La., 45–46
Norms: of plantation system, 13, 22–23, 34; and slave marriages, 30
Notary publics, 2, 52
Nuestra Señora de la Asunción (cafetal), 130
Nuestra Señora del Rosario (cafetal), 111–13
Núñez, Juan Bautista, 99–100

O'Farril, Rafael, 197 (n. 1)
Olabe, Petrona, 138–39
Oliva, José, 104
Orta, José Ignacio de, 67
Oviedo, Esteban Santa Cruz de, 156–58

Padrinazgo, 33–34, 194 (n. 32)
Padrón, Marcos, 90
Palenques (remote fugitive slave settlements): court redress and flight to, compared, 2; and slaves' holdings, 39; and slave rebellions, 44; and urban slaves, 45; slaveholders' characterization of, 66, 68; accounts of, 168–69. *See also* Maroons; Runaway slaves
Palomino, Antonio Abad, 95–96, 198 (n. 15)
Paula, Francisco de, 123

Paula, Justo, 140
Paula Sánchez, Francisco de, 131
Paulo Congo, Francisco de (alias Boticario), 123–24, 200 (n. 14)
Paz Mariartu, Salvador de la, 132
Peiton, Tomás, 174, 175–76
Peñalver, Agustina, 102
Pérez, Francisco, 156
Pérez, José, 189
Pérez, Luisa, 110
Perserverancia (cafetal), 26
Peru, 63
Pichardo (ingenio), 189
Pichardo, Esteban, 27
Piedra, Luis, 113–14
Pineiro, Nicolás, 141
Piñeiro, Toribio, 145–46
Piñero, Emilio, 100–101
Plantation infirmaries: and slave children, 30–31; and slave code, 49–50, 64–65, 75, 78, 83; and slave grievances, 108; and effects of punishments, 154
Plantation slave community: treatment of, as machine, 23–24, 34; structure of, 23–29; hierarchy of subordination within, 24, 29; newly arrived versus experienced slaves in, 29, 31; and slave families, 29–36, 40; meetings between members of different, 31, 34, 36; and barracks system, 34–36, 39; freedoms within, 35, 36, 39; and company store, 39; and violence, 43; conflicts within, 121–23
Plantation system: hegemony of, 4–7; sociodemographic impact of, 11–15; social relations within, 15, 20–23; and spatial distribution of housing, 23; informal structure of, 23–29; balance of power in, 27; and commerce, 36–40; capitalism compared to, 39–40; and labor demands, 41; continuity in, 43
Planter class: history of slave societies presented by, 1; norms established by, 34; and barracks system, 34–36; hostility toward taverns, 37; and slaves' holdings, 38–39
Polo, Carlota, 102–3, 198 (n. 26)

Polo, Merced, 92–93
Ports: and commerce, 36; and runaway slaves, 45
Portuondo, Vicente, 169
Portuondo Congo, Bartolomé, 169
Pozo Hernández, Rafael, 101
Prado, Miguel, 191, 203 (n. 14)
Prado Ameno, Marqués of, 121
Prieto, Carlos, 85–86
Public opinion, and slave rights, 42
Puerto Príncipe, Real Audiencia (Royal Court) of, 33
Punishments: and free blacks' treatment, 14; contramayorals' administration of, 25; and slave code, 50–52, 64, 66, 67–71, 84; and slaves' grievances against mayorals, 106, 107, 109, 116–17, 119, 120, 199 (nn. 2, 8); slaves' uprising against, 132–35, 200 (n. 20); and master/slave relations, 145–52; as motive for runaway slaves, 166, 167, 168–69, 170

Quesada, Petronila, 138–39
Quesada Congo, Antonio, 143–44, 201 (n. 13)
Quiqutis, José, 110
Quisi, Sandi, 175

Railroads, and commerce, 36
Rancherías, slaveholders' characterization of, 66
Real Audiencia (Royal Court) of Puerto Príncipe, 33
Real Congo, Pedro, 139–40
Real Consulado de Agricultura y Comercio (Royal Consulate for Agriculture and Commerce), 38
Recreation, and slave code, 49, 65, 82
Regla de Ocha, 33
Regla de Palo, 33
Regulation of 1765, 5
Regulation of 1842: and slave children's care, 30–31; and barracks system, 34–36; and slaves' holdings, 38
Regulation of Valdés, 38
Religious instruction, and slave code, 48, 49, 56, 57, 80

Rendón, Benigna, 98
Rendón, Juan Ignacio, 97
Residence trials, and slave code, 53–54, 196 (n. 2)
Respeto, Dionisia, 88
Reyes, Cirilo, 188
Ribero, Antonio, 109–10
Rivero, Pepe Martín, 101
Roca, Dolores, 101–2
Roca, Teresa, 101–2
Rocafort, Blas, 153
Rodríguez, Florencia, 146–50
Rodríguez, Joaquín Ceferino, 168
Romeu, Francisco, 103
Roque, Jacinto, 33
Ros, Francisco, 163, 202 (n. 4)
Rosario, José del, 122–23, 200 (n. 13)
Rosario Gangá, María del, 125–26
Royal Decree of February 28, 1789, 47, 49
Rubio, Josefa, 86
Rufina, María, 95–96
Ruiz, Cándido, 162, 190, 191
Ruiz, Francisco, 127–28, 129
Ruiz, José, 162
Runaway slaves: contramayorals' communication with, 27; and slaves' holdings, 39; motives and incentives of, 44–46, 105–6, 159, 164, 166, 167, 168–69, 170; collaborative network supporting, 45; and slave code, 53; conflicts with fellow slaves, 123–27. *See also* Maroons; Palenques
Rural areas: slave labor in, 4, 11; restructuring of holdings in, 5; demographic trends in, 9; kin networks in, 33, 34; and slaves' visits with other farms, 36; and taverns, 37; and slaves' commerce, 39; runaway slaves in, 45
Rural slaves/urban slaves relationship, and kin networks, 33, 40

Sabanazo (cafetal), 176
Sagarra, Juan Bautista, 151–52
Saint-Domingue (modern Haiti), 6, 8, 38
Sáinz, Ramón, 146–50
Salas, Mamerto, 143, 201 (n. 12)

Salas, Pablo Antonio de, 188
Sánchez, Antonio, 97
Sánchez, Santiago Ramón, 87
Sánchez y Sánchez, Ángela, 98
Sánchez y Sánchez, Juana, 98
San Fernando (ingenio), 153–56, 201 (n. 3)
San Fernando de Peñalver, Countess, 124
San Francisco (ingenio), 165
San Isidro (ingenio), 165
San Joaquín (ingenio), 121–22
San José (ingenio), 123–24, 189, 190
San Juan (ingenio), 155
San Juan de Manacas (cafetal), 115–17
San Lorenzo (ingenio), 186
San Matías (ingenio), 122–23
San Miguel (ingenio), 184, 203 (n. 12)
San Rafael (ingenio), 184, 187, 203 (n. 12)
San Ramón (ingenio), 190
Santa Ana (ingenio), 188
Santa Cruz, María Magdalena, 137–38
Santaella, María de la Concepción, 137, 138
Santa Teresa (ingenio), 119–21
Santería, 33
Santiago de Cuba, Cuba, 6, 10, 41
Santísima Trinidad (ingenio), 166–67
Santo Domingo de Domingo Aldama (ingenio), 126–27
Santo Tomás (cafetal), 166, 167
Sateliens, Lorenzo, 171–73, 202 (n. 10)
Satrán del Sabanazo (cafetal), 172
Scott, Rebecca J., 2
Serrano, Francisco, 156–58
Serrudo, Bernardo, 115–16, 117
Settlement patterns, and plantation system, 11–15
Sexual division of labor, 28, 49, 65, 81
Siete Partidas, 47, 196 (n. 1)
Slave children: mothers' care of, 28, 31, 75, 78–79, 81, 83; and plantation infirmary, 30–31; and slave code, 50, 75, 76, 77, 80–81
Slave code: and mayordomos, 47, 49, 50, 51–54, 78, 82; and slaveholder abuses, 47, 51–52, 62–64, 67–73, 84; and holidays, 48, 49, 56, 57, 63, 65, 67, 80; and religious instruction, 48, 49, 56, 57, 80; and syndics, 48, 50, 51–54, 68; and food provisions, 48, 57–58, 63, 74, 76–77, 80; and clothing provision, 48, 57–58, 63, 74, 77, 80; and housing, 49; and age of slaves, 49, 50, 81; and slaves' holdings, 49, 56–57, 59, 75, 79, 81; and slave occupations, 49, 58–62, 65, 74–75, 77–78, 79, 81; and recreation, 49, 65, 82; and plantation infirmaries, 49–50, 64–65, 75, 78, 83; and marriage, 50, 65, 75, 82, 83; and slave children, 50, 75, 76, 77, 80–81; and slaves' obedience, 50, 80, 84; and chronic illness, 50, 81; and punishments, 50–52, 64, 66, 67–71, 84; and disciplinary measures, 50–52, 66; and slave rosters, 52, 71; and residence trials, 53–54, 196 (n. 2); and slaveholders' economic interests, 55–56, 58, 60, 63, 68, 71–73, 79; Valdés's survey on, 74–76; and pregnancy, 75, 76, 77, 78–79; excerpts from revision of, 80–85; and tools, 81–82; and slaves visiting other farms, 82
Slave families: affirmation of, 3; separation of, 29, 31, 32, 78; and plantation slave community, 29–36, 40; and marriage, 30–31, 50, 65, 75, 82, 83; composition of, 31; and proceedings on attempted suicide, 85–86; and theft of slave woman, 87; and suits against siblings, 88–89; and petitions for freedom of family members, 89, 90–96, 97, 98, 102–4, 197 (nn. 7, 11), 198 (nn. 12, 15, 26), 198–99 (n. 28); and petitions for change in master, 90, 96–97, 99–100, 197 (n. 6), 198 (nn. 16, 23); and petitions to redeem unborn children, 91, 94, 102, 197 (n. 8); and petitions seeking visitation with children, 91–92, 99–100; and petitions for freedom of prospective wife, 94–95; and petitions for revised coartación, 98, 100–102, 198 (nn. 21, 25); and complaints against master and husband, 99, 198 (n. 22); and appraisal of family members, 101–2, 198 (n. 25); and charges on unjust enslavement, 103–4; conflicts within, 125–26. *See also* Kin networks
Slaveholders: defense against abuse

allegations, 47, 62–64, 67–73, 121, 145–46; on slave code's effect on commerce, 55, 60, 71; on economic consequences of slave code, 55–56, 58, 60, 63, 68, 71–73, 79; and religious instruction in slave code, 56, 57; on holidays, 56, 57, 63, 65; and slaves' holdings, 56–57, 79; on food and clothing requirements in slave code, 57–58, 63, 76–77; on slave occupations, 58–61, 77–78, 79; on punishments, 64, 66, 67–71; on plantation infirmaries, 64–65, 78; on slave rosters, 71; on barracks system, 78

Slave labor, and hegemony of plantation system, 4–7

Slave men, 8–9, 31. *See also* Slave women

Slave occupations: slaves' advocating improvement in, 2; slaves' protests concerning, 22; and slave code, 49, 58–62, 65, 74–75, 77–78, 79, 81

Slave population, 8–11, 41

Slave quarters. *See* Housing

Slave rebellions: results of, 1; and mayorals, 22; and kinship networks, 31; and barracks system, 34; and slaves' holdings, 39; ethnic causes of, 43–44; stereotypes of, 44; and runaway slaves, 44–46; planning of, 46; slaveholders' characterization of, 66–67, 68; rewards for discovering plans for, 84; on cafetals of Matanzas, 171–76; in Mariel area, 176–80, 203 (n. 11); on El Triunvirato, 180–87; general insurrection aborted, 187–91, 203 (n. 14)

Slave resistance: forms of, 1, 2; consequences of, 21, 22, 194 (n. 15); contramayorals' role in, 27; and age of slaves, 28; authorities' fears of, 34; and norms of planter class, 34; and cart drivers, 36; and slaves' holdings, 38, 39; and colonial legal system, 42; and coartación, 42, 43

Slave rights: and law enforcement, 3; and small holdings, 37–38; and colonial legal structure, 40, 42–43; and travel to countries without slavery, 161–64

Slave rosters, 52, 71

Slaves: letters of, 1; illiteracy of, 1–2; psychological profile of, 2–3; mortality rates of, 9; living conditions of, 9, 20, 22; as percentage of population, 10–11, 12; communication networks of, 36, 39; cultivation of small plots by, 37–39, 59; fear of dogs, 106, 108, 131, 199 (n. 1); conflicts over debt collection, 121–22; conflicts with runaway slaves, 123–27; solidarity among, 127–35

—free hired help's relations with: and production needs, 15; and violence, 20–21; and hierarchical principles, 23; benefits to slaves in, 37

—holdings of: sale of goods from, 37–39; and slave code, 49, 56–57, 59, 75, 79, 81; supplementing food with, 76; caring for, 76, 78

See also Age of slaves; Plantation slave community; Runaway slaves; Slave children; Slave families; Slave men; Slave women

Slave trade, 7–8

Slave women: population of, 8–9; and food preparation and laundry, 28; care of slave children, 28, 31, 75, 78–79, 81, 83; and regulation of slave occupations, 49, 65, 81; masters' abuse of, 146–50, 156–58. *See also* Slave men

Sobrado, Juan Pablo, 91, 197 (n. 8)

Socarrás, Felipe, 104

Socarrás, Juana, 103–4

Songuito (cafetal), 170

Sorzano, Gabriel Segundo, 115, 117

Spain, 7, 9, 31, 161–62

Suárez, Ildelfonso, 200 (n. 18)

Suárez, José Ildelfonso, 202 (n. 7)

Suazo, Juana Evangelista, 96–97, 198 (n. 16)

Suicide: slaveholders' views of, 67; attempts, 85–86; threats of, 153; in response to punishments, 154, 155; rulings of, 200 (n. 10)

Sumidero rebellion, 31, 46

Syndics (legal advocates): role in court proceedings, 3; and slave rights, 42, 43; and slave code, 48, 50, 51–54, 68

Tacón, Miguel, 202 (n. 7)
Taitas (venerated black leaders), 27–28
Tamayo, Narciso, 169
Taverns, 37
Taylor (cafetal), 173
Taylor, Samuel, 202 (n. 10)
Télles, Juan, 32
Tobacco production, 4, 6, 61
Toca, Rafael de, 120
Toledo, Juan Gualberto, 87, 197 (n. 2)
Torre, José de la, 115
Tosca, Pablo de, 171–73
Toscano, Antonio, 106, 107–8
Trade policy, liberalization of, 4–5, 7
Transmigration, 66, 197 (n. 30)
Transportation and commerce, 36
Trapiches (sugar mills), 4
Traveling peddlers, 37, 39
Tribal antagonisms, 25–26
Trinidad, Cuba, 6, 10

Unzaga, Diego Francisco de, 85–86
Urban areas: slaves of, 4, 40–41, 43; demographic trends in, 9; free blacks in, 14; cabildos de nación in, 32; kin networks in, 33; runaway slaves in, 45
Urrutia Gangá, Matías, 136–37, 200 (n. 1)

Valdés, Gerónimo, 34, 74–76
Valdés, José, 97
Valdés, Merced, 164
Valenzuela, Juana, 99, 198 (n. 23)
Valerio, Manuel, 99–100, 198 (n. 22)

Varona, Agustín José, 201 (n. 12)
Varreiro, Diego, 176–77
Vega, Francisco de la, 140
Veguerí, Juan Pedro, 94
Venezuela, 164
Verdugo, Domingo, 152–56
Viera, Ramón, 127–28
Vildóstegui, Matías, 105–6, 107, 108
Villalón, Manuel, 169
Villanueva (cafetal), 170
Villaurrutia, Wenceslao, 197 (n. 1)
Violence: effect on plantation community, 15, 20–21, 22; in master/slave relations, 20–21, 145–60; and contramayorals' role, 24–25; and plantation slave community, 43; and urban slaves, 43; and slaveholders' characterization of slave rebellions, 67
Viví, Gregorio, 199 (n. 7)
Vuelta Arriba (cafetal), 175–76

Webster (cafetal), 173, 176
Witchcraft: and plantation slave community, 27; accusations of, 33; and slave rebellions, 189–90. *See also* Brujos
Working conditions of slaves. *See* Slave occupations

Yucatecans, 9

Zacanini, Nicolás, 166, 167
Zayas, Antonia, 168
Zayas, Antonio María de, 101, 198 (n. 25)

www.ingramcontent.com/pod-product-compliance
Lightning Source LLC
Chambersburg PA
CBHW030110010526
44116CB00005B/186